BRITISH EXPERIMENTAL
TURBOJET
AIRCRAFT

Other titles in the Crowood Aviation Series

BRITISH
EXPERIMENTAL

TURBOJET
AIRCRAFT

Barry Jones

All artwork by the author

The Crowood Press

First published in 2003 by
The Crowood Press Ltd
Ramsbury, Marlborough
Wiltshire SN8 2HR

www.crowood.com

British Library Cataloguing-in-Publication Data
A catalogue record for this book is available from
the British Library.

ISBN 1 86126 621 9

Typefaces used: Goudy (*text*), Cheltenham (*head-ings*), Univers Condensed (*captions and boxes*).

Typeset and designed by
D & N Publishing
Lowesden Business Park, Hungerford, Berkshire.

Printed and bound in Malaysia by Times Offset (M)
Sdn. Bhd.

Acknowledgements

Trawling through the 23-year span covered by this book has been exciting, but I readily admit that it might not have been so but for the assistance freely given by many people, two of whom sadly left us before its completion. In particular I give my grateful thanks to *Aeroplane*'s staff, Adrian Balch, the late R. B. 'Bee' Beamont, Cranfield University Press, Neville Duke, Ian Frimiton, the late A. E. 'Ben' Gunn, the Handley Page Association, Harry Holmes, Derek James, Philip Jarrett, Tricia Jones, Ben May, Michael Oakey, Stanley 'Olly' Oliver, Dennis Robinson and Michael Stroud.

Contents

Introduction

The adaptation of the gas turbine into a practical means of powering an aeroplane presented the designer with entirely new vistas into which to channel his ambitions and theories. He is by his very nature an enterprising breed, so that, with the constraints of the propeller eliminated, there appeared virtually limitless boundaries of speed, range and operating altitudes to be explored.

It was the innovative approaches to these factors that made the era covered by this book – 1941 to 1964 – so special. It was one in which the numerous companies' engineers, aerodynamicists, metallurgists and systems designers had to run in order to keep up with one another, as never before.

The Society of British Aircraft Constructors (SBAC) staged its first display in June 1932. As the industry's 'shop window', it became an annual event until 1937, after which the international political climate worsened and the Society's members had their true abilities put to the test in no uncertain way by World War Two. Resumed in September 1946, the Shows annually featured new types on a scale never to be repeated, until 1962, when the financially ruinous impracticality of competition between so many British manufacturers generated a contraction, and the resultant company mergers only justified a biennial display. The first of these, from 7 to 13 September 1964, ended a fortnight before the final aircraft described in this volume first flew.

A multitude of weird, impractical and over-ambitious projects poured off the drawing boards, but the realities of walking before running prevailed and the subjects of this book are the experimental aircraft that either flew or were in an advanced state of construction before the industry's *bête noire*, the politician, intervened. The order of appearance in the book has been determined by the date of the maiden flight made by the first prototype or, in the case of the cancelled projects, the dates scheduled for the first flight. Each aircraft was produced as an experimental type, which

Fairey's first delta design, the FD.1, banks hard to port to display the defunct rocket motor housing under the rear fuselage, which was used as a braking parachute housing. Author's collection

was not intended for production in its original guise. Inevitably there are borderline cases, such as Hawker's various explorations that led to the Sea Hawk, Hunter and Harrier, and Supermarine's single-engined experimental programmes that culminated in the Swift and twin-engined trials that produced the Scimitar. However, these early first steps justify inclusion.

Many of the avenues that were initially explored and for which types were produced, were found to be cul-de-sacs, with the result that the programmes were quietly abandoned and donated to aeronautical history. Nothing is gained by questioning these ambitious programmes in retrospect. It is the fact that today's aircraft designs are computer-generated, making them so visually comparatively similar, that makes the 23-year period covered here such an exciting era. I hope the reader will consider this volume confirms such an assertion.

Barry Jones
May 2003

PART ONE

1941 to 1950

CHAPTER ONE

Gloster E.28/39

The British Pioneer

The circumstances whereby the Gloster Aircraft Company was projected into the vanguard of British turbojet aviation are quite complicated.

While Frank (later Air Cdre Sir Frank) Whittle was at the RAF College, Cranwell, he collaborated with J. H. McC. Reynolds in researching piston-engine supercharging, and on 23 July 1931 they filed a joint patent to cover their findings. The two officers went their individual ways after leaving Cranwell, but maintained contact through correspondence. Alongside his flying career in the RAF, Whittle worked in his spare time on gas-turbine aeroplane propulsion and, despite a frustrating lack of official interest, set up the Power Jets company in 1936 to develop the WU (Whittle Unit) turbojet engine.

By 1939, Wg Cdr Reynolds was the Air Ministry's overseer at the Gloster Aircraft Company, situated at Hucclecote in Gloucestershire. (When it was first founded, on 5 June 1917, it was registered as the Gloucestershire Aircraft Company Limited, but the long and virtually unpronounceable county name became a problem when export orders started to be received, so the company was officially renamed the Gloster Aircraft Company Limited on 11 November 1926.) He had been following Whittle's researches with the WU engine over the years and realized that eventually an aeroplane would be required to prove Whittle's theories in practice.

With his position at Hucclecote, Reynolds was aware of the whole company's activities. The shop floor was occupied with the tail-end of Gladiator orders from overseas customers and the production of 200 Henley aircraft for Hawker Aircraft. The company was a co-member, with Hawker and Armstrong Whitworth, of the Hawker Siddeley Group, and in August 1938 the foundations for a vast new 'shadow' factory had been laid down on the other side of the airfield site, to handle the mass production of the Hawker Hurricane. (By March 1942, 2,750 Hurricanes had been handed over to the RAF and the production of 3,330 Hawker Typhoons was completed by November 1945.)

However, activity on the shop floor was not mirrored in the Design Office. This was engaged with designing single- and twin-engined fighters to meet Specifications F.5/34 and F.9/37, respectively, neither of which progressed beyond the prototype stage. Gloster's Chief Designer, Harry P. Folland, had left the company in 1937, to form his own Folland Aircraft Limited and his successor was Wilfred George Carter, who had been Chief Designer at Hawker Aircraft for two years before transferring to Hucclecote to join Folland's team in 1925.

With the capacity available within Carter's team in mind, Reynolds set up a meeting between the designer and Whittle, which was held at Hucclecote on 28 April 1939. The company's Chief Test Pilot (CTP), Flt Lt P. E. G. 'Gerry' Sayer, together with his deputy, Michael Daunt, were also introduced to Whittle. George Carter and Frank Whittle quickly formed a good relationship, such that the company's latest design, to meet Specification F.18/37, was presented at the meeting. This was a twin-boom fighter powered by a Napier Sabre engine and Whittle considered the configuration to be ideal for the WU turbojet in place of the Sabre.

The start of it all. Whittle's original WU (Whittle Unit), that was first run on 12 April 1937, at the Rugby works of British Thomson-Houston. Author's collection

Dr D. R. Pye, the Director of Scientific Research, had been acquainted with the Carter/Whittle meeting and decided to visit Whittle's Power Jets Limited at their Lutterworth works. He went there on 30 June 1939, armed with a natural inclination to treat the whole project with an air of scepticism, but the WU performed perfectly at nearly 16,000rpm and the Director became an instant convert to the whole concept. On his return he reported to the Air Ministry his opinion that an airframe to test-fly the WU should be ordered as soon as possible.

Contract SB/3229

The combination of Whittle and Carter's complete understanding of what was required, together with the immediate availability of a substantial portion of Gloster's design team, prompted the issuing of Contract SB/3229 to the company, for the design and construction of a turbojet-powered aircraft to Specification E.28/39, with the company designation G.40. The Air Ministry's enthusiasm for the project extended to them requiring the design to be a fighter, as well as a flight-test machine for the new source of propulsion. Whittle's earlier thoughts of the F.18/37 twin-boom design being adapted for the purpose had waned, principally because there was uncertainty about the effects of the engine's jet efflux on the tailplane positioned between the two booms. Therefore a completely new design was called for.

The Gloster Type G.40

Because the Air Ministry wanted a fighter, the new design had space on the drawings for four Browning .303in machine-guns, together with 2,000 rounds of ammunition, but the true convictions of both Carter and Whittle were very doubtful about the fighter aspect, considering the limited thrust available from the engine. These feelings were expressed to Whitehall and, on the strength of George Carter's belief that a twin-turbojet design was required to fulfil the fighter role, it was accepted that a new design, with the company Type number G.40, would be an aircraft specifically produced to evaluate turbojet propulsion and Specification E.28/39 was raised to cover the project. Two prototypes were ordered,

to which serial numbers W4041 and W4046 were allocated.

Carter's design team produced an uncomplicated low-wing monoplane with a nose intake, the cockpit raised above the ducting to the WU, and an 81gal (368ltr) fuel tank between the cockpit and the mid-positioned engine, which had a straight-through jet-pipe exhausting at the fuselage rear. Two wing designs were to be produced, one featuring an NACA 23012 section and the other employing an EC1240 section, which was dubbed the 'high-speed' wing. The fuselage was fabricated as an all-metal monocoque clad with a light metal alloy stressed skin, with the two-spar mainplanes and tail unit treated likewise, while the elevators, rudder and ailerons were fabric-covered. This form of construction had already been applied to Gloster's F.5/34 fighter design and its basic wing planform, together with the fin/rudder configuration, was carried forward to the E.28/39. To compensate for the absence of propeller slipstream, both the rudder and elevators were designed on the large side and the all-metal hydraulically operated split trailing-edge flaps were similarly generous in area.

Construction Begins

In February 1940, when metal was first cut and the construction of W4041 started, tricycle-undercarriage experience in Britain was rather limited. General Aircraft had produced a modification to their ST.25 Monospar in August 1938, to meet an Air Ministry contract, in order to evaluate the configuration and de Havilland were working on a one-off tricycle-undercarriaged variant of their DH.94 Moth Minor. But Whittle had doubts as to whether his engine could produce enough power to lift the rear of a tail-wheeled aeroplane within the required distance to get airborne so, with the engine already basically an unknown factor, Carter decided to 'go for broke' and the G.40's layout incorporated a tricycle undercarriage with very short legs, which was designed and manufactured by Dowty Equipment Limited at Cheltenham. The steerable nose-wheel was operated by the rudder pedals and retracted rearwards, while the main wheels retracted inwards into housings in the wings, which consequently required bulging to the upper and lower skin panels due to the thin wing section. The whole sequence was hydraulically operated by an accumulator pre-charged

to 1,500lb/sq in, and a bottle of compressed-air was provided for the emergency lowering of the undercarriage. The boldness of Carter and Whittle's selection of a tricycle undercarriage can be appreciated when it is realized that both Willy Messerschmitt and Ernst Heinkel, who at the time were designing Germany's first turbojet-powered aeroplanes, did not take this radical step.

Although construction started at Hucclecote, the building of the large Hawker Siddeley shadow factory on the site, together with Gloster's existing works, made the whole complex a prime target for Luftwaffe attention. Consequently, in the summer of 1940 all work on the E.29/39 was transferred to a commandeered section of Regent Motors in Cheltenham (now buried under the foundations of a shopping precinct), under the management of Gloster's experimental department's superintendent, Jack Johnstone.

Power Jets constructed a special engine, the W1X with an output of only 750lb (340kg) thrust, which was really a rebuild of the original WU, to be used for taxiing trials and the positioning of auxiliary systems. As it was believed that the heat created by the rear bearings when at maximum power would need dissipating, a radiator was installed on either side of the intake ducts leading to the engine bay.

Taxi Trials

With the NACA 23012-sectioned wing installed and all systems preliminarily checked, W4041 was transported from Cheltenham to Hucclecote soon after dawn on Monday 7 April 1941, and in the late afternoon Gerry Sayer started up a turbojet engine fitted in an airframe for the first time in Britain. Hucclecote was still suffering from the effects of the winter and the W1X needed winding up to 12,000rpm before the aircraft would make its first movements. Sayer then gave way to Whittle for a few taxiing runs, but while he, Carter and Sayer appreciated that the soft ground conditions were not conducive to satisfactory taxi trials, observers to the occasion were a little disappointed that W4041 did not charge away like a Grand Prix car. The day was rounded off by the obligatory official photographic session.

The following day was dryer and Hucclecote's ground hardened enough for genuine taxi runs to be undertaken. Adjustments were made to allow the engine to run at

15,000rpm and Whittle made the initial run before handing over to Sayer. The next three weeks were taken up with a series of taxi trials, during which the W1X's speed was increased to 16,000rpm and several short hops were made due to the undulations on the airfield's surface. With the trials completed to everyone's satisfaction, W4041 was again prepared for road transportation. Besides Regent Motors, Gloster had requisitioned a garage section of the family motor engineering firm of E. R. Crabtree, also in Cheltenham, and the aircraft was delivered there for further work to be incorporated. It was appreciated that a longer-stroke nose-wheel would be required for a satisfactory take-off and this was fitted before full undercarriage retraction tests were carried out. The aircraft also required a camouflage paint finish and the then-current Dark Green/Dark Earth scheme was applied, with the underside painted bright

yellow. Type A.1 fuselage and wing roundels, together with equal-sized red/white/blue bands on the fin, brought it up to date so far as the national insignia was concerned. Also, a new system had recently been introduced, whereby serial numbers on important aircraft were given a 'G' suffix to denote that they required guarding whenever 'away from home'. Consequently, the first E.28/39 became W4041/G.

Flying Begins

It had already been recognized that Hucclecote's grass runway was unsuitable for G.40 flight trials and, because secrecy was of paramount importance Cranwell, with its 3,300ft (1,000m) hard runway in the unpopulated, open spaces of Lincolnshire and with only No. 3 OTU as a resident unit, was selected. Early in May 1941,

W4041/G was taken by road to the base where, coincidentally, Whittle had first consigned his theories to paper years before. At Cranwell, with the 860lb-thrust (390kg) W1 flight engine installed, the first E.28/39 was prepared for its maiden flight which commenced, with 'Gerry' Sayer at the controls, at 19.40hr on 15 May. A speed of 240mph (390km/h) was attained during the seventeen-minute flight, with the aircraft behaving quite conventionally, and although there was a slight over-sensitivity of the elevators, the flight was rated as being very successful.

Further flights were made over the succeeding two weeks, during which 300mph

On 10 May 1941, W4041 (before it was given the /G suffix) was given its Design Certificate for Flight Trials, three days after taxiing trials had commenced at 20.00hr on 7 April. Derek James

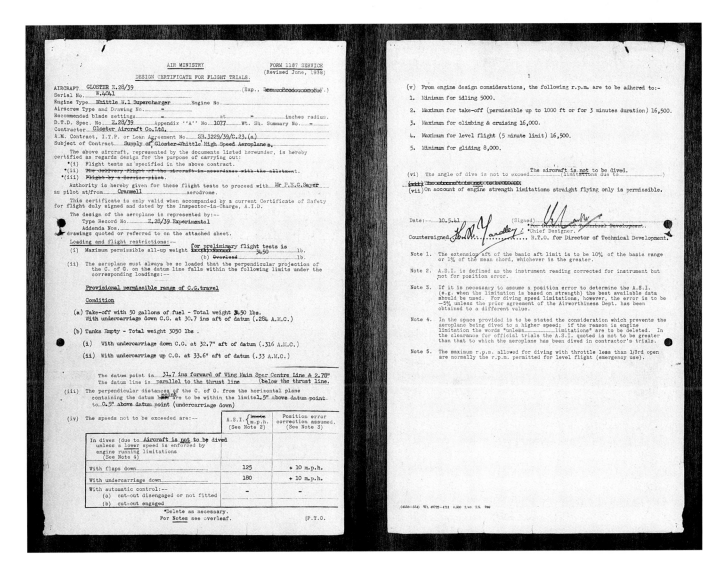

It seems amazing that the only record of the E.28/39's maiden flight was made on an amateur cine camera, from which this is a very grainy still. Derek James

decrease in atmospheric pressure at high altitude, but although the CTP reported that the W1A was a smoother-operating engine than the W1, the aircraft was grounded after the sixth flight, as the exhaust cone had wrinkled due to heat, while the clearance between the turbine blades and the shroud ring had reduced to below safety limits. Power Jets remedied the defects, and ten days later flying from Edge Hill was resumed. (During this period, the author was living in Banbury and much cycling was done over the 9 miles to Edge Hill, in order to get glimpses of the aircraft. Besides its quietness, the lasting impression is how small it looked.)

Further delays occurred two flights later when a turbine blade failed in flight, which produced vibrations serious enough for Sayer to reduce the engine to 10,000rpm and return to base. On completion of repairs, test flying was again resumed, with a series of high-altitude trials that commenced on 2 June. Troubles with the barostat's relay piston seizing up at 30,000ft (9,000m) were followed four days later by further vibrations and a complete flame-out due to a bearing failure through loss of oil feed. Sayer again brought the E.28/39 back

(480km/h) was exceeded on several occasions and an altitude of 25,000ft (7,600m) was reached. It was confirmed that, with a full fuel load, a maximum endurance of fifty-six minutes was attainable. Then it was back to Hucclecote for a detailed inspection, together with the removal of the W1 engine and the installation of a W1A, producing 1,160lb (530kg) static thrust.

From 15 August 1941, service camouflage for fighters – and so far as officialdom was concerned, the G.40 came into this category – was changed from Dark Green/Dark Earth to Dark Green/Ocean Grey. Type C.1 roundels were introduced, which had a reduced thickness of the white and yellow bands, together with a thinner width of white on the fin bands. W4041/G received the new colour scheme during its period of inspection at Hucclecote, as well as the prototype-aircraft marking of a yellow 'P' within a yellow circle aft of the fuselage roundel on each side, which had been promulgated in an Air Ministry order of 11 July 1941.

The Oxfordshire Era

Cranwell was too far from Gloster's works to make it viable as a lasting site for their experimental turbojet aircraft, so a search for an alternative was made and No. 21 OTU's base at Edge Hill, 9 miles north-west of Banbury in Oxfordshire, was selected. Being roughly equidistant between Hucclecote and Power Jet's facility at Lutterworth, Edge Hill was far more convenient that Cranwell, so late in January 1942 W4041/G

was again loaded onto a transporter, this time bound for the Midlands.

New taxiing trials with the W1A engine installed began on 4 February, before Sayer resumed full flight trials. A barostat had been fitted at the same time as the new engine, which automatically reduced fuel flow to compensate for the

In 1944, W4041/G was at RAE Farnborough and had acquired small stabilizing fins on its tailplane to correct slight instability encountered at higher speeds, together with the grey/green camouflage scheme introduced into Fighter Command on 15 August 1941. The shape of the stabilizing fins was altered slightly at a later date. Author's collection

to Edge Hill, but this time it was a dead-stick landing, which confirmed that the aircraft's basic aerodynamics were sound.

It was three and a half months before another W1A, with a modified oil system, arrived for installation and on 27 September 1942 the aircraft first flew with the replacement engine, for a demonstration before a visiting delegation of officials from the United States. However, the flight had to be aborted immediately after take-off, once again due to high-pressure oil-feed fluctuations. This time the under-side of the port wing came into contact with Edge Hill's tarmac on landing and was damaged. In retrospect, the summer of 1942 was not the happiest time for the E.28/39 project. Thoughts that things could only get better were dashed, however, when Gerry Sayer was killed in early October, when the Hawker Typhoon that he was flying collided with another, and both aircraft crashed into the North Sea.

Sayer's deputy, Michael Daunt, now became Gloster's new Chief Test Pilot. He had been fully appraised of the E.28/39's progress throughout the test flying, so his having to step into the breach at such short notice did not affect the programme so much as was first feared, and he made three preliminary handling flights on 6 November, after the damaged port wing had been repaired. The oil-flow problem had been cured by a combination of increasing the bore of the system's pipelines and applying substantial lagging as protection against the drop in temperature at high altitude.

This is thought to be W4046/G, the second prototype, here with its engine maintenance panels removed to reveal its W2/500 engine, which delivered 1,760lb (800kg) static thrust. The combustion chambers are surrounded by a substantial heat-shroud.
Author's collection

Second Prototype

Completion of W4046/G had been a rather lengthy process, due to the late arrival of the first Rover-built W2B flight engine. This 1,200lb-thrust (540kg) unit arrived early in February 1943 and towards the end of the month the aircraft, fitted with the EC1240 'high-speed' wing, was transported to Edge Hill for flight-testing. By this time, W4041/G had been transferred to RAE Farnborough, where the Establishment operated it under the security codename 'Weaver'.

Michael Daunt was fully occupied in preparing the first prototype of Gloster's twin-engined F.9/40, forerunner to the Meteor, for its maiden flight. E.28/39 flight testing was therefore put in the hands of John Grierson, who had joined the

company in 1941 as a production flight test pilot for the sub-contracted Hurricane and Typhoon programme, before becoming a member of Gloster's experimental test pilot team. W4046/G was his first prototype and it initially presented him with a brake-over-heating problem, due to the high idling thrust of the W2B. This was overcome so that, on 1 March 1943, he took the aircraft into the Oxfordshire air for the first time and followed this with a second flight on the same day. A dozen more sorties were flown during the next two weeks, and on 17 April he flew from Edge Hill to de Havilland's Hatfield airfield to give an impressive demonstration to no less a dignitary than the Prime Minister, Winston Churchill.

Farnborough Testing

On 3 May, W4046/G was flown to the RAE by another member of the experimental test pilot team, John Crosby-Warren, to join W4041/G for engine development flying. A new W2B/23 engine (later named the Welland), producing 1,526lb (692kg) thrust, was tested over a fifty-hour flight programme, which included trial maximum endurance sorties at 35,000ft (11,000m) under the jurisdiction of the Establishment's newly-formed Turbine Flight. A team of RAE pilots took part in

the programme, including the Flight's CO Sqn Ldr Douglas Davie, the RAE's Commandant Gp Capt Allen Wheeler, and Wg Cdrs Wilson, McClure and Macracken. After much 'string pulling', Frank Whittle obtained permission to fly W4046/G, but on the appointed day, the aircraft was declared unserviceable and was to remain so for what was officially stated 'an indefinite period'. Were they trying to tell Whittle something?

Troubles and Disaster

Near the end of July 1943 (when it is presumed that Whittle was otherwise engaged), flying was resumed and on the 27th, Wg Cdr McClure had a flame-out at 6,000ft (1,800m). He was very relieved when the recently installed relight switch operated successfully. Three days later, on 30 July, Sqn Ldr Davie applied full aileron at 35,000ft (11,000m), whereupon W4046/G yawed violently and the pilot was thrown straight through the canopy. His oxygen mask was torn off in the process and partial unconsciousness occurred during the ensuing 10,000ft (3,000m) free fall until his parachute deployed. He sucked oxygen from the emergency bottle to keep himself awake during the long descent and was lucky to eventually touch down with nothing more serious than frostbite in one hand. W4046/G hit terra firma much harder and was completely destroyed. The later investigation came to the conclusion that the aileron had probably jammed due to differential thermal contraction at the high altitude.

When photographed at Bentham, W4041/G had the EC1240-section wing, but no stabilizing fins, and it was carrying its title on the nose, as displayed at the Science Museum, London.
Author's collection

And Then There Was One

W4041/G had left the RAE in the late spring of 1943 and returned to the manufacturer, where a W2/500 engine was installed. This initially produced 1,700lb (770kg) thrust, which was later increased to 1,760lb (800kg). Michael Daunt undertook the first test flight with the new engine before handing the task of development flying to John Grierson. The Oxfordshire connection was maintained, but this time at No. 16 OTU's base at Barford St

John, 5 miles the other side of Banbury from Edge Hill. Gloster had been granted the use of half a T.4 hangar for F.9/40 testing while the company's airfield at Moreton Valence had its runway strengthened, and Grierson shared the facility for E.28/39 testing. An EC1240-section wing was delivered on 30 June to be fitted to the aircraft, and the maiden flight with the new mainplane was made on 6 July.

As F.9/40 test flying had now taken precedence over the E.28/39, the W2/500 was removed from W4041/G later in the

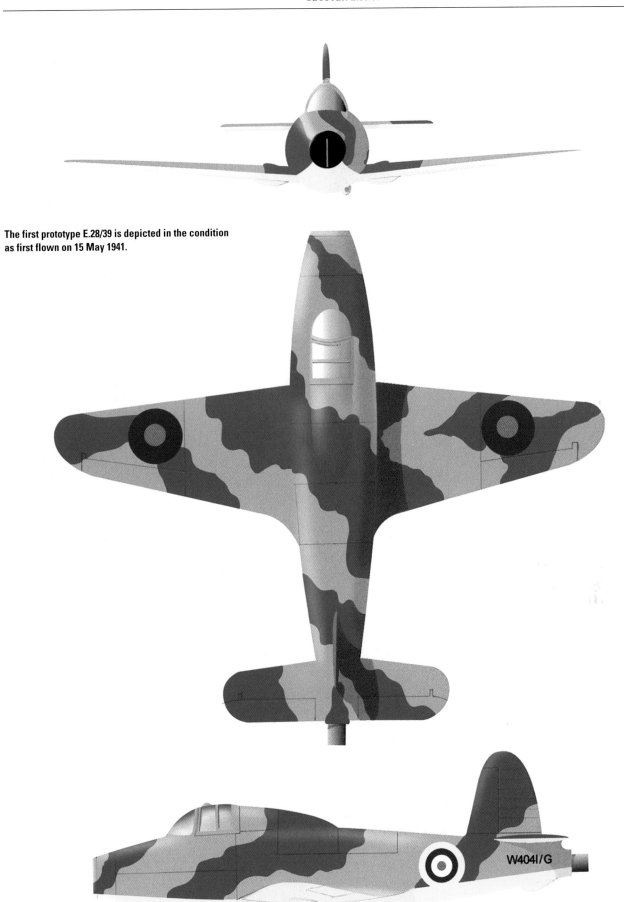

The first prototype E.28/39 is depicted in the condition as first flown on 15 May 1941.

summer of 1943, to be returned to Hucclecote for installation in an F.9/40 prototype, which goes to show how few turbojet engines were available at that time. The first E.28/39 prototype remained at Barford for many weeks before a replacement engine was delivered, and once it was installed the aircraft's test flying was taken over by RAE Farnborough. Modifications were made to the cockpit canopy and small stabilizing fins were fitted on the tailplane, to overcome the inherent directional instability which, while being acceptable in the high intensity testing programmes of the preceding years, was now considered worth curing at the more leisurely pace of the RAE. As the Meteor was now in full production, test flying of W4041/G became rather academic.

The name 'Pioneer' has been associated with the aircraft over the years, but this was never officially recognized by the manufacturer, the Ministry of Aircraft Production (MAP) or the Air Ministry. Gloster's Type number, G.40, has similarly grown out of use and the Specification number E.28/39 has universally been accepted as the aircraft's title. Another interesting fact is that the aircraft is one of the very few types that did not go to the A&AEE at Boscombe Down during some part of its development flying.

A certain amount of flying to provide aerodynamic statistics was made by the RAE, with the last flight being carried out on 20 February 1945. Its final move, to the Science Museum at Kensington, was made on 28 April 1946, and fifty-six years after its maiden flight the first E.28/39 is still on display, to substantiate Britain's early participation in the turbojet-powered era.

In 1980, this bronze plaque was erected on the site of the gateway to the former Gloster Aircraft Company's factory and airfield at Hucclecote, but sadly is there no longer. Derek James

Technical Data – Gloster G.40	
Dimensions:	Span 29ft (8.8m); length 25ft 3¾in (7.6m); height 9ft 3in (2.7m)
Powerplants:	W4041/G: One Power Jets W1X turbojet, producing 750lb (340kg) thrust, for taxiing only; one Power Jets W1 turbojet, producing 860lb (390kg) thrust; one Power Jets W2/500 turbojet, producing 1,700lb (770kg) thrust (this was later increased to 1,760lb (800kg) thrust; one Power Jets W2/700 turbojet, producing 2,700lb (1,220kg) thrust installed at RAE in March 1945. W4046/G: One Rover-built W2B turbojet, producing 1,200lb (544kg) thrust; one Rover-built W2B turbojet, producing 1,526lb (692kg) thrust
Weights:	Empty, approximately 2,890lb (1,310kg); loaded, approximately 3,750lb (1,700kg) NB: Weights changed with different engines installed
Performance:	Maximum speed with W1 engine 310mph (500km/h), with W1A 388mph (624km/h), with W2/500 460mph (740km/h), with W2B engine 476mph (766km/h); normal service ceiling 32,000ft (9,750m); maximum altitude reached 41,600ft (12,680m)
Production:	Two aircraft built to Specification E.28/39, with serial numbers W4041/G and W4046/G

CHAPTER TWO

De Havilland DH.108

The Tailless Trio

By December 1942 the British push in the Middle East, under General Montgomery, had started, but that was then about the sum total of British success in the war, apart from the Battle of Britain. Throughout the country's industries, design, manufacture and finance were totally concentrated on munitions, so it does indicate a mammoth slice of optimism that, in that month, the MAP should set up a committee, under the chairmanship of Lord Brabazon of Tara, to deliberate about civil air transport's requirements once the war was over.

The Brabazon Committee

As may be imagined, numerous meetings were convened without any form of decision being made, for the question 'how long will the war last?' was very much 'how long is a piece of string?'. However, in the summer of 1944, the British Overseas Airways Corporation (BOAC) did make a number of recommendations as to the type of aircraft that they would like to see being produced by British manufacturers for their operations

A section of their proposals centred on a paper written by Sir Geoffrey de Havilland on the prospects for the turbojet-powered commercial airliner, and these were embodied in the proposition submitted by the Committee's Type 4A (which became the de Havilland Comet). Naturally, with his company having a thriving engine division under Major Frank Halford, which already had its first indigenous turbojet, the Goblin, in production, Sir Geoffrey's arguments carried considerable weight and an eager design team led by

Ronald Bishop was given the go-ahead to come up with a realistic turbojet-powered long-range transport aircraft.

The Type 106 Design

The company Type number 106 was allocated to the project and, as the propeller did not feature in any requirements, some pretty radical ideas had been tossed around de Havilland's Project Office by the end of 1944. A layout based on the twin-boom configuration of the company's Vampire turbojet-powered fighter and a rear-engined canard type were among the proposals, as was a tailless design with swept wings. The Brabazon Committee issued its final report to the Ministry of Supply (MoS) in the late summer of 1945, and the Ministry was so impressed by the idea of a tailless DH.106 that an official aircraft recognition wall-chart was produced, depicting such an aircraft.

De Havilland appreciated that their swept-wing tailless project would require much research into the aerodynamics of this layout, and so they proposed that a small single-seat experimental aircraft would be required to investigate all aspects of this DH.106 design; the MoS strongly approved of such a prudent approach. The

company gave the experimental aircraft the design number DH.108 and the Ministry issued Specification E.18/45 to cover the design and construction of two prototypes under contract number SB.66562, the first to investigate low-speed characteristics, the other to be a high-speed trials aircraft.

The DH.108 is Born

In the interests of economy and as it was to be the swept wing that was to be evaluated, the design was based around the Vampire F.1 fuselage nacelle. English Electric's works at Preston was handling the building of a total of 300 Vampires under licence, so the tenth and forty-fifth fuselages from the first contract for 120 aircraft were taken off the production line for turning into the two swept-wing trials aircraft. The two fuselage nacelles were transported by road to de Havilland's works at Hatfield but one, VN856/TG283 (*see* below), went on to the RAE at Farnborough for a week. It was back at Hatfield by the beginning of October 1945 and construction of the two experimental aircraft got under way.

Their serial numbers on the Vampire line had been TG283 and TG306; however, the Ministry considered that new serials should be bestowed on them, so that TG283

The first prototype, TG283, on its maiden flight above the Woodbridge airfield on 15 May 1946. It is not known whether the undercarriage was kept down throughout the flight or had been lowered here while on the approach. *Aeroplane*

The wing tip-protecting skids and fixed leading-edge slats are discernable as TG283 crosses the airfield boundary road, with the lights set at red. *Aeroplane*

became VN856 and TG306 became VN860. The thinking behind this renumbering is difficult to ascertain, but then, it is probably better not to: before the end of construction the serial numbers VN856 and VN860 were cancelled and the two DH.108s reverted to the original numbers as allocated on the Preston production line. The two VN serials became void and were never reallocated to any other airframes.

Construction Begins

The new all-metal wings for TG283 were mated to the fuselage nacelle at the existing pick-up points. It featured a leading-edge sweepback of 43 degrees, with 25 degrees of sweep on the trailing edge, and the total span was 39ft (11.8m). The tall single fin, with a 51 degree leading-edge sweep, carried a conventional tip-balanced rudder, that operated in conjunction with the wing's elevons.

Although the undercarriage was also straight off the Vampire production line, the main wheels were actuated to retract inwards. Like the fighter's, the DH.108's fuselage nacelle had no ejector seat and was unpressurized, but its rear end was lengthened to take the single fin and was recontoured to meet up with the large

wing-root fairings. The question of there being no ejector seat was raised by the MoS, but when it was pointed out that the cockpit was basically of wood construction, so that the redesign and construction necessary to accommodate such a seat would cause considerable delay to the trials programme, the Ministry said no more on the subject. The work to create the first DH.108 was carried out in record time, and when TG283 emerged from the assembly shop in April 1946, this was only seven months from the time when the two fuselage nacelles arrived from Preston.

The RAE's Warning

Farnborough had been aware of de Havilland's work on an unconventional tailless design and expressed their opinion that there was considerable theoretical evidence to prove that such a configuration could enter into a 'Dutch roll' at low altitude. This would result in a wing drop with a loss of control at the stall, thereby inducing a spin from which, they considered, there would be little chance of a recovery. In view of this information from the well-respected Establishment, de Havilland incorporated large Handley Page slats on the leading edge, which were

locked in the open position. Cylindrical housings were fitted on each wing tip to take anti-spin parachutes and a small skid was attached under each housing, to protect the wing tips during uneven landings.

The DH.106 is Revised

During the time of the DH.108s' construction, Ronald Bishop and his design team came to the conclusion that a tailless configuration for a long-range civil airliner was fraught with potential problems, to a point where the whole conception bordered on the impractical, bearing in mind the limited experience in this field at that time. Therefore, it was literally back to the drawing board and the airliner design took on a more conventional appearance; the swept wings were retained, but at a reduced angle of sweep. While the design hardened to a more orthodox fuselage and tail assembly, it was during the prototype's construction that the name Comet was resurrected from the record-breaking DH.88 racer of the 1930s. On 27 July 1949, the gracefully proportioned prototype G-ALVG had its first flight.

First DH.108

Although the airliner's shape had changed, de Havilland proceeded with the experimental prototypes. The view was taken that swept-wing experience in Britain was very sparse, and while a certain amount of data obtained from the 108s could be incorporated in the Comet's trials programme, it would be valuable for the company's DH.110 all-weather fighter project, which was in the embryonic stage. On a more national level, research into swept-wing behaviour and handling would be of value to the aircraft industry in general.

TG283 was fitted with a de Havilland Goblin 2 centrifugal-flow turbojet, delivering 3,100lb (1,400kg) thrust, receiving air via the bifurcated wing-root intakes already proven on the Vampire. On roll-out, the aircraft's finish was overall matt silver, with Type C roundels on the upper and lower wing surfaces, but with none on the fuselage. The fin flash was red and blue, without any dividing white stripe, positioned above the regulation yellow 'P' in a circle adjacent to the engine's orifice. At that time, de Havilland had a strange anomaly with their presentation of serial numbers: a diagonal stroke was inserted between the prefix letters and the number on early production Vampire F.1s, but no official reason has ever been gleaned. This system was carried into the DH.108 fuselage nacelle, but the under-wing presentation was conventional, without the stroke.

Woodbridge

During World War Two, the increase in operational sorties flown by Allied bombers during the day and night offensive meant that even if the percentage of losses remained constant, a greater number of aircraft would be returning in a damaged condition. Experience had shown that aircraft often managed to reach the British coastline, but were unable to make it to their bases further north.

Consequently, in 1942 special emergency-landing airfields were constructed near the east coast, at Carnaby, Manston and Woodbridge. Each had a 3,000yd-long (2,740m) runway that was a very generous 250yd (230m) wide, with considerable additional under- and over-shoot areas at either end. The Woodbridge site, being in the middle of a dense coniferous forest area in Suffolk, was ideally situated from a security point of view which, while not being necessary in wartime, was certainly advantageous now, when an experimental aircraft, cloaked in secrecy, required to be test-flown.

A few days after TG283 was rolled onto de Havilland's dispersal area at Hatfield and underwent preliminary systems checks, it was dismantled to be taken by road into the depths of Suffolk. The rapid re-assembly and further systems checks carried out by a de Havilland Working Party meant that by the second week of May the aircraft was starting taxiing trials. With Geoffrey de Havilland Jnr, the company's Chief Test Pilot (CTP) and son of the founder, at the controls, the first DH.108 made some preliminary hops on 14 May.

Maiden Flight

The following day, Wednesday 15 May 1946, Britain's first swept-wing aircraft took to the air. The CTP carried out a trouble-free half-hour flight and on landing expressed complete satisfaction with the maiden flight of such an unorthodox aircraft. Further flights were made over the next four days, before TG283 returned to Hatfield on 19 May, for the future full flight-test programme to be carried out from its home base.

With typical impetuosity and without any reference to the constructors, the Under-Secretary at the MoS referred to the aircraft as the Swallow. The name became a colloquial title on the shop floor at Hatfield, but so far as de Havilland management was concerned, the aircraft was the DH.108, and was always referred to as such in all company literature and advertising.

As flying experience was gained, the RAE's anticipated low-speed instability did not materialize and speed was increased to the 300mph (480km/h) maximum imposed by the fixed leading-edge slats. An early lesson learned was that the elevon flying control layout on a tailless aircraft meant that it required a greater landing speed compared with more conventional aircraft. This was because the elevons were in the raised position to increase the angle of incidence and depress the wingtips, thereby reducing the usable wing area, which created a loss of lift from the outer sections. But these new characteristics were quickly mastered.

Second Prototype

Specification E.18/45 covered two airframes and they were both put in hand at roughly the same time. However, with the second aircraft, TG306, being for trials at the high-speed end of the flight envelope, a considerable number of modifications had to be implemented compared with TG283. In particular, the wing leading-edge sweep was increased by 2 degrees, to 45 degrees, and Handley Page retractable slats replaced the fixed units on the first aircraft. Additional wiring for fully automatic recording instrumentation was fitted and a Goblin 3, producing 3,300lb (1,500kg) thrust, was installed.

Geoffrey de Havilland brings the first prototype close to the camera, to display the individual way that de Havilland inserted a slash between the serial's letters and figures. This was unique in the first batch of Vampire F.1s, from which the first two DH.108 centrebodies were taken. Author's collection

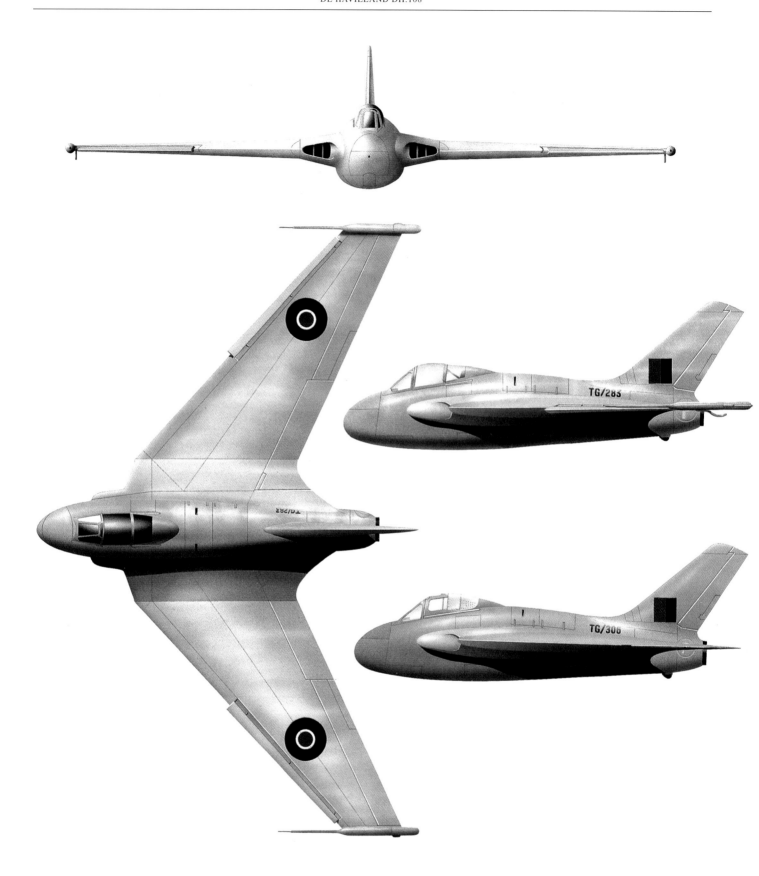

Three-view of the first DH.108 TG283, built to investigate slow-speed characteristics. BELOW: **Side view of the second prototype TG306 in the configuration for its attempt at the world's air-speed record.**

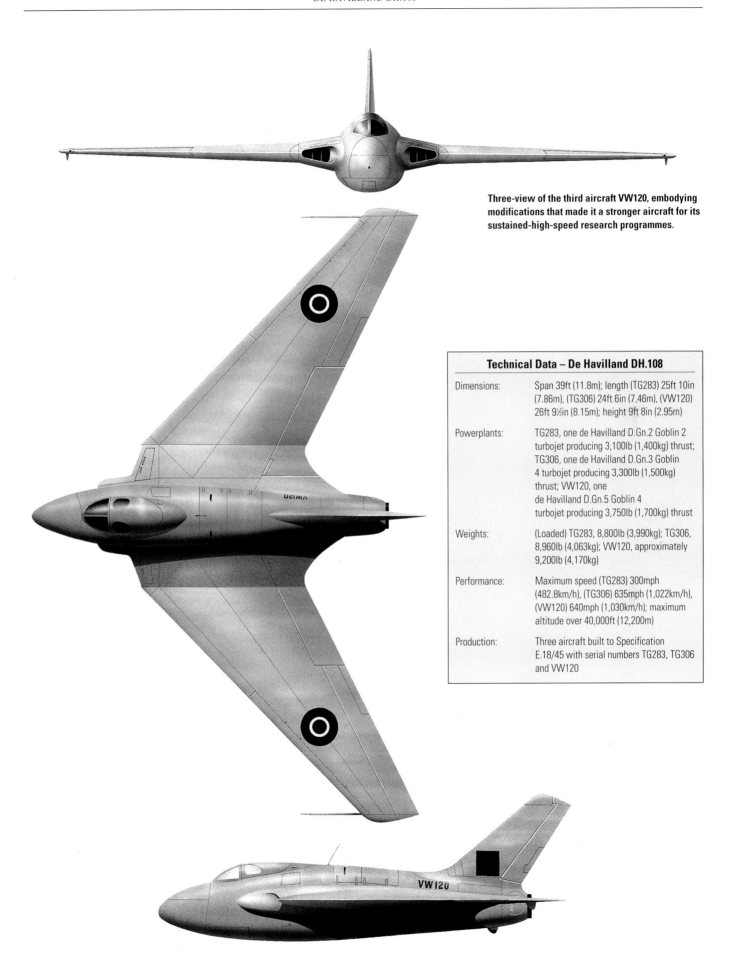

Three-view of the third aircraft VW120, embodying modifications that made it a stronger aircraft for its sustained-high-speed research programmes.

Technical Data – De Havilland DH.108	
Dimensions:	Span 39ft (11.8m); length (TG283) 25ft 10in (7.86m), (TG306) 24ft 6in (7.46m), (VW120) 26ft 9½in (8.15m); height 9ft 8in (2.95m)
Powerplants:	TG283, one de Havilland D.Gn.2 Goblin 2 turbojet producing 3,100lb (1,400kg) thrust; TG306, one de Havilland D.Gn.3 Goblin 4 turbojet producing 3,300lb (1,500kg) thrust; VW120, one de Havilland D.Gn.5 Goblin 4 turbojet producing 3,750lb (1,700kg) thrust
Weights:	(Loaded) TG283, 8,800lb (3,990kg); TG306, 8,960lb (4,063kg); VW120, approximately 9,200lb (4,170kg)
Performance:	Maximum speed (TG283) 300mph (482.8km/h), (TG306) 635mph (1,022km/h), (VW120) 640mph (1,030km/h); maximum altitude over 40,000ft (12,200m)
Production:	Three aircraft built to Specification E.18/45 with serial numbers TG283, TG306 and VW120

Because of the projected higher speeds, the cockpit canopy was reinforced with heavier metal framing, thereby reducing the glazed area by approximately 25 per cent. This whole programme of modification meant that TG306 was roughly three months behind the first prototype, and it was rolled out from the Hatfield assembly shop in early August 1946. At this time it too had anti-spin parachute housings at its wing-tips, but these were later discarded. The aircraft's finish was very similar to that of its predecessor, even to the diagonal stroke in the serial, but there the similarities finished. Geoffrey de Havilland Jnr handled its maiden flight on 23 August and quickly found that the second DH.108 was decidedly faster than TG283. At the time of this flight, the first prototype had been heavily tufted on the upper wing surface, prior to a new trials programme.

The second prototype, with its original cockpit canopy, at the 1946 SBAC Display, in company with a Vampire F.1, Bristol Freighter, Hamilcar Mk X and Bristol Buckmaster. The retractable leading-edge slats are in the open position. *Aeroplane*

Display and Disaster

On 12 and 13 September 1946, the Society of British Aircraft Constructors (SBAC) held its first post-war display. Handley Page's airfield at Radlett in Hertfordshire was the chosen venue and de Havilland's CTP demonstrated a fine selection of aerobatics with the second prototype which, considering it was only three weeks since the maiden flight, showed the company's great confidence in their unconventional design. The aircraft had already been flown at speeds in excess of the official World Speed Record of 614mph (988km/h), which had been achieved by Gp Capt (later Air Cdre) E. M. Donaldson in Gloster Meteor F.4 EE549 on 7 September of that year. De Havilland believed that TG306 could raise this speed by a considerable margin.

Therefore, after the Radlett display the aircraft went back into Hatfield's workshops to receive a series of modifications prior to an official record attempt. Alterations were made to the cockpit canopy by installing 50 per cent more metal framing and the wing-tip anti-spin parachute housings were removed. All panel joints were smoothed off to reduce drag and the whole airframe was given a gloss re-spray. A trials programme was established and the official south coast course near Tangmere, over which the Meteor flew, was to be used. During the third week in September, de Havilland Jnr made several

practice flights and the end of the month was chosen as the time to make the record attempt.

In the evening of 27 September, the company's founder watched his son take off from Hatfield for a simulated record run over the Thames Estuary. The schedule was for a high-speed run to be made at 10,000ft (3,000m), followed by a dive to the lower prescribed record attempt altitude. The CTP entered the dive but at 6,500ft (2,000m) the aircraft was seen to break up into several large pieces, which plummeted into the mud flats of Egypt Bay, near Gravesend. The fact that TG306 was not equipped with an ejector had no bearing on the pilot's death, for the break-up was so fast, and the ejector seats of that era were far removed from the sophisticated units of today. So Sir Geoffrey de Havilland had lost a second son in a flying accident involving a de Havilland aircraft, for his elder son John had been killed in an air-to-air accident while piloting a Mosquito in 1943.

A large proportion of TG306's wreckage was recovered and, as it was established that there was no engine failure, it was concluded that the loads induced on the airframe on approaching a speed of approximately Mach 0.9 had led to a complete structural failure. During the thirty-six days it had flown since the first take-off, TG306 had shown that an aircraft of

that configuration had great potential as a research vehicle and consequently, the MoS ordered a replacement aircraft under contract number 6/AFTC/1067/CB.6(a).

DH.108 Number Three

Many of the lessons learned through TG306 test flying were embodied in its replacement. A Vampire F.5 fuselage nacelle was taken as the basis and a more pointed nose cone, which had already been proven to be beneficial on Vampire F.1 TG281, was incorporated during the assembly of the third prototype. This aircraft was also intended for high-speed research and it was decided that this time an ejector seat would be installed. A new sliding canopy, with a lower profile plus a curved windscreen, had already been designed, so the lowering and extending further forward of the cockpit floor to accommodate the new seat, was a logical step. Glazing in the new canopy was reduced to the minimum required for safe vision (and to avoid claustrophobia), in order to maintain rigidity.

The 45-degree leading-edge sweep was retained and the Handley Page slats were made fully automatic. The fuselage was extended by 2ft 3in (0.68m) in order for it to receive a Goblin 4, rated at 3,750lb

(1,700kg) thrust. The serial VW120 was applied and a silver finish with national markings as applied to the two earlier aircraft, but de Havilland's fetish for the diagonal stroke had finally been excised.

First Flight

Following roll-out in mid-July 1947, systems checks and taxiing trials were carried out at Hatfield by the company's new Chief Test Pilot. Geoffrey de Havilland's successor was John Cunningham, who joined the company with a brilliant war record and on 24 July he took the third DH.108 for its maiden flight. His deputy, John Derry, was to share the aircraft's trials programme and this also included the flying routine at the 1947 SBAC Display, again held at Radlett. The success of test flying over the succeeding months encouraged the company's founder to consider entering VW120 into competitive events.

Record and a Bang

On 27 February 1948, Supermarine's Assistant Chief Test pilot, Mike Lithgow, flew an Attacker naval fighter over a 100km (60 mile) closed-circuit course in the New Forest, at an average speed of 564.88mph (909km/h), but Sir Geoffrey was convinced that VW120 could better this. He approached the MoS, technically the aircraft's owner, and they agreed to such a record attempt being made as a joint venture with de Havilland. A pentagonal course was laid out starting and finishing at Bell Bar, near Hatfield. The flight course would be via the Hertfordshire villages of Puckeridge, Arlesey, Sundon and Redbourne; this was actually 150m greater

TG306, showing the strengthened cockpit canopy fitted for the closed-circuit speed record attempt in 1946 and its leading-edge slats retracted. *Aeroplane*

than the required 100km which, the company was at pains to point out, would cost approximately 1mph (1.6km/h) in the recorded speed.

In the evening of Friday 12 April 1948, Derry flew VW120 around the course to raise the record to 605.23mph (947km/h), thereby bettering the Attacker by over 40mph, and this was using an engine that produced 1,350lb (612.2kg) less thrust than the Attacker's Rolls-Royce Nene.

Research flying continued throughout the summer of 1948 and the aircraft was scheduled for a flying slot on the final two days of that year's SBAC Display, which was to be held at the new venue of the RAE's airfield at Farnborough. Ever conscious of good publicity, de Havilland considered that VW120 was capable of exceeding Mach 1, and when better than during 'Farnborough week'? On Thursday 9 September, Derry took the aircraft for a high-altitude test flight. From above 40,000ft (12,000m),

he put VW120 into a dive and the angle of descent was increased to near vertical, by which point the pilot was getting no response from the controls. Power was reduced and gradually control response was regained, so that the aircraft was levelled out just above 20,000ft (6,000m). During the dive, Mach 1.04 was registered and supersonic flight was achieved for the first time in the United Kingdom, with the resultant sonic boom being heard over a large radius. A check of the instruments after landing showed a slight error in their registering, which meant that Derry's true speed had been Mach 1.2. The press coverage given to the achievement resulted in John Derry's exhilarating display at Farnborough two days later being even more

VW120 shows its pointed nose and revised windscreen as it taxies across the Hatfield grass. *Aeroplane*

ABOVE: **A pair of record-breakers. The third DH.108 was the first British aircraft to exceed Mach 1, achieved in a dive on 6 September 1948. Behind it is the Ghost-powered Vampire TG287, in which John Cunningham attained a new World altitude record of 59,446ft (18,119m) on 23 March 1948.** Author's collection

RIGHT: **The third prototype is towed out for the start of the SBAC Challenge Trophy Race held at Elmdon on 1 August 1949. Flown by John Derry, it lapped the course at 488mph (785km/h), coming in third.** Aeroplane

rapturously reported and the aircraft, together with its pilot, received what modern jargon would rate as 'star status'. Then it was back to the serious routine of precise research flying, until August 1949.

The 1949 SBAC Challenge Trophy Race was held at Elmdon, which today is submerged into the complex of Birmingham International Airport. De Havilland entered Vampire F.3 VV190, with John Cunningham at the controls, and John Derry flying VW120. The race was held on 1 August and Hawker's 'Wimpy' Wade won, flying the P.1040 prototype VP401. Cunningham came second and Derry third. The moist atmospheric conditions

prevailing on the day created visible shock waves emitting from the DH.108, which was the first time that such phenomena, so regularly generated by aircraft today, had been witnessed in Britain.

The Tailless Farewell

Nearly three weeks after the Elmdon race, on 19 August 1949, VW120 was transferred to full MoS ownership and based at RAE Farnborough. There it joined TG283, which had been with the Establishment for some time. This meant that de Havilland's handling of the two aircraft was dis-

continued, but the MoS ownership was rather short-lived. On 15 February 1950, VW120 crashed near Birhill in Buckinghamshire, killing RAE pilot Sqn Ldr J. S. R. Muller-Rowland DSO, DFC. Although the aircraft was fitted with an ejector seat the pilot did not use it, and the suggested cause of the accident as a failure of the oxygen supply may be substantiated by his not ejecting.

Three months later, TG283 also crashed, claiming the life of the pilot, Sqn Ldr G. E. C. Genders AFC, DFM. The three DH.108s contributed much useful data in those early days of swept-wing research, but it was at considerable human cost.

CHAPTER THREE

Saunders-Roe SR.A/1

The Water-Borne Fighter

Whether the concept of a flying-boat fighter was ever a viable proposition is debateable, but in 1944 'it seemed a good idea at the time'.

During World War Two, in May 1942, Kawanishi of Japan flew the N1K1 Kyofu float-plane fighter prototype and a small number were built before the project was cancelled. Similarly, in Britain the Blackburn Roc was originally designed as a twin-float seaplane fighter to Specification 26/36 and three examples were produced before the idea was discarded, for the aircraft to become a rather unsuccessful land-based fighter. Also, three Spitfire VBs and an LF IXB were converted to a float-plane configuration, but again the practical difficulties outweighed the concept. Blackburn also projected a fighter with a retractable hull, under the designation B.44, but this did not progress beyond the drawing board.

However, with the advent of the turbojet engine, which did not require a great propeller thrashing away either in front of or behind it, the idea of a flying-boat fighter seemed more promising. With a flying boat lineage going back to Sam Saunders' building the 'Bat Boat' for T. O. M. Sopwith in 1913, and only interrupted by the land-based A.10 fighter of 1928, the A.22 Segrave Meteor of 1930 and the Spartan range built in the early 1930s, Saunders-Roe was totally marine-oriented. Sir Alliott Verdon Roe gave up his shares in A. V. Roe Limited in 1928, to join the board of S.E. Saunders Limited, thereby forming Saunders-Roe Limited, which took on the recognized abbreviated name of Saro, although it was not an officially registered title. During World War Two the company was heavily involved in manufacturing Walrus and Sea Otter amphibians under contract to Supermarine.

A Concept is Aired

In the winter of 1943, Sir Arthur Gouge resigned from the board of Short Brothers to become vice-chairman of Saro. His was a dynamic personality, which was also steeped in the flying-boat tradition, and in the turbojet he saw an ideal power source for a single-seat flying-boat fighter. He tendered a projected company design to the MAP, emphasizing the ability of such a fighter to operate from inland waterways, as well as sheltered coastal installations. The suggestion has been expressed that Gouge had the Far East theatre of operations in mind for the project, but this has never been officially substantiated and the internal fuel capacity of the aircraft as designed would have been inadequate for the 'island-hopping' operations into which the Far East conflict progressed. But that is not to say that the aircraft could not have been adapted for such a role: adaptations of existing aircraft to fit varying and differing roles are still very prevalent today.

After Ministry-suggested amendments had been implemented into the design by Saro, the company was given the go-ahead to proceed with the project and the issuing of a contract was assured.

The hull of the SR.A/1 was designed to ride high in the water, as can be seen in this early take-off shot. Once lift had been achieved, the aircraft levelled out as it left the water. Author's collection

Contracted

Specification E.6/44 was written around the design, which carried the company designation SR.44, until a new SBAC nomenclature system was introduced into the industry and Saro's flying-boat fighter was re-designated the SR.A/1. Legend has it that the aircraft was colloquially known as the 'Squirt' within Saunders-Roe, but this has never been officially recognized.

The construction of three prototypes, allocated serial numbers TG263, TG267 and TG271, was contracted in May 1944. The MAP insisted that the final design was to be kept to a minimal practical size and was to have a service operating altitude that made a pressurized cockpit mandatory. It was obvious that the aircraft could not be single-engined, given the power that turbojets were producing at that time, but the diameters of the centrifugal-flow engines that were in production, Rolls-Royce's Derwent and Nene and de Havilland's Goblin, were considered too great for the side-by-side installation proposed for the SR.A/1, so at an early stage in the final design it was established that axial-flow engines would be required.

The Engines

With both Rolls-Royce and de Havilland's engine division firmly into centrifugal flow, only Metropolitan-Vickers (Metrovick) recognized that the axial-flow engine, with its smaller overall diameter, would give the aircraft designer more flexibility in terms of the size of a project to meet an operational requirement. They also had the added advantage of many years' experience in the field of industrial turbines. The axial-flow engine for aeronautical requirements was a logical step.

In 1942, only a year after its first bench-run, the Metrovick F.2 passed a Special Category Test for flight clearance. The first Lancaster prototype, BT308, was modified to become the engine's flying test-bed, with the F.2 fitted in the rear turret position, fed by a large dorsal intake built into the fuselage, between the twin fin/rudder assemblies. BT308 first took to the air with this installation on 29 June 1943, and on 13 November the engine became a prime power plant for the first time, when the third F.9/40 prototype, DG204/G, had its maiden flight from the RAE's airfield at Farnborough, powered by F.2s.

An improved variant, the F.2/4A, was designated the M.V.B.1 Beryl, before an example was installed in the rear of Lancaster B.II LL735 for test flying in 1945, and in 1948 a pair of Beryls powered Meteor IV RA490 for its SBAC Display appearance. Saro considered the Beryl, producing 3,250lb (1,470kg) thrust, to be the ideal engine for their SR.A/1 project, with the side-by-side installation of a pair of them enabling a narrow fuselage cross-section to be maintained, plus a fairly small oval-shaped nose air intake.

The Design Takes Shape

During the war, Saunders-Roe's design and production facilities were dispersed to various localities. Their main design department was at Beaumaris on the island of Anglesey, and this was the birthplace of the initial SR.A/1 concept. When the conflict ended on 8 May 1945 and the threat of air raids was finally eliminated, the design team relocated to another island site, East Cowes on the Isle of Wight.

The SR.A/1 being a flying-boat, the principal element to be perfected was the hull shape and Chief Designer Henry Knowler's early aspirations centred around a slim planing surface, in order to keep drag, in both the water and the air, down to a minimum. However, calculations showing that longitudinal instability could be a hazard determined that a more conventional hull with a length/beam ratio of 6:1 should be designed. The air intake was positioned high up in the nose and, in order to minimize the risk of water entering the nose section, a 10in (25cm) extension of the intake nozzle was designed to operate when the retractable floats were lowered. Such prudence was, in reality, found to be unnecessary and the actuating mechanism was only installed in the third aircraft, for a limited period of its life.

The wing-mounted floats were carried on struts that arced through 90 degrees inwards for retraction, while the floats themselves rotated through 180 degrees so that their planing surface was within the structure of the straight-tapered wing and their top-sides protruded below the wing's lower skin surface.

At the rear end of the planing surface, a small rudder was fitted for manoeuvring in the water at slow speeds, before the aerodynamic rudder became effective. This was controlled from the cockpit and

became locked in a central attitude once the aircraft was airborne. In order to keep the nose clear of water ingress at all times, the aircraft's hull enabled it to float in a tail-down attitude and the large two-spar single fin was constructed integral with the rear fuselage. The lower rear fuselage surface was swept sharply upwards to keep it clear of the water, with a broad fin/rudder assembly carrying the tailplane at the halfway-up point, to keep it clear of water spray and jet efflux.

The side-by-side Beryl installation was sited below the shoulder-mounted wing, with the jet-pipes positioned aft of the wing trailing edge and towed out at 5 degrees to the centreline. The single-seat cockpit was equipped with a Martin-Baker ejector seat, the first SR.A/1 prototype received the first production Mk. 1 seat. A sliding Triplex raised bubble canopy enclosed the whole pressurized cockpit and provision was made for an armament of four 20mm Hispano cannon, with about 800 rounds per gun, in the nose above the air intake. Underwing hard-points to carry bombs or rocket projectiles were incorporated in the wing's design, but during the whole of their lives, no armament or combat loads were ever fitted to any of the aircraft.

Construction Begins

The main components of all three aircraft were manufactured at Beaumaris and in Saro's leased building at Eastleigh, which is now absorbed into Southampton Airport. Assembly was scheduled to be carried out at the company's main facility at East Cowes.

Being water-borne, the aircraft was much larger than land-based single-seaters of that era. The majority of the structure was manufactured from light alloy, with the wing main spars and their attachment booms being of extruded aluminium alloy. The cockpit section was armour-plated and pressurized to 3.5psi. The two Beryls were installed in a substantial engine bay, which was entered via a large hatch aft of the cockpit; a fixed internal ladder enabled engineers to descend into the bay to undertake engine maintenance. Two fuel tanks were fitted into each wing, giving the aircraft a total capacity of 426gal (1,917ltr) and an attachment point was fitted under each wing to take a 140gal (630ltr) external 'slipper' tank.

Flying surfaces, including the flaps, were hydraulically operated and an electrical

circuit actuated the flap selection gear, the canopy sliding mechanism and the onboard fire extinguishing system.

When the outboard stability floats were lowered, the wing's inner structure was revealed; when retracted, the floats arced through 180 degrees, for the planing surface to be inside the wing and their top surface forming a neat fairing under the wing outer skin. Derek James and *Aeroplane*

Maiden Flight

In early July 1947, TG263 went down the East Cowes slipway and got its feet wet for the first time. Two years earlier, Geoffrey Tyson, who had previously been a test pilot with Short Brothers, had joined Saunders-Roe as their Chief Test Pilot, a post that he was to hold until his retirement nine years later. He started taxi trials in the morning of 16 July and found the aircraft to be so vice-less that he decided to make the maiden flight that evening. After a remarkably short take-off run, TG263 lifted off the surface of the River Medina that divides East Cowes from the yachting Mecca of Cowes. On landing, Tyson's only reservation concerned a slight directional snaking. As his previous experience at Shorts' involved their large C-class Empire flying boats, it is quite understandable why he found the much lighter SR.A/1 so eager to get airborne.

During subsequent flights made during July, turbulence was located at the leading edge of the fin/tailplane joint and a small acorn fairing was installed, which provided the remedial effect. The rudder horn-balance was slightly reduced to eliminate a minor tendency to roll and an even shorter take-off procedure was perfected by retracting the wing floats to reduce drag as soon as the aircraft attained lateral stability. The only mishap that occurred was in

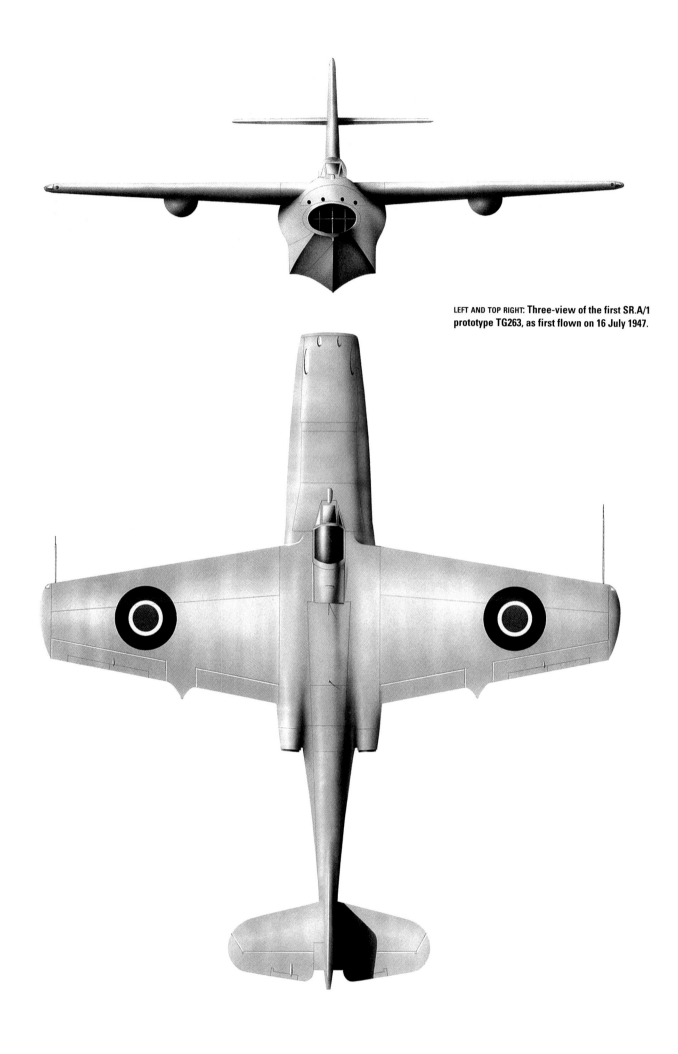

LEFT AND TOP RIGHT: **Three-view of the first SR.A/1 prototype TG263, as first flown on 16 July 1947.**

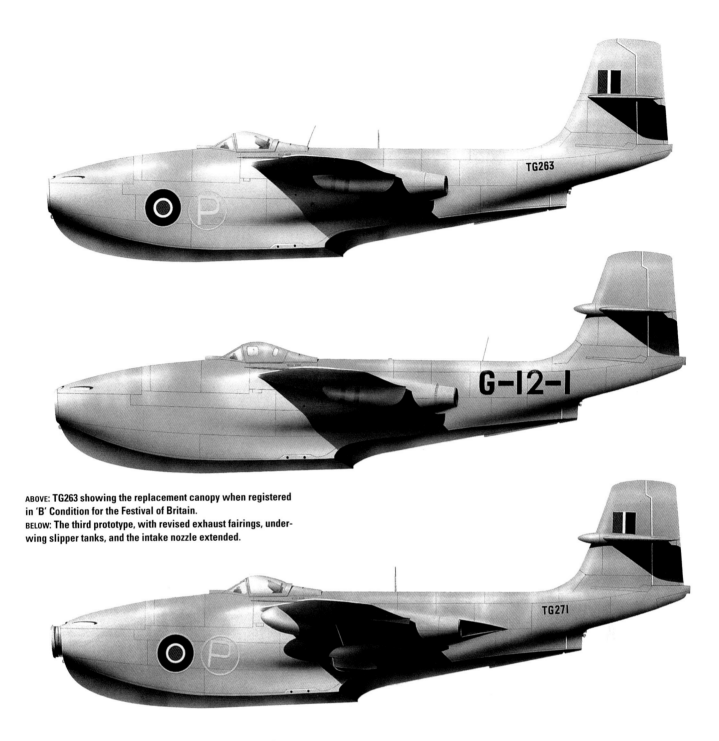

ABOVE: **TG263 showing the replacement canopy when registered in 'B' Condition for the Festival of Britain.**
BELOW: **The third prototype, with revised exhaust fairings, underwing slipper tanks, and the intake nozzle extended.**

Technical Data – Saunders-Roe SR.44/SR.A/1	
Dimensions:	Span 46ft (14m); length: 50ft (15.24m); height 16ft 9in (5.10m)
Powerplants:	TG263, two Metropolitan Vickers M.V.B.1 Beryl turbojets, each producing 3,250lb (1,470kg) thrust; TG267, two Metropolitan Vickers M.V.B.2 Beryl turbojets, each producing 3,500lb (1,590kg) thrust; TG271, two uprated Metropolitan Vickers M.V.B.1 Beryl turbojets, each producing 3,850lb (1,750kg) thrust
Weights:	Empty 11,262lb (5,107kg); loaded, without external fuel tanks, 16,255lb (7,372kg); maximum loaded, approximately 19,250lb (8,730kg)
Armament:	(Projected) Four Hispano Mk 5 20mm cannon, with 800 rounds per gun; two 250lb or two 1,000lb bombs, or eight 60lb rocket projectiles underwing mounted
Performance:	(TG271) Maximum level speed 512mph (824km/h); normal service ceiling 43,000ft (13,000m)
Production:	Three aircraft built to Specification E.6/44, with serial numbers TG263 (G-12-1 for a time), TG267 and TG271

The first prototype had a bullet fairing installed at the fin/tailplane junction fairly early in its flight trials, and the reinforced cockpit canopy had been fitted by April 1951, when this photograph was taken. *Aeroplane*

May 1948, when the transparent cockpit canopy parted company with the rest of the aircraft while in flight. Its replacement was of metal construction, with one small, and one even smaller, glazed area on each side; the aircraft still retains this canopy.

It has to be said that, considering the SR.A/1 was such a radical design as far as fighters went at that time, and the Beryl's only previous installation as a prime mover had been in Meteor RA490, the early test flights were comparatively trouble-free. The absence of a Service requirement for such an aircraft does not detract from its aerodynamic success.

The Second Prototype

Construction of the second aircraft had followed about nine months behind TG263 and during April 1948, TG267 was first launched into the River Medina. The horn-balance and acorn fairing changes made on the first prototype were incorporated in aircraft number two, which was also painted an overall Titanine silver, with Type C roundels, plus the regulation yellow 'P' in a circle. Metrovick M.V.B.2 Beryls, each producing 250lb (113kg) more thrust than TG263's engines, were installed and on 30 April, Geoffrey Tyson took the second prototype for its first flight, which was completely trouble-free. Manufacturer's flight trials continued throughout the summer, before TG267 left East Cowes.

The Marine Aircraft Experimental Establishment (MAEE) was transferred from its long-established base at Felixstowe during World War Two, to Helensburgh on the River Clyde. After the cessation of hostilities, a gradual return to Felixstowe was made and in autumn of 1948, TG267 was handed over to the Establishment for evaluation.

SR.A/1 Number Three

Four months after the second prototype, TG271, the third and last aircraft, was completed. Tyson completed his 'hat-trick' of SR.A/1 maiden flights on 17 August when he flew the aircraft for the first time. Power was provided by a pair of uprated M.V.B.1 Beryls, each giving 3,850lb (1,760kg) static thrust at sea level. A fully transparent cockpit canopy was fitted, as well as the linkage between the intake nozzle extension and the floats. The dive recovery flaps, on the wing under-surfaces behind the main spar, were also fully operable. TG271's wing floats were modified by having the planing surface aft of the step slightly more upswept, which required the wing trailing-edge fixed fairings, that covered the floats when retracted, to be slightly deeper.

At various times during its testing life, TG271 carried a pair of under-wing external 'slipper' tanks, although it is thought that this was purely to evaluate their aerodynamic shape and the handling of the aircraft with them installed. Whether they were plumbed in to be used as additional fuel tanks is uncertain.

Extensive engine test equipment was fitted to the third SR.A/1 and it is believed that modifications made to the area around the jet efflux were incorporated as a part of these tests. The two Hawker P.1052 research prototypes had 'pen nib'-shaped fairings on their fuselages, encompassing their Rolls-Royce Nene 2 exhaust outlets; a similarly shaped fairing was fitted on each side of TG217 during a part of its test programme.

Up-Side-Downs and Down

Three weeks after its first flight, TG271 was presented at the 1948 SBAC Display which was held at Farnborough for the first time. This was the SR.A/1's first and only appearance at the annual event, but it was certainly memorable.

Naturally, with Farnborough being devoid of lakes or rivers, each day's demonstration was a flying-only appearance, operated from East Cowes. The aircraft's agility was displayed to full effect during its routine, and for its finale each day, Geoffrey Tyson flew down the full length of Farnborough's main runway, from the 'black sheds' to Laffan's Plain, inverted a couple of hundred feet above the 2,000yd (1,830m) ribbon of tarmac. A special inverted-flight fuel valve delivered 18gal (81ltr) of fuel, to last for just one pass per day. The demonstration lives high in the SBAC Display's folklore.

In 1949, the Commanding Officer of the RAE's Aero Flight at Farnborough was Lt Cdr Eric Brown, who was also the Establishment's senior naval pilot and has the distinction of having flown more types than any other test pilot. On 12 August he took up Saunders-Roe's invita-

tion to visit East Cowes and fly TG271. He is on record as stating that the aircraft was surprisingly easy to manoeuvre in the water, although he found the virtual disappearance of forward vision until nearly at take-off speed rather disconcerting. About eighteen seconds after opening the throttles, the aircraft lifted into the air and following a dive made at a recorded speed of 550mph (890km/h), he observed that the deceleration provided by the airbrakes was very satisfactory.

Lt Cdr Brown was informed by radio of a shift in wind direction prior to landing, but the flat calm appearance of the water's surface encouraged him to approach at 110mph (180km/h) for a light touchdown and settlement in the water. Immediately before manoeuvring towards the aircraft's

berth, he saw a large baulk directly in his taxiing path and TG271 struck it with an enormous crash. The chunk of timber ricocheted out from under the planing bottom, hitting the starboard float with sufficient velocity to break it right off the wing, making its tip dip below the surface. The aircraft then cart-wheeled, before skimming along the surface in an inverted attitude.

In the early hours of Sunday 17 June 1951, TG263 landed in Woolwich Reach on the River Thames, carrying the 'B' Condition registration G-12-1. It was towed up river and moored off the South Bank, to become an exhibit in the British Gas Turbine Week of the Festival of Britain.
Author's collection

A Dramatic Rescue

Water poured into the cockpit area and, although he managed to clear his safety straps, together with his parachute, the pilot could not surface as he kept hitting the wing. As Saunders-Roe's recovery launch approached the inverted wreck at high speed, Geoffrey Tyson dived, fully clothed, into the water to rescue the RAE's CO, which he did in the nick of time: as they were being hauled into the launch, TG271 disappeared into the depths of the River Medina for ever. Before it sank, observers reported seeing two large holes forward of the main planing step.

The unfortunate experience did not deter Lt Cdr Brown from giving his opinion that the SR.A/1 was very enjoyable to fly and 'was a unique aircraft of unexpected quality'.

Another Disaster

One month later, Sqn Ldr K. A. Major of the MAEE was rehearsing, in poor weather, for a forthcoming Battle of Britain Day air display; these were annual events that were held at many RAF stations in those days. The precise reason for what happened during this rehearsal has never been fully determined, but TG267 dived into the North Sea off Felixstowe, broke up and sank, claiming the life of the MAEE pilot. The fact that he did not eject points to the crash being quite unexpected and the subsequent recovery of the wreckage did not add any further data to the episode.

With the sinking of the two aircraft, the whole SR.A/1 programme also sank. TG263 was put into storage and, following Metropolitan Vickers' decision to discontinue turbojet engine work for the aircraft industry, the Beryl also disappeared. The three flight engines for the SR.A/1, plus five spares, the one tested in Lancaster LL735 and the two fitted in Meteor RA490 remained the sum total of the engine's production.

Swansong

Armstrong Siddeley took over the remains of Metrovick's aero-engine work but, having their own Sapphire axial-flow turbojet in production here, as well as in the United States as the J65, there was no room for anything inherited from another manufacturer. They did make a loose suggestion that the remaining SR.A/1 could be converted to take a single Sapphire 3, but when the economics of the work required to redesign the hull were made apparent, this idea sank as quickly as had TG267 and TG271.

The Korean War brought about a slight resurgence in the flying-boat fighter concept and TG263 was brought out of storage in November 1950 to undergo new hydrodynamic trials. However, the disappearance of the Beryl programme meant that new engines would have to be selected. The resultant work to accommodate them, whatever they were, was considered financially and work-wise too much for Saunders-Roe to undertake, particularly as there would be no guarantee of a production order at the end of it.

Close-up of the ring of vortex generators around the jet outlet, seen on TG263 when it was displayed, on its beaching trolley, at Cosford in the 1980s. Author's collection

TG263's re-emergence did, however, encourage having it as an exhibit at the 1951 Festival of Britain. A new B-condition registration, G-12-1, was bestowed upon the aircraft and Tyson flew it to Woolwich Reach, from where it was towed upriver to the South Bank site at Waterloo where the Festival was to be held. Following the Festival's closure, the aircraft was presented to the College of Aeronautics at Cranfield in Bedfordshire.

While the SR.A/1 was at Cranfield, the starboard Beryl was removed, to power Donald Campbell's attempts at the World water speed record in *Bluebird*. Campbell broke the record several times, though *Bluebird*'s Beryl was replaced by a Bristol Siddeley Orpheus for his final attempt on the record, which ended with his fatal crash on Coniston Water in 1967.

In 1966, G-12-1 joined Skyfame's museum at Staverton, outside Cheltenham, and twelve years later it became a part of the Imperial War Museum's collection at Duxford. The B-condition registration was cancelled as the aircraft reverted to its original TG263 serial and carried Service markings once more. By 1994, the first SR.A/1 had moved to the Southampton Hall of Aviation, and is still there at the time of writing.

In the late 1940s, both *Aeroplane* and *Flight* carried Saunders-Roe advertising artwork on their covers. A painting, depicting SR.A/1-type operational flying-boat fighters returning to base in a peaceful lagoon, carried a caption stating that the base's runway had just been bombed. Eric Brown may have considered that a good load of logs would have put the base out of commission! Saunders-Roe's SR.A/1 programme was unique, with nothing like it ever being attempted by any other manufacturer. In the United States, Convair produced their XF2Y-1 Sea Dart delta-wing fighter with hydroskis, which first flew on 9 April 1953, with as much genuine ambition as Saunders-Roe had five years earlier. This project also sank without trace.

CHAPTER FOUR

Hawker P.1040, P.1052, P.1072 and P.1081

When first rolled out, VP401, the first prototype P.1040, had a wrap-round windscreen and rectangular heat shields aft of the jet-pipe outlets. Author's collection

Kingston Goes Propless

Hawker Aircraft first flew their Hurricane monoplane fighter on 6 November 1935 and delivered the first production aircraft to the Royal Air Force in December 1937. Their great rivals, Supermarine, had their first monoplane fighter, the Spitfire, airborne on 5 March 1937 and the RAF took delivery of its first of the type in December 1938. By the time that World War Two broke out, the RAF had 400 Hurricanes and 270 Spitfires officially in service.

It therefore seems rather surprising, considering how Sydney Camm, Hawker's Chief Designer, working in the company's Project Office at Kingston-upon-Thames, was so forward-thinking in the mid-1930s, that he did not approach the turbojet era until Specifications F.43/46 and F.44/46 were issued. Supermarine, on the other hand, had answered the call for a new turbojet fighter to meet Specification E.1/44, which eventually went into production

for the Royal Navy as the Attacker (*see* Chapter Seven).

No doubt the principal reason for Hawker's relatively late start with turbojet-engined designs was the fact that the company was up to its eyes with Typhoon and Tempest production, with the Fury hot on their heels. These were the fastest single-engined fighters in service at that time, with the promise that later Sabre, Griffon and Centaurus engines would provide the aircraft with even greater performance.

The Powerplant

In 1944, Rolls-Royce drew up plans for a new centrifugal-flow turbojet with a design rating of 4,000lb (1,800kg) thrust. It was considered capable of being developed to provide a much greater output that would place it as the most powerful turbojet engine in the world. It featured the double-sided impeller of the Derwent,

but was physically larger, being 6½in (16.5cm) greater in diameter, nearly 14in (35.5cm) longer and weighing over 300lb (140kg) more than its predecessor.

With an MAP contract covering the design and manufacture of prototype engines firmly in hand, the company's Barnoldswick section produced the B.40 design, with an output of 4,200lb (1,900kg) static thrust. On 27 October 1944 a refined variant, the RB.41, was first bench-run, when it surpassed the company's ambitious hopes by giving an output of 5,000lb (2,300kg) thrust. The engine was put into production in 1945 as the Nene, to power the Supermarine Attacker, and Sydney Camm saw it as being the ideal power plant around which to design Hawker's first turbojet fighter.

Test flying of the Nene was carried out with Lancastrians VH742 and VH737, while Vickers Viking VX856/G-AJPH was converted to have a pair, in order to evaluate civil airlines operating with turbojet aircraft. But an agreement with the MAP and the Treasury determined that Nene production would be on a limited scale, with around only 1,000 units being built, the eventual service installations of the engine being in the Attacker and the Hawker Sea Hawk, which grew out of the P.1040 programme. The second Armstrong Whitworth AW.52, the Avro Tudor Mk 8, all six Avro Ashtons, early Supermarine Type 510 and Type 535 swept-wing research aircraft and Boulton Paul's little P.111 delta-wing research aircraft were all powered by the Nene, and the second prototype Canberra was fitted with two for test flying, as an insurance against development of the more powerful Rolls-Royce Avon hitting a major snag. This was the sum total of the engine's applications in the United Kingdom.

However, before the engine went into production, the British Labour Government, as part of the 1946 Anglo-Soviet Trade Agreement, made a present of six Nenes to the Mikoyan-Gurevich design bureau. It was soon copied and put into production as the RD-45F, without any consideration of a licence agreement with Rolls-Royce, and a later development by V.K. Klimov as the VK-1 powered the many thousands of MiG-15 fighters built to various configurations.

The P.1040 Airframe

The first Hawker jet, the P.1035 was initially a private venture. With so much of their design work in the Tempest and the Fury being centred around an elliptical wing with square tips, it was logical that Camm's initial thoughts for a turbojet-powered aircraft should involve a similar wing plan-form, and the P.1035 project was in essence a Fury with wing-root intakes, the cockpit positioned further forward and a long jet-pipe exhausting at the rear. But it was already being appreciated that, with the long jet-pipe, there was a considerable loss of thrust and Hawker's drew up plans for a bifurcated jet-pipe with an outlet on each side of the fuselage, aft of the wing-root trailing edge. In collaboration with Rolls-Royce, they patented the layout.

Camm may have entered the turbojet age behind Supermarine, but his designs were far more graceful and visually appealing. A refining of the P.1035 project brought about the P.1040. The upper and lower centre-section surfaces of the

straight-edged, tapered wing, blended into a sleek fuselage, with its cockpit sited far forward under a transparent one-piece canopy, ahead of which was a curved windscreen. Wing-root intakes in either side of the leading edge centre-section supplied air to the Nene installed aft of the engine equipment bay behind the cockpit. The bifurcated jet-pipes allowed the main fuel tank to be fitted between them, with a smaller slipper-tank situated between it and the engine's circle of combustion chambers.

From rectangular exhaust fairings on either side of the jet-pipes, the rear fuselage tapered sharply to meet a gracefully curved fin/rudder assembly, to which a straight tapered tailplane was attached either side halfway up its height. The tricycle undercarriage featured Hawker's familiar wide-track main wheels, which retracted inwards, with the nose-wheel retracting forwards into the nose-cone.

Rebuff and Acceptance

Because of the unorthodoxy of the design, only tentative interest was expressed by the Air Staff, together with the Admiralty, but this was encouragement enough for Hawker to go ahead and manufacture a prototype on a private venture basis. However, after metal had initially been cut at the end of 1945, the Air Ministry opined that the brochure performance of the P.1040 did not show sufficient improvement over the Meteors in service

to justify financing the aircraft's trials programme. So far as they were concerned, the aircraft was a non-starter.

However, the Admiralty's attitude was quite the opposite and they expressed enough enthusiasm for Specification N.7/46 to be issued, to cover the continuation of the prototype already being built, plus two more to be evaluated as a naval fighter to succeed the Attacker. A fourth airframe was to be built for structural testing. Hawker Aircraft were delighted, and component and sub-assembly manufacture went ahead at Kingston. From there they were to be transported to the company's large works at Langley in Buckinghamshire for final assembly.

The Prototype Emerges

In early August 1947, the graceful first P.1040 was rolled out. It was unpainted and minus the cockpit canopy when Hawker's Chief Test Pilot Bill Humble taxied the aircraft for the first time over the grass airfield, seated on a Malcolm ejector seat. (This was a short-lived design built by ML Aviation of White Waltham.) Systems checks were carried out but Langley only had a grass runway and the factory's future was too uncertain, due to the expansion of nearby Heathrow, for a concrete runway to be constructed. Therefore, with everything checked as far as possible, with the cockpit canopy installed, an overall silver finish with C-Type national markings, the obligatory yellow prototype 'P' between the

Sqn Ldr Trevor 'Wimpy' Wade takes the aircraft for an early air-to-air photocall, but the jet-pipe heat shields had been modified to a 'pen-nib' shape. *Aeroplane*

fuselage roundels, and the serial VP401, the aircraft was prepared for transportation by road to the A&AEE's vast complex at Boscombe Down, where it would start initial flight trials.

First Flight

VP401 arrived at Boscombe Down towards the end of August 1947 and Bill Humble carried out more detailed taxiing trials before taking the aircraft into the air for the first time on 2 September. Three days later, the P.1040 was transferred to Farnborough for the continuation of test flying.

Later in September, a modification was made to the windscreen, in that it was changed to a flat surface, to alleviate the distortion encountered during early flights. The rectangular heat shields aft of the jet-pipes had been found to induce vibration, so a redesign – giving a more streamlined and 'pen-nib' appearance – was put in hand. A bullet fairing was fitted at the intersection of the fin and tailplane in order to raise the critical Mach number.

As the SBAC Display was held at Radlett, as in the previous year, the testing was not compromised by Farnborough being taken over for the annual event and, in fact, it was in September 1948, when the RAE's airfield was first used for the Display, that VP401 made its first public appearance.

By that time the first P.1040 was viewed principally as a research vehicle to establish the type as a suitable RN fighter. Provision

had been made at the design stage for a four-cannon armament in the nose, but this was not installed in VP401. The second and third prototypes, VP413 and VP433, were fully 'navalized', with folding wings, cannon armament, arrester hook, plus a name, Sea Hawk. VP413 also undertook carrier landing trials on HMS *Illustrious*, but the development of the Sea Hawk into an operational aircraft falls outside the sphere of this narrative.

On 1 August 1949, Sqn Ldr Trevor 'Wimpy' Wade flew VP401 in the National Air Races at Elmdon, to win the SBAC Challenge Cup at a speed of 510mph (820km/h). One month later, with its work in the N.7/46 programme completed, it returned to Kingston for conversion into the P.1072, which will be featured later in this chapter.

P.1052

While P.1040 trials were proceeding through 1948, Hawker began construction of their first aircraft for research into the aerodynamics of swept wings. To meet Specification E.38/46, two flying prototypes were ordered, under the designation P.1052, with a third structural test airframe. As the P.1040 design concept was firmly established, the new aircraft featured an identical fuselage and tail assembly. A new wing had a 35-degree sweep on its leading edge and deeper, but shorter, air intakes for the proposed Nene RN.2, which was rated at 5,000lb (2,300kg) static thrust. The first

prototype, VX272, came out from the company's new shop at Kingston in the autumn of 1948, with a natural metal finish and similar markings to VP401. It was disassembled for going by road to Boscombe Down where, after reassembly and taxiing trials, it was given its maiden flight in the hands of Trevor Wade on 19 November.

The second P.1052, VX279, followed five months later. It too went to Boscombe Down, from where Wade made the first flight on 13 April 1949. Exactly one month later, on 13 May, he flew VX272 to establish a new London-to-Paris record. The 221 statute miles (336km) were flown in 21 minutes 27 seconds, giving an average speed of 617.9mph (994.3km/h), thereby clipping nearly seven minutes off the former record made by a Meteor T.7.

A Catalogue of Mishaps

The RAE received VX272 at Farnborough in June 1949 and VX279 went to the A&AEE for an assessment at the request of the Royal Australian Air Force (RAAF). They found the aircraft pleasant to fly, with good acceleration at high altitude. A level speed of 592mph (953km/h) was attained at 25,000ft (7,600m), but it was considered that the elevators were too heavy during turns of Mach 0.9 and the Nene's thrust was inadequate to sustain turns at that speed.

Towards the end of September 1949, VX272 suffered a failure of the fuel pump drive and the resultant forced landing

By early 1948, the distortion created by the original wrap-round windscreen had been eliminated, with the fitting of a new flat-glass-framed screen. *Aeroplane*

ABOVE: Hawker's first turbojet prototype attended the 1948 SBAC Display, now moved from Radlett to Farnborough. It stands beside RA490, the Metrovick Beryl-powered Meteor F.4, with the Avro Tudor Mk 8 VX195 in the background. Author's collection

BELOW: VP413, the second prototype P.1040, became the first N.7/46 for the Royal Navy, which went into production as the Sea Hawk. It had fully folding wings and provision for an arrester hook, which was installed at a later date than this photograph. Derek James.

caused damage that took until March 1950 to repair. Test flying was resumed, but on 24 July a partial undercarriage failure during landing put the aircraft back into the works for another repair, which took over a year. On its first flight following completion of the repair, a failure of the undercarriage retraction system resulted in VX272 having to be repaired for the third time.

Mixed Histories

At this point, the lives of VX272 and VX279 become rather entwined. Tests on the structural airframe had indicated that a strengthening of the wing spars and main spar fuselage frames should be implemented. This was applied to VX279. Also, it had been the intention for some time to

install a swept all-flying tailplane on the P.1052, but this had been a rather protracted affair and it had not been introduced so far.

However, the continuing interest by the RAAF led to VX279 being returned to Kingston for modifications to accept a new Rolls-Royce engine, the Tay. This required a complete redesign of the whole rear fuselage, so the aircraft's existing strengthened rear fuselage was grafted onto VX272, with the additions of an arrester hook for future deck-landing trials, together with a large bullet fairing fitted at the fin/tailplane intersection to improve handling at higher Mach numbers. (The future career of VX279 is described under 'P.1081', see p.38.)

The long-stroke undercarriage oleos developed for production Sea Hawks were

fitted to VX272. The A&AEE had reported in its assessment that deck-landings were considered entirely feasible, so trials on HMS *Eagle* commenced, although they were really only of academic interest. For the trials the aircraft acquired the then-current Royal Navy colour scheme of Sea Grey and Duck-egg Green. However, on completion of its association with the Navy, a swept tailplane was at last installed and the aircraft went to RAE Farnborough for flight trials. These continued over a three-month period, until VX272 once again became the victim of a crash landing and, although repairs were put in hand, the aircraft's useful flying days had come to an end. On completion of the repairs, VX272 was given the Instructional Airframe number 7174M, to spend a considerable time at both Cardington and

ABOVE AND RIGHT: VX272 was the first prototype P.1052, a P.1040 fuselage with a 35-degree swept wing. When it was initially flown, in 1948, it was in an overall metal finish, with service roundels but no fin flashes; later it was painted in Fleet Air Arm colours. *Derek James and author's collection*

BELOW: The second prototype P.1052, VX279, was resplendent in Hawker's special colour, referred to as 'duck-egg green'. *Author's collection*

Colerne in this capacity. After numerous revisions to its paint finish, it reverted to its VX272 serial before being passed to Cosford's Aerospace Museum, as it was known in the 1970s. Today, VX272 is held by the Fleet Air Arm Museum at RNAS Yeovilton, but is not on display at the time of writing.

The P.1072

Hawker certainly got good mileage out of their original N.7/46 and E.38/46 airframes. In October 1945, the MAP had intimated an interest in having the P.1040 powered by a rocket motor, although no such power plant existed and the idea was quietly shelved with the Royal Navy's firm commitment to the N.7/46 with its Nene. The manufacturers themselves had examined the rocket-propelled idea and had designed such an aircraft under the designation P.1047. But again, the absence of a suitable rocket motor brought about the cancellation of the project.

At Last, a Rocket Motor

In 1947, Armstrong Siddeley began work on a rocket motor, with a designed output of 2,000lb (900kg) thrust. Designated the Snarler ASSn.1, the motor was fed with liquid oxygen combined with water/methanol, and had an all-up-weight of only 215lb (98kg). Development was also put in hand to replace the water/methanol by ordinary turbojet fuel. The Snarler was viewed as an auxiliary power source to increase an aircraft's rate of climb, and not as a prime mover. The MAP renewed its interest in the scheme and, with VP401's constructive input into the N.7/46 programme ended, the aircraft was earmarked for modification to take a Snarler.

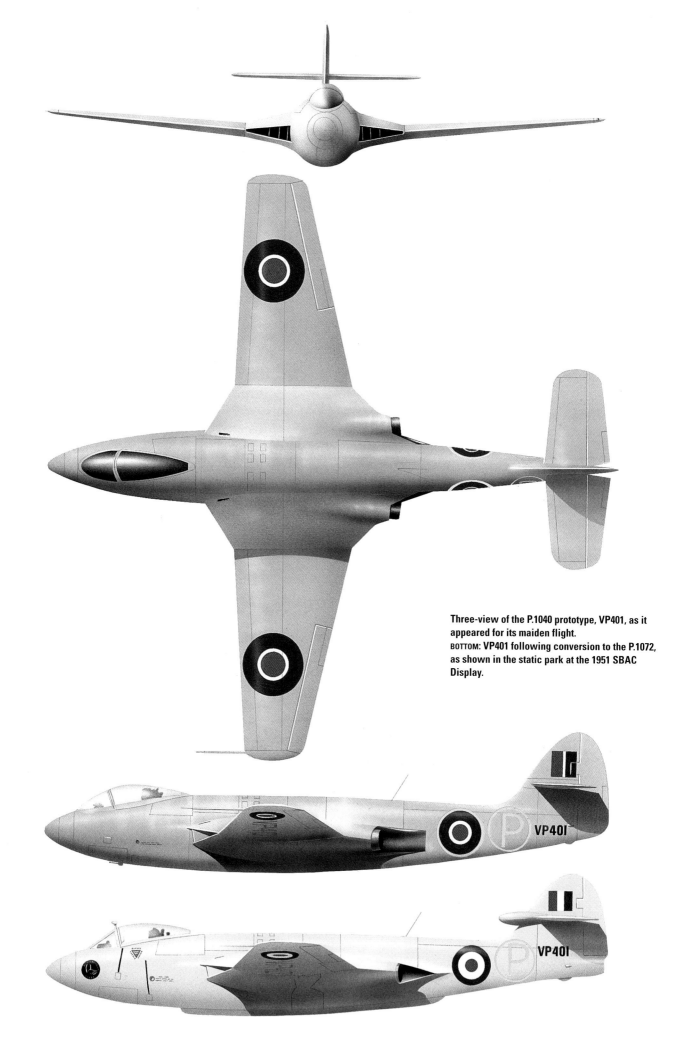

Three-view of the P.1040 prototype, VP401, as it appeared for its maiden flight.
BOTTOM: VP401 following conversion to the P.1072, as shown in the static park at the 1951 SBAC Display.

VP401

VP401

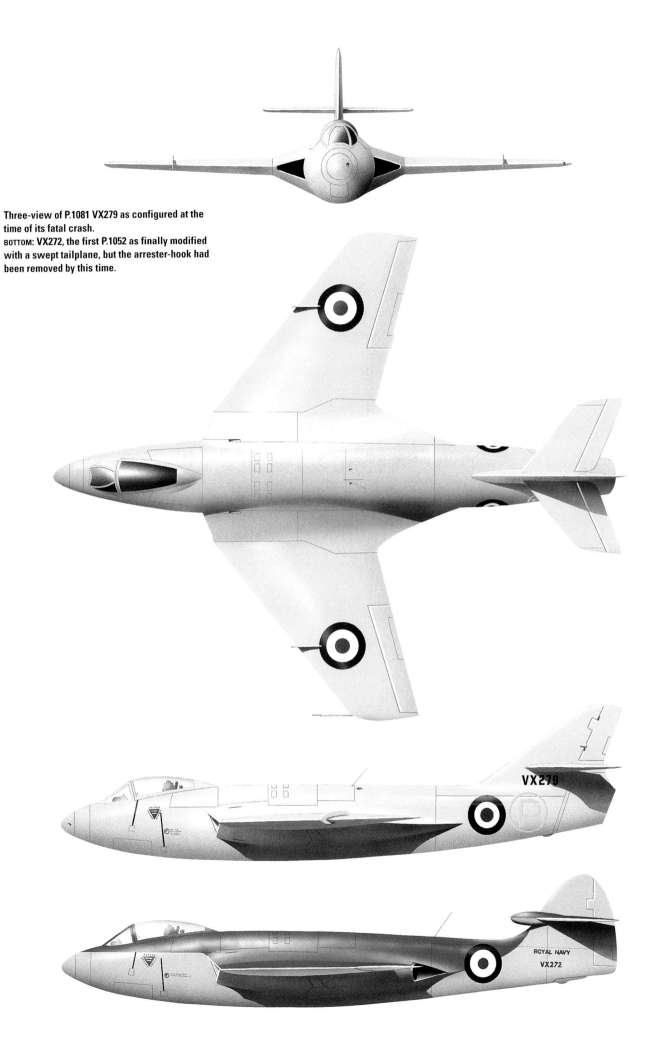

Three-view of P.1081 VX279 as configured at the time of its fatal crash.

BOTTOM: VX272, the first P.1052 as finally modified with a swept tailplane, but the arrester-hook had been removed by this time.

VX279

ROYAL NAVY
VX272

The first P.1040 was modified in 1949 to become the P.1072, with an Armstrong Siddeley rocket motor in a redesigned rear fuselage and a modified fin/rudder assembly. Author's collection

VP401 returned to Kingston in September 1949 for this work to be put in hand. The rocket motor was installed in the rear fuselage extremity, under the tail assembly. The fin area was increased but the rudder was actually reduced. An external rear-view mirror placed above the windscreen enabled the pilot to monitor the rocket motor's activity.

A Revised Fuel System

New internal fuel tanks were installed. The forward fuselage slipper tank was modified to hold 75gal (338ltr) of liquid oxygen and an additional tank was sited further aft to carry 120gal (540ltr) of water/methanol. Together, the new tanks reduced the aircraft's kerosene capacity by about 50 per cent. During the conversion, VP401's Nene RN.1 was replaced by an RN.2, developing 500lb (230kg) more thrust. The plumbing for the Snarler was routed in an external under-fuselage pipe, covered by a fairing that gave the appearance of the aircraft having a ventral keel. The rocket motor's endurance was 2.75 minutes, during which its 2,000lb (900kg) thrust augmented the Nene's 5,000lb (2,300kg) output, to produce a considerable amount of power.

New Designation, but a Short Life

With all these revisions, VP401 ceased to be a P.1040 and was given the new designation P.1072. As such, the aircraft had its maiden flight on 16 November 1950 on the power of the Nene alone, to be ferried to Armstrong Siddeley's test facility at Bitteswell in Leicestershire. On 20 November, the Snarler was fired in flight for the first time, giving the aircraft a dramatic increase in climbing speed.

However, the Nene/Snarler combination was short-lived. Hawker's CTP, 'Wimpy' Wade and his assistant, Sqn Ldr Neville Duke, both flew the aircraft three times before, on 19 January 1951, when Duke was relighting the Snarler the unit exploded, setting the tail unit on fire. The pilot immediately shut the rocket motor down and made an emergency landing at Bitteswell on the power of the Nene.

Inspection of the damage showed it not to be as severe as feared and a repair was completed in just over a month. But during this time, official policy on rocket motors had changed. The reheat abilities of turbojet engines had been developed to a point where they were a much more viable proposition, and no further finance was forthcoming for the P.1072 project. Consequently, the Snarler was never used again and VP401 had three years of unproductive flying on Nene power, together with being a rather pointless static exhibit at the 1951 SBAC Display, before being scrapped in the autumn of 1954.

The P.1081

VX279's return to Kingston was sponsored by the continuing RAAF interest in a Hawker replacement for their Meteor F.8s and by Rolls-Royce's Tay RTa.1 development of the Nene. The principal improvement over the latter was the Tay's reheat facility, which was foreseen as providing 20 per cent more power. Furthermore, its construction made much more use of magnesium alloys, in order to reduce the all-up-weight.

With the Tay having reheat, Hawker's bifurcated jet exhausts had to go, so a new layout for VX279 involved a completely new fuselage aft of revised wing fairings,

with a straight-through jet-pipe exhausting via a large diameter orifice, and a new swept tail assembly sitting above the outlet. The whole revision was accomplished in six months and, as this was well in advance of Rolls-Royce's progress with the Tay, VX279 retained its Nene RN.2 with a long tailpipe, in order to obtain flight data for the new configuration. The former second prototype P.1052 now became the Hawker P.1081 and it followed the well-worn path to Boscombe Down, resplendent in an overall glossy pale green colour scheme. Trevor Wade gave the aircraft its first flight on 19 June 1950 and development test flying proceeded at a concentrated pace, with just a week's break to have a daily flying slot at that year's SBAC Display.

Improving the Performance

Although the installed Nene's thrust was well below the design output of 6,250lb (2,830kg) envisaged for the Tay, VX279 was attaining Mach 0.89 in level flight at 36,000ft (11,000m) and close to 700mph (1,130km/h) at sea level. This was an improvement of 40 per cent over the Meteor F.8, attained with considerably less power. It was considered that this would be sufficient to keep Australian interest alive.

Flight testing indicated that directional stability could benefit from an increase in fin area, and a modification was made that faired the fin trailing edge into the fuselage rear end, above the jet-pipe outlet. Large wing fences were fitted to the wing top surface at approximately 60 per cent span, to cure airflow turbulence over the outer wing.

The Death Knell

Rolls-Royce's November 1950 cancellation of the whole Tay programme, in favour of their new AJ.65 axial-flow engine (later to become the Avon), put paid to Hawker's ambitions of an Australian contract. The P.1081 with a Nene did not hold favour with the RAAF: they wanted a good swept-wing fighter to equip their squadron engaged over Korea, to give them some semblance of parity with the MiG-15. The requirement was met by their Common-wealth Aircraft Corporation manufactur-ing the North American F-86 Sabre under licence, but the Korean conflict was over before it could make any contribution.

As the CA-27, the aircraft was powered by an Avon turbojet, so Rolls-Royce did not lose out in the P.1081 affair. However, with their Australian aspirations ended, Hawker was forced to terminate the P.1081 programme and VX279 was hand-ed over to RAE Farnborough in January 1951, to further the Establishment's high-Mach-number trials. Hawkers were only five months away from having the first prototype P.1067 completed; therefore VX279 could not contribute anything to that programme – the P.1067 became the Hunter, so the company was not exactly on the bread-line when the Australian cancellation was announced.

Hawker's first aircraft with all its flying surfaces swept was VX279, the P.1081 created by major surgery on the second P.1052 prototype. Author's collection

The RAE's holding of VX279 was rather short-lived. On 3 April 1951, the aircraft crashed and Trevor Wade was killed in the accident. He had ejected, but at too low an altitude and his body was still strapped in the Malcolm seat when he was found. The reason for VX279's loss has never been 100 per cent established.

On 25 June 1950, VX279 was displayed at the Brussels Air Show. Three days earlier, it had landed at Heathrow for a fuel 'top-up' as seen here, prior to flying to Maelsbruck, then Antwerp. Aeroplane

Observers heard a sonic boom just before the aircraft came into view, so it is believed that a transonic dive was being flown. Following Wade's ejection, with the weight of the pilot, seat and canopy gone, the drag generated by the open cockpit induced a levelling-out, so that the P.1081 crash-landed with comparatively little damage: this certainly underlines the stability of the aircraft's basic aerodynamic shape, as well as its structural strength.

So ended Hawker's preliminary steps in the era of the turbojet. That the Hunter was the eventual resounding success that it was is due in no small measure to the data obtained from the earlier aircraft. Also, the Royal Navy's 434 production Sea Hawks, the sixty-four that were ordered by West Germany and twenty-four for the Indian Navy, prove that the whole programme was fruitful. But like too many other aviation projects over the years, it had a human cost.

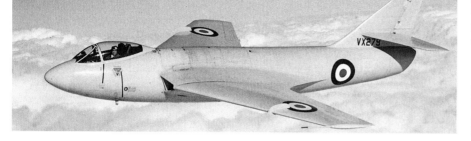

In its final configuration with wing fences, VX279 is flown by 'Wimpy' Wade, shortly before his untimely death when the aircraft crashed on 3 April 1951.
Derek James

Technical Data

Hawker P.1040

Dimensions: Span 36ft 6in (11.12m); length 37ft 7in (11.44m); height 8ft 9in (2.66m)

Powerplant: One Rolls-Royce Nene RN.1 turbojet producing 4,500lb (2,000kg) thrust

Weights: Empty, approximately 7,800lb (3,500kg); loaded, approximately 10,000lb (4,500kg)

Performance: Maximum speed 600mph (970km/h) at 36,000ft (11,000m), or 580mph (930km/h) at sea level; service ceiling 44,500ft (13,600m)

Production: One aircraft built as private venture, with serial number VP401 (two later aircraft built to Specification N.7/46, with serial numbers VX272 and VX279 do not apply)

Hawker P.1052

Dimensions: Span 31ft 6in (9.60m); length 37ft 7in (11.44m) with straight tailplane, 40ft 3in (12.26m) with swept tailplane

Powerplant: One Rolls-Royce Nene RN.2 turbojet producing 5,000lb (2,300kg) thrust

Weights: Empty 9,450lb (4,290kg); loaded 13,488lb (6,120kg)

Performance: Maximum speed 592mph (953km/h) at 25,000ft (7,600m); service ceiling 45,000ft (13,900m)

Production: Two aircraft built to Specification E.38/46 with serial numbers VX272 and VX279

Hawker P.1072

Dimensions: Span 36ft 6in (11.12m); length 37ft 7in (11.44m); height 8ft 9in (2.66m)

Powerplants: One Rolls-Royce Nene RN.2 turbojet producing 5,000lb (2,300kg) thrust and one Armstrong Siddeley Snarler ASSn.1 liquid-fuel rocket producing 2,000lb (900kg) thrust

Weights: Empty 11,050lb (5,000kg); loaded 14,050lb (6,370kg)

Performance: Maximum speed at sea level 581mph (935km/h); climb 500ft/min (150m/min); service ceiling 44,500ft (13,560m)

Production: One P.1040 converted, with serial number VP401

Hawker P.1081

Dimensions: Span 31ft 6in (9.60m); length 37ft 4in (11.37m); height 13ft 3in (4.03m)

Powerplant: One Rolls-Royce Nene RN.2 turbojet producing 5,000lb (2,300kg) thrust

Weights: Empty 11,200lb (5,080kg); loaded 14,480lb (6,570kg)

Performance: Maximum speed at sea level 694mph (1,116km/h); service ceiling 45,600ft (13,900m)

Production: One P.1052 converted, with serial number VX279

CHAPTER FIVE

Armstrong Whitworth AW.52G and AW.52

Baginton's Flying Wings

The company Sir W. G. Armstrong Whitworth Aircraft Limited (AWA) was formed at Whitley, north-west of Coventry, in 1921. In 1935 the company became a member of the newly formed Hawker Siddeley Aircraft Co. Ltd together with Hawker Aircraft Ltd, A. V. Roe & Co. Ltd and the Armstrong Siddeley Development Co. Ltd. With the Gloster Aircraft Co. Ltd joining the consortium a little later, the Hawker Siddeley Group (HSG) was established.

Also in 1935, AWA acquired a large area of land on a plateau above the village of Baginton, a couple of miles south-east of Whitley, which today is part of Coventry Airport. Factory space was built and with this additional facility the company was able to produce larger aircraft in larger numbers. This enabled Imperial Airways to operate AWA's Argosy, Atlanta and Ensign airliners over many different routes. Smaller aircraft such as the Siskin and Atlas were supplied in quantity to the RAF.

Then, when Specification B.3/34 was issued by the Air Ministry for a heavy bomber, AWA's experience with their large airliners enabled them to produce a prototype of their AW.38 design within two years. Named the Whitley in recognition of AWA's origins, the aircraft went into large-scale production, and by the time that the last aircraft went down the line in 1942, no fewer than 1,737 had been built.

AWA's next indigenous design was the AW.41 Albermarle, whose production was affected by a shortage of materials, but was nevertheless the first British operational aircraft to be equipped with a tricycle undercarriage. With the large capacity available at AWA's two plants, the HSG nominated the company to build Lancasters and Lincolns for Avro under licence. After World War Two, the company was given responsibility for the development and production of all night-fighter variants of the Gloster Meteor, followed by Sea Hawk production, together with all the Armstrong-Siddeley Sapphire-powered Hunter F.2s and F.5s.

Laminar Flow

The company had established a reputation for being prepared to tackle the unorthodox aspects of aviation, fostered by their pioneering work in the development of all-metal aircraft, involving the use of high-tensile steel. It was this reputation that brought AWA, in the early 1940s, into the research being conducted by the Royal Aircraft Establishment concerning airflow over the wings of high-speed monoplanes. The term 'laminar flow' was coined, meaning the design of wing sections that had a large percentage of their surface free from turbulence. To further this, it was found that the wing section was only as good as its surface finish.

AWA's Chief Designer, John Lloyd, expressed his desire to design and construct a full-size wing portion and in November 1942, the Directorate of Scientific Research (DSR) department at the MAP awarded a contract to the company to cover this work. The wing portion would be passed to the National Physical Laboratory (NPL) for wind-tunnel tests and when these were made, the results proved to be very promising. Profile drag was reduced to 50 per cent of normal value, with laminar flow being maintained over nearly 60 per cent of the chord.

A Flying-Wing Bomber

The company wanted to put the principle into practice. Their AW.49 twin-boom design was quickly discarded in favour of a bomber project, given the type number AW.50. This would be a flying-wing of 120ft (36.5m) span, powered by four Metrovick

On the approach, the AW.52G, built of plywood and spruce with a 'Plymax' skin, displays its generous flap area. *Aeroplane*

F.2/4A Beryl axial-flow turbojets. The Directorate of Technical Development (DTD) formed a Tailless Advisory Committee, and a close liaison with them was maintained by AWA's design office.

With the crew compartment, weapons bay and engines designed to be buried within the wing, it was considered prudent to evaluate the handling of such a profile by building a one-third scale glider, allocated type number AW.51. During the bomber's design development, the wingspan was reduced to 112ft (34.14m) and the crew compartment was moved into a central nacelle; this amendment required the glider design to be altered and a new company type number was bestowed upon it, AW.52G. However, the end of World War Two brought about a vast rash of cancellations throughout the aircraft industry and Armstrong Whitworth's flying-wing bomber was included, mainly because it was considered too radical a design.

Flying Trials

However, the evaluation of laminar-flow wing sections was considered an ongoing piece of research and, although the NPL tests had given encouragement, it was thought necessary to confirm them in practice. Hawker Hurricane IIB Z3687 was allocated to AWA, to assist in the practical testing of the laminar-flow wing. The company designed and manufactured a set of test wings, which were fitted as replacements for the aircraft's standard outboard ones. Chief Test Pilot Charles Turner-Hughes gave the aircraft a maiden flight with the new wings on 23 March 1945.

The very comprehensive flight-test programme that he and his assistant, F. R. Midgley, flew was augmented by several RAE test pilots, to confirm that in practice the findings of the NPL wind-tunnel tests were not entirely dependable. Each slight undulation in the wing's surface had to be filled and carefully rubbed down. The everyday adhesion of insects and the dirt that prevailed in the industrial Midlands, which had never before been considered, now took on a far greater importance, for they were found to reduce the wing's laminar-flow characteristics by a considerable margin. A satisfactory answer to these problems had to be sought, if the tests were to be continued.

As well as AWA's testing, the RAE's Professor A. A. Griffiths had designed a

laminar-flow section, with boundary-layer sections employed on both upper and lower surfaces. (These use a system of ducts in the wing and vacuum pumps to improve the airflow.) A test wing was fitted on Meteor F.3 EE445 and, besides RAE pilots, AWA's Sqn Ldr Eric Franklin took part in a nine-month evaluation of the project. Reluctantly it was decided that the wing did not totally fulfil Professor Griffith's expectations.

The two small windmills supplied the drive to pumps that generated boundary-layer suction through slots in the wing upper surface. *Aeroplane*

The Flying Scale-Model Glider

As the AW.50 had been received with a certain amount of scepticism, the company's design team introduced a civil airliner variant with the same laminar-flow planform. The AW.52G was starting to take shape on the Baginton Oak site (which is now a part of Air Atlantique's engineering facility) and therefore, if it was to be of any value relative to the handling of a full-size aircraft, military or civil, their design should be kept close to the glider's configuration, which was now established.

Financing the project was a big issue so, in the interests of economy, the glider was constructed mainly of plywood and spruce. The wing skinning material was a bonding of 22SWG dural sheeting to plywood, called 'Plymax'. The in-tandem two-seater cockpit for the pilot and observer had a raised, well-glazed canopy. The vertical

fin/rudder assemblies on each wing tip were elliptical in shape, and again in the interests of keeping costs down, the tricycle undercarriage was fixed. A small windmill was attached to the leading edge of each mainwheel leg fairing, to drive the pumps that would generate boundary-layer suction, through a series of slots in the wing's upper surface, just ahead of the elevons.

The wing itself had an area of 443sq ft (41.15sq m) and featured a leading edge sweep of 34 degrees, with the trailing edge swept at 22 degrees. The whole aircraft was finished with a glossy grey top surface and yellow underside. C-Type military and prototype markings were carried, with the serial number RG324 positioned on the port wing's upper surface only, adjacent to the canopy.

The Glider Flies

During AWA's expansion in 1943 they acquired facilities at Bitteswell, north of Rugby, sharing the airfield with Nos 18 and 29 OTUs, which in November 1944 were superseded by No. 105 OTU. The company used the base for the assembly and test flying of licence-built Lancaster bombers. The completed AW.52G was rolled out at Baginton near the end of February 1945, to be transported to Bitteswell for flight

The serial RG324 was only carried on the port side of the wing's upper surface. The apparatus behind the port trailing edge recorded data on airflow over the wing at various levels. Author's collection

BELOW: The root thickness/chord ratio of 15 per cent is quite evident here, as is the crew's raised, well-glazed compartment and the wing tip anti-spin parachute housing, which was duplicated on the starboard side. Author's collection

BOTTOM: The first AW.52 prototype had its mandatory photo session before its TS363 serial had been applied. Author's collection

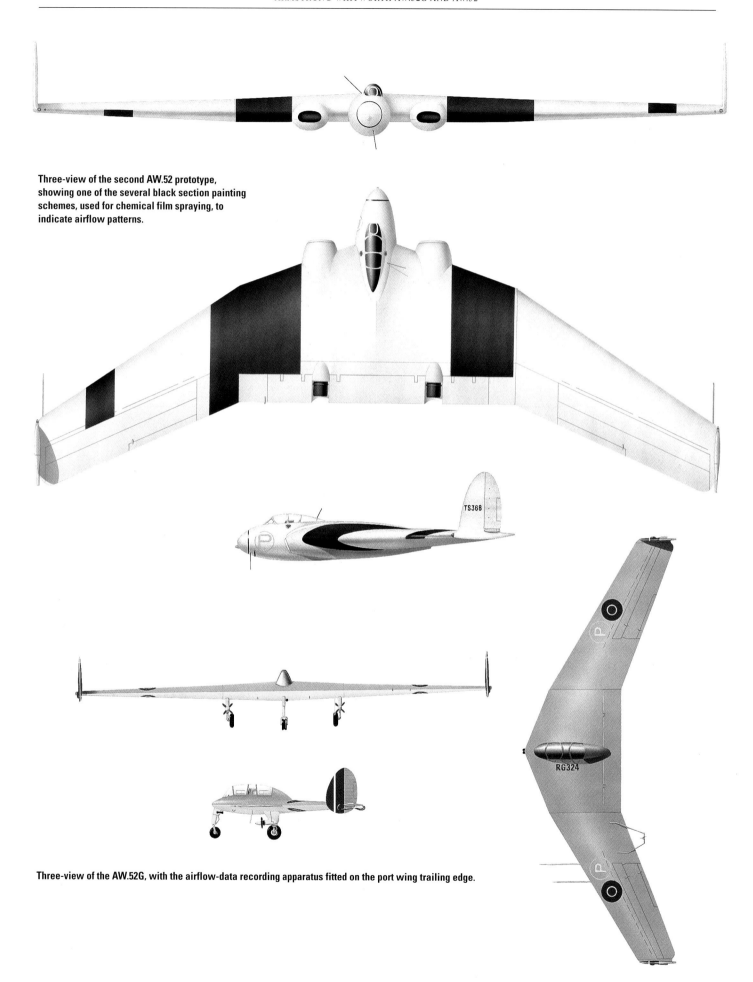

Three-view of the second AW.52 prototype, showing one of the several black section painting schemes, used for chemical film spraying, to indicate airflow patterns.

Three-view of the AW.52G, with the airflow-data recording apparatus fitted on the port wing trailing edge.

testing. The last production Whitley Mk V, LA951, was assigned as the glider's tug and on 2 March, with Charles Turner-Hughes at the controls, RG324 was towed into the air for the first time. A maiden release was made at 12,000ft (3,700m) and a 25-minute free flight was accomplished, with the aircraft handling perfectly. In fact, during its whole eight-year life, the only modification required was a reduction of the elevon control-ratio gearing.

Test flying of RG324 was carried out from both Bitteswell and Baginton. The glider attended the 1946 SBAC Display at Radlett with LA951 as its tug, but later in its life, Lancaster B.1 PA366 took over from the Whitley and releases up to 20,000ft (6,000m) were made, enabling free gliding for over 30 minutes. Test flights of this duration were able to supply a large amount of data.

The Airborne Forces Experimental Establishment (AFEE), who had considerable glider experience, as well as Boscombe Down, both had the aircraft on their inventory for varying periods, but by 1953 its useful life was completed and it returned to Baginton for display as a 'gate-guardian' and at various other locations on the airfield. Exposure to the elements was far from perfect for the glider and its wooden structure was sorely affected. Foresight as to aircraft preservation was not a very prevalent commodity in those days, so RG324 was eventually consigned to the bonfire.

The Big Brother

Although the glider made a very valuable contribution to the low-speed characteristics of the flying-wing concept, it was obvious that a larger, powered aircraft would be required to enlarge the test-flying envelope. While still hanging onto the civil airliner as a viable design, AWA would be unable to finance such a project and Treasury backing was not available. An aircraft with a wingspan of at least 160ft (50m) would be required, because it was only at this size that the wing could be deep enough to enclose the passenger accommodation. However, officialdom's interest in the design was not completely dead. The Ministry of Supply issued Specification E.9/44 to cover the design and production of two scaled-down, powered flying-wing research aircraft. AWA considered that they stood a better chance of the whole project going through

ABOVE: **TS363 flies over a snow-covered landscape during an early test flight in the winter of 1947–48.** Derek James

BELOW: **The dull weather at the 1948 SBAC Display belies the fact that TS363 was painted an overall vivid gloss white.** *Aeroplane*

if it was suggested that the aircraft be designed to carry a 4,000lb (1,800kg) load of mail or freight, as a high-speed courier with a range of about 2,000 miles (3,200km). Whitehall smiled broadly!

The design, given the company number AW.52, was established as a twin-engined flying-wing, with the first prototype, TS363, being powered by a pair of Rolls-Royce Nene RN.2s, each delivering 5,000lb (2,300kg) thrust. The second aircraft, TS368, would have two Rolls-Royce Derwent 5s, each rated at 3,500lb (1,600kg) thrust. As the two research aircraft were to be only about half the size of the proposed airliner, it could not be a pure flying-wing. The two-man crew would have to be situated in a central nacelle, with the centrifugal-flow engines in bulged housings, whereas in the airliner design everything and everybody was carried in the wing. Therefore, to the purists, the AW.52s were not perfect 'flying-wings', but they have always been referred to as such.

The wing's construction followed the pattern established with the NPL test section, in being built from the outside inwards. The engineers on the shop floor took time to get used to drawings showing the spar booms decreasing in chord but increasing in thickness, as they progressed towards the tips. But construction proceeded at a creditable pace, considering the unorthodox design.

The AW.52G's wing-sweep angles were maintained on the larger aircraft, with the centre-section trailing edge again having no sweep at all. A large constant-chord Fowler flap extended the full length of the centre-section, with two semi-circular ducts to accommodate the engine jet-pipes. Generously sized elevons that could operate in unison or differentially, were fitted, and each wing tip blended upwards into an elliptical fin, carrying a rudder that was biased to operate over a range of 10 degrees inwards and 30 degrees outward.

In a tailless aircraft, the change of trim required when the flaps are lowered has to be counteracted. On the glider and the AW.52, a 'corrector' surface was built into the wing ahead of each elevon, extending from about 50 per cent of the chord to about 70 per cent. The nose-down pitching moment that occurred when the flap was lowered was automatically corrected by the 'corrector' moving upwards. These movements were approximately 4 degrees upwards, when the flap was down at the 20 degrees required for take-off and a further 2 degrees was required when the flap was lowered for landing. The 'correctors' were also able to be operated independently over a range of 6 degrees for longitudinal trim when the flap was not in use.

Eight fuel tanks, two in each centre-section outboard of the engines and two in each outer wing section, holding a total of 1,700gal (2,000ltr), gave a designed operating range of 2,100 miles (3,400km). The pressurized crew compartment, with its long, glazed canopy, was off-set to port of the centreline. The pilot was provided with a Martin-Baker Mk 1 ejector seat, but the radio operator/navigator, who was positioned behind and below the pilot, was required to evacuate via the crew entry hatch in an emergency.

The Finish

Both the Hurricane and the glider had illustrated that a satisfactory laminar flow could only be achieved if the outer skin surface was unmarked. Every precaution was taken during the construction of the two AW.52s, with Alclad sheets received from the manufacturers having fabric doped on each, in order to protect the surface from scratches or damage during transit. During the building of the aircraft, this fabric was partly lifted where drilling was required and was not fully removed until each prototype had been fully assembled. To maintain this smoothness, both AW.52s were painted overall one colour (white) and national markings were omitted, as it was considered that these could affect the airflow. Just the serial number

was painted on the outer surface of each fin and the prototype yellow 'P' was carried on the central nacelle, beneath the cockpit canopy.

TS363 was rolled out from the Baginton assembly shop on 1 April 1947 and initial taxiing was conducted on the airfield's grass runway. Then, as if to nullify all the care taken during its manufacture, the aircraft was dismantled and taken by road for static display at that year's SBAC Display, being held at Radlett. It was reassembled for the event, then on 12 September, with the display over, TS363 was again dismantled for transportation to Boscombe Down. At the A&AEE's vast airfield, the aircraft was reassembled once more and constructive taxiing trials were started. During these, it became noticeable that the aircraft was very sensitive in pitch.

First Flight

A couple of short hops were accidentally made during the taxiing when the nose had not been lowered in time. It was a twitchy aircraft and adjustments had to be made to the control settings, as cutting the engines had been the only means of getting the nose down after uncontrollable lifting occurred. These were satisfactorily completed during the second week of November, so that on the 13th, the company's new CTP, Eric Franklin, gave TS363 a maiden flight that lasted twenty minutes. This was actually extended by a couple of minutes for, on returning to the A&AEE's runway and despite having a large flap area, with its maximum deflection of 40 degrees, plus long-travel oleo legs, the aircraft floated above the tarmac for a considerable distance before eventually touching down. Large all-wing aircraft showed a reluctance to be reacquainted with terra firma.

Four days later, the aircraft had its second flight and this nearly ended in disaster, as the nose-wheel would not lock down. However, a satisfactory touchdown was achieved and it was found that the aircraft was easier when ground manoeuvring with the nose jack not completely extended.

A Sensitive Aircraft

The continuation of the extreme sensitivity in pitch, except in very smooth air, required TS363's return to Baginton in December 1947, for modifications to be incorporated. These only partially cured the problem and the flight trials during 1948 produced another complication, wing flexing. In spite of these problematic phenomena, a considerable number of hours were flown by the aircraft and it is to the credit of the pilot that an exhilarating programme was flown each day at that year's SBAC Display, being staged at Farnborough for the first time.

A Pair, for a While

TS363 was joined by the second aircraft, TS368, at that event. It had made its maiden flight from Baginton on 1 September, but because it had not completed the ten hours in the air that was required before an aircraft could be included in the flying programme, it flew down to Farnborough to appear as a static exhibit. With its two Derwent 5s, the second prototype was just over 50mph (80km/h) slower than TS363, although it was nearly 850lb (385kg) lighter. Furthermore, its rate of climb was only half the 4,800ft/min (1,460m/min) of its stablemate. The two aircraft had the same overall glossy white finish, and apart from the serial number, the only way to tell them apart was the more oval shape of the Derwent's air intakes on TS368.

The two aircraft were subjected to a concentrated test flight programme for eight months after their Farnborough outings. But on 30 May 1949, AWA test pilot J. O. 'Jo' Lancaster was flying TS363 solo, when on reaching 320mph (515km/h) for the first time there was a violent pitch oscillation. He quickly descended to 3,000ft (900m) without there being any

The second prototype, TS368, was fully painted when it had its roll-out photo session in September 1948 – although the external markings were restricted to the serial and prototype circle, as it was thought that roundels on the wings might affect their laminar-flow properties. Author's collection

The intakes feeding TS363's Nene engines were deeper than those on the Derwent-powered TS368. *Aeroplane*

improvement in the aircraft's behaviour, so he earned his place in aviation history by being the first British pilot to evacuate an aircraft in an emergency by means of an ejector seat. He made a safe parachute descent into the Warwickshire village of Long Itchington, and TS363 became more stable after the exit, to make a reasonable crash landing a few miles away at Leamington Hastings. The principal damage to the aircraft was generated by the two Nenes being torn from their mountings.

Limitations

By this time, the whole flying-wing airliner project had been discarded and, as TS368 was still airworthy to continue general research into the handling of flying wings, TS363 was scrapped. As was to be expected, with the two aircraft being of the same configuration, they had the same flying characteristics and, after extensive checks had been made on TS368's structure, the aircraft was cleared to resume flying, but was limited to not exceeding 300mph (480km/h).

AWA continued trials with the aircraft until October 1950, when it was assigned to RAE Farnborough, to assist in their laminar flow research. During these trials, airflow plotting was monitored by spraying a thin film of chemicals over various portions of the wings. To assist in this programme, designated portions were painted black, so that the chemical stain showing its flow and therefore the airflow over that

part of the wing, could be reviewed upon returning to Farnborough. These trials were conducted at a very leisurely pace for over three years, before the whole programme was discontinued.

The Curtain is Lowered

TS368 remained at Farnborough until March 1954 and was occasionally flown, but not for any specific trial. Then in May, it was taken to the Proof and Experimental Establishment (PEE) at Shoeburyness

in Essex to end its life as a target for the range of armaments being perfected at the time.

The stability and control of tailless aircraft were not fully improved until the advent of the artificial stabilizer that is now commonplace. Laminar flow, while being a good principle, has its limitations when applied to large wings, for the practicality of keeping a flying surface free of foreign bodies to produce a perfect airflow, in the everyday environment in which both civil and military aircraft operate, is well-nigh impossible.

Technical Data	
Armstrong Whitworth AW.52G	
Dimensions:	Span 53ft 10in (16.39m); length 19ft 4in (5.9m); height 8ft 4in (2.56m)
Performance:	Ceiling 20,000ft (6,100m)
Production:	One aircraft built initially as a private venture, but operated as part of Specification E.9/44, with serial number RG324
Armstrong Whitworth AW.52	
Dimensions:	Span 90ft 11in (27.72m); length 37ft 3½in (11.35m); height: 14ft 4½in (4.40m)
Powerplants:	TS363, two Rolls-Royce Nene RN.2 turbojets, each producing 5,000lb (2,300kg) thrust; TS368, two Rolls-Royce Derwent 5 turbojets, each producing 3,500lb (1,600kg) thrust
Weights:	(TS363) 19,662lb (8,917kg) empty, 34,154lb (5,956kg) loaded; (TS368) 19,185lb (8,700kg) empty, 33,305lb (15,104kg) loaded
Performance:	Maximum speed at sea level (TS363) 499mph (803km/h), (TS368) 448mph (721km/h); normal service ceiling (TS363) 50,000ft (15,240m), (TS368) 45,000ft (13,716m); maximum range 2,130 miles (3,430km)
Production:	Two aircraft built to Specification E.9/44, with serial numbers TS363 and TS368

CHAPTER SIX

Gloster E.1/44

Gloster's Nene Machine

With the principle and practicality of Frank Whittle's engine established through Gloster's E.28/39, the company progressed to designing a Service fighter based on the new power source. Because it was recognized that the existing engines had fairly limited thrust, the company's Chief Designer, George Carter, drew up plans for a twin-engined aircraft. Specification F.9/40 was issued covering twelve prototypes, which was later reduced to six, but finally finished as eight. Tooling-up also began for the quantity production of the RAF's first turbojet fighter, as the company was convinced that the prototypes would confirm the potential of their design.

However, engines due from Rover, who had taken over production of Power Jet's W.2B and de Havilland Engines' H.1, were far behind schedule. Both the Ministry of Aircraft Production and Gloster were becoming very anxious about the situation. Gloster's project office had drawn up a single-engined fighter design, based on the assumption that turbojet thrust outputs were bound to improve.

The Contingency Design

Because of the engine situation, the company approached the MAP early in 1942, asking if their new design could be considered as a contingency plan against the engine manufacturer's further lapse in supplying power plants for their F.9/40s. The Ministry welcomed the suggestion and Specification E.5/42 was drawn up around Gloster's proposal. The fact that the specification had an 'E' prefix emphasized the MAP's consideration that the design was an experimental aircraft, but it was a start, which had official approval. As things turned out, both engine manufacturers delivered flight engines, as did Metropolitan Vickers, and the F.9/40 progressed through the development stages to become the Meteor.

Nevertheless, Gloster's design team forged ahead, refining their single-engined project and de Havilland's H.1 or H.2 were the engines around which the E.5/42 was developed. With the Meteor having been put into large-scale production in the summer of 1942, the MAP started having reservations as to whether the E.5/42 might prejudice the company's being able to meet the Meteor's order deadlines. They put forward the suggestion that Armstrong Whitworth, being a fellow Hawker Siddeley Group member, could be better placed to handle detailed design work. This did not go down at all well at Gloster Aircraft: as they were quick to point out, they had more turbojet aircraft experience than the rest of the industry put together.

Refinements Galore

The Group was fortunate in having the dynamic Sir Frank Spriggs as its Chairman and he left the Ministry in no doubt that it was a Gloster project and that company should see it through. Two months later, officialdom reluctantly conceded and the E.5/42 stayed with its sire.

By the beginning of 1943, the design office issued a performance table indicating that, with an armament of two 20mm Hispano cannon, plus provision for two more, the aircraft would have a service ceiling of over 48,000ft (15,000m) and a level-flight speed of not less than 490mph (790km/h) at 30,000ft (9,000m). At the altitudes forecast, a pressurized cockpit was essential and it was considered that the H.2 engine's power output would enable all figures to be met. Despite the 20mm cannon installation indicated in the design performance figures, which would be sited under the front fuselage, no E.5/42 or subsequent E.1/44 ever received any armament whatsoever.

A 1:4.5 scale model of the aircraft was tested in the RAE's low-speed wind tunnel and on the strength of the results, coupled with the announced performance figures,

Gloster received a contract for the manufacture of three prototypes, given the serial numbers NN648, NN651 and NN655. Of these, NN648 would be purely an aerodynamic test airframe, with no inbuilt provision for further development.

The company's experimental works were based at Bentham, some 3 miles east of the main Hucclecote site. It was here that the majority of F.9/40 work had been done and where initial E.5/42 work would be undertaken. However, modifications and refinements to the design kept pouring out from the design office to such an extent that by the spring of 1944, the aircraft was a vastly different one from that originally projected. It was considered that the aircraft now had little resemblance to the requirements laid down in Specification E.5/42 and therefore a revised contract was issued to Gloster, to cover the production of three prototypes to Specification E.1/44.

The New Aircraft

During the two years of E.5/42 refinement, Rolls-Royce had taken their original Derwent turbojet and redesigned it into a new engine, the Nene. This was due to be bench-run for the first time in October 1944, but even before that, all indicators pointed to the Nene being potentially the most powerful turbojet in the world at that time. This prophecy was substantiated in November 1945, when the engine was type-tested at 5,000lb (2,300kg).

The H.2 was now discarded and a single Nene was chosen as the power plant for the E.1/44 and, this now being a new design, the original three serial numbers in the NN range were cancelled, never to be reallocated. The three new aircraft were allotted serial numbers SM801, SM805 and SM809. Also by this time, the SBAC had issued a standardization of numbering throughout the industry. These were prefixed with a letter denoting the company, which in the case of Gloster was 'G', and each company would designate an alphabetical character

to a design, starting with 'A'. Development of an original design would be indicated by a number, starting with '1' so that, under the new system, the E.1/44 carried the company designation GA.1. The name Ace was also bestowed upon the aircraft, but somehow this seems to have evaporated and the GA.1 was never officially referred to by this name.

Victims of Development

With all the revisions, the Nene as the engine plus a stream of specification modifications that seemed to change almost every week, the two airframes already on Bentham's shop floor, SM801 and SM805, got to a stage where it was impossible to incorporate all the desired alterations. Consequently, all work on these aircraft was suspended and the third airframe, SM809, became the first prototype E.1/44, with the company designation GA.2 (the first development of the 'GA' under the SBAC system). The construction of this aircraft commenced in the autumn of 1944.

In January 1945, Gloster received a contract for three additional GA.2s, given serial numbers TX145, TX148 and TX150. All were to be powered by a single Rolls-Royce Nene RN.2 turbojet. A year later, two pre-production contracts were issued to the company, each covering the building of twenty additional aircraft. The first batch was to be numbered VP601 to VP620 and the second, VR164 to VR183. These pre-production aircraft would receive the company designation GA.4. To illustrate the vacillations of the Ministries of that era, barely a week after receiving the second pre-production contract, Gloster was informed that it had been cancelled. Serials VR164 to VR183 died with the cancellation, never to reappear.

A Pedestrian Pace

One thing that the MAP did not get wrong was their opinion expressed in 1942 as to Gloster's ability to handle the E.1/44 programme alongside full-scale Meteor

The first prototype SM809 was photographed in various degrees of primer in July 1947, which is possibly just as well, for it was irreparably damaged in a road accident while being transported to Boscombe Down later in the month. Author's collection

ABOVE: **When the second prototype was completed it showed that, compared with SM809, the rudder had been modified by the removal of the horn balance. One wonders what a Dutch Harvard was doing at Moreton Valence!** Derek James

RIGHT: **This close-up view of the second prototype's rear end shows the modified rudder and the anti-spin parachute housing between it and the Nene's jet-pipe.** Derek James

production. SM809's construction was afforded very little priority and it was three years later, in July 1947, before it was rolled out from the assembly shop. However, the GA.2 as a production aircraft under the heading GA.4 was designed with subcontracting strongly in mind. The all-metal fuselage consisted of five sub-assemblies and the wings, with a single high-tensile-steel main spar, were designed in four sections.

The End of SM809

In an unpainted condition, SM809 posed for an official photographic session shortly after roll-out, and by the end of July it was dismantled for transportation by road to A&AEE Boscombe Down for a scheduled maiden flight. Then fate took a hand.

Somewhere between the Gloster works and Boscombe Down, the transporter jack-knifed while negotiating a steep hill and the aircraft was damaged beyond repair. One strange thing about this accident is the fact that it does not appear to have been included in any police, county or A&AEE records. Besides the destruction of the two Supermarine B.12/36 bomber prototypes during construction, in an air raid on 26 September 1940, the demise of SM809 is the only case of a prototype being destroyed before its maiden flight – apart from the destruction undertaken over the years, with official blessing, in the form of cancellations!

A New Urgency

Suddenly, with SM809 being a write-off, the E.1/44 programme was awarded an air of urgency and that element of Gloster Aircraft was galvanized into action. The second airframe, TX145, now became the official first prototype and work on its construction was accelerated so that only eight months later, at the beginning of March 1948, it was ready to follow its predecessor's road to Boscombe Down – with the aim of making the whole journey intact this time. The official photographs were taken before its departure, with the aircraft resplendent in an overall silver finish, with

C-Type service markings and the obligatory prototype 'P'. Its physical appearance was identical to SM809's, apart from the absence of the rudder horn balance carried on the first aircraft, and the serial.

The sturdy-looking, wide-tracked undercarriage supported a rotund fuselage with an air intake for the Nene on either side, aft of the cockpit, and an anti-spin parachute housed at the base of the fin/rudder assembly, above the jet outlet. Both wings and tailplane, each with straight, tapered edges, were mid-set on the fuselage. The main wheels retraced inwards into housings within each wing and the nose-wheel retracted rearwards into the nose. An internal fuel capacity of 428gal (1,926ltr) was carried in fuselage tanks.

Airborne, at Last

Having arrived safely at Boscombe Down, TX145 had its maiden flight on 9 March 1948, in the hands of W. A. 'Bill' Waterman. He had joined the company two years previously for development test flying, and this was his first prototype sortie. He expressed general satisfaction with the aircraft's handling, and in subsequent flights TX145 confirmed the company's design performance figures. A good rate of climb was achieved and 620mph (1,000km/h) was attained early in the test programme.

New Tail

However, as the trials envelope was extended, the handling started to generate criticism and close attention to the problem seemed to indicate that the tailplane was

affected by turbulence. A model of a newly designed tail assembly was tested in a Farnborough wind tunnel and the results confirmed that the new configuration would cure the handling problem. The new tail featured a much taller fin/rudder and the tailplane was situated roughly halfway up the fin. A bullet fairing at the intersection smoothed the airflow around the area.

So good were the RAE's test results that the new tail unit was incorporated during the building of the next GA.2 prototype, TX148, although it was already in an advanced state of construction. The aircraft, which was the second prototype but the third airframe, was completed by January 1949 and, with company confidence restored, was taken by road to the A&AEE's airfield to make a successful maiden flight. Besides the new tail unit, TX148 differed from TX145 by having slightly larger air intakes and a braking parachute housing that extended well aft of the jet tailpipe. The external finish was the same as its predecessor's apart from the national markings, which had reverted to the pre-war even-thickness red, white and blue roundels, together with even-thickness tail markings.

The new tail made a huge difference. The handling was found to be so superior and the new assembly so successful, right from the first take-off, that it was decided to introduce it into the Meteor production line. The Meteor T.7's fuselage was 30in (76cm) longer than earlier marks', which enhanced longitudinal stability compared with the F.4. The F.8 under development would also have the longer fuselage, housing an additional 94gal (427ltr) fuel tank and a relocated ammunition bay. But, once the fuel in this tank had been used and the ammunition bay emptied, pitch control

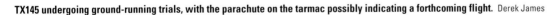

TX145 undergoing ground-running trials, with the parachute on the tarmac possibly indicating a forthcoming flight. Derek James

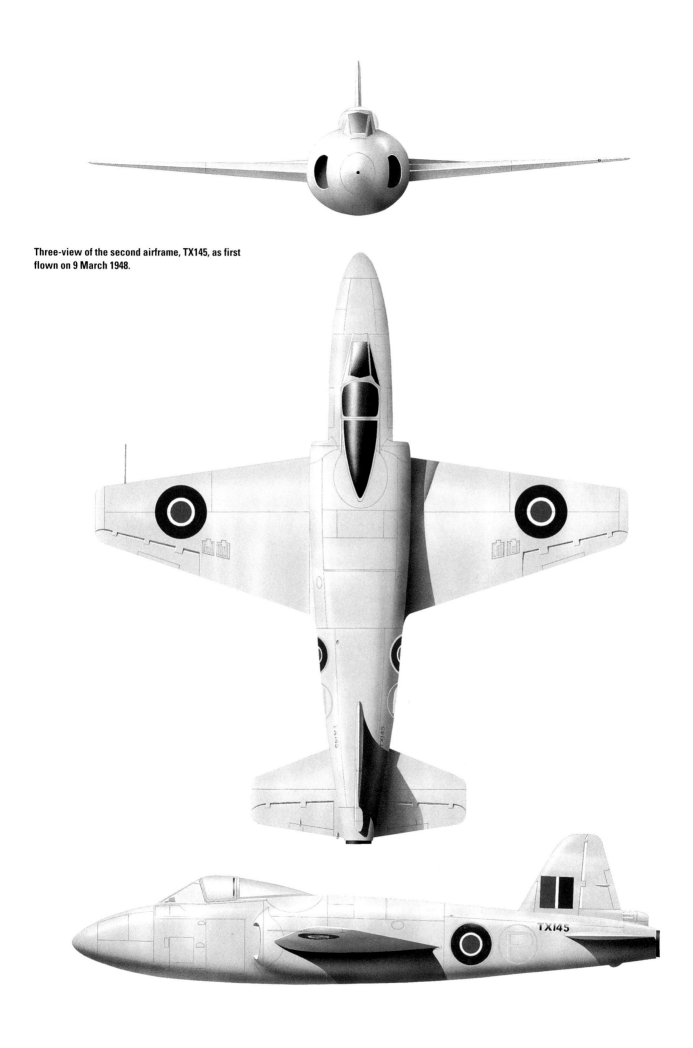

Three-view of the second airframe, TX145, as first
flown on 9 March 1948.

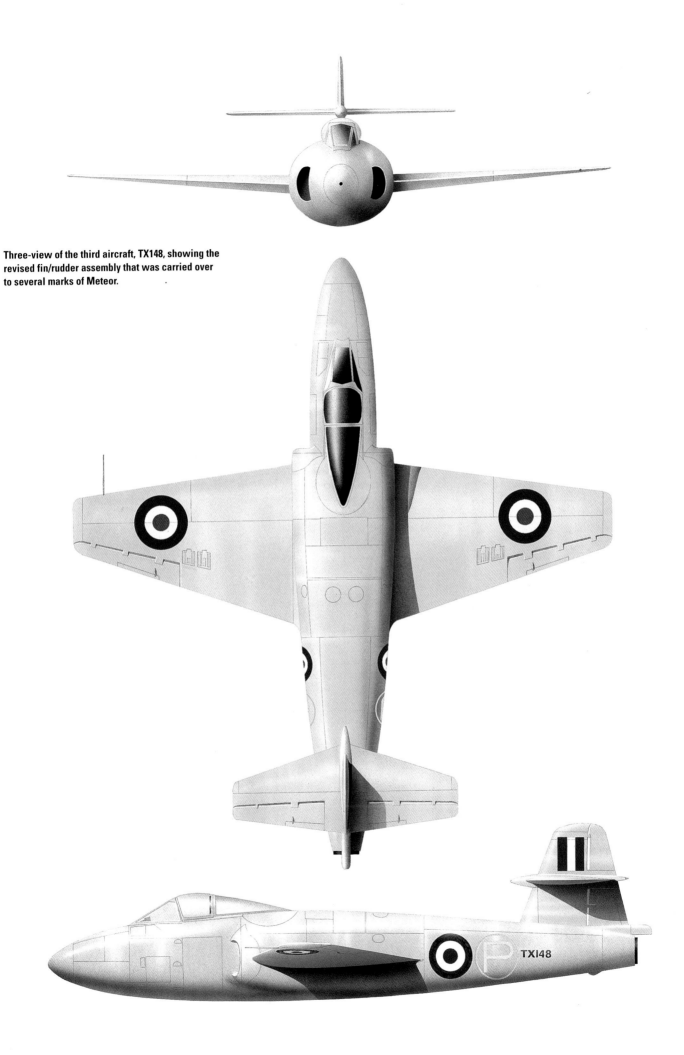

Three-view of the third aircraft, TX148, showing the revised fin/rudder assembly that was carried over to several marks of Meteor.

TX148

became problematic. The new E.1/44 tail design was adapted for installation on the Meteor and tests on trials aircraft RA382 proved to be so successful that the modification was carried into the Meteor F.8 production line, from the 101st aircraft. The preceding 100 aircraft, rolled out with F.4 tail units, were modified retrospectively; similarly, the T.7s under construction were fitted with the new tail, and those already built were modified.

The third prototype, TX148, featured the redesigned fin/rudder assembly, which was so successful that it was introduced into the Meteor F.8 production line at an early stage. Philip Jarrett

The Paradoxical Solution

In designing the new tail assembly for the GA.2, however, Gloster drew up the aircraft's death warrant. Adapting the unit for the Meteor made such an improvement to that type that the GA.2's performance was now only marginally better than its stablemate's. Furthermore, it was considered that the Meteor had a far greater development potential than the GA.2, a fact that was to be confirmed by the photographic reconnaissance and night-fighter variants of the Meteor that evolved, not to mention the many trials and test-bed adaptations that proved so vital to aviation research in many parts of the world over the years.

The first GA.4 pre-production contract for twenty aircraft was cancelled, even though components had already been produced. Therefore, with the type's future as a Service fighter now virtually non-existent, TX145 was transferred to the RAE in mid-December 1949. Two months later, on 14 February 1950, TX148 joined it at Farnborough, where the two aircraft were used by the Establishment for a variety of trials programmes, which included flying control systems research and the testing of numerous braking parachutes.

With this programme completed, TX150 appears to have been abandoned until 14 April 1956, when it was sold to the College of Aeronautics at Cranfield. It was taken by road to the College, in the sectional state that existed after the structural test programme, and remained in this condition for several years. By then, the College had no further instructional use for the sections and TX150 was eventually scrapped.

Rolls-Royce had starting developing its first axial-flow turbojet, the AJ.65, in 1946 and it went into production as the Avon, which proved to be the most important single element in the whole of the British aircraft industry in the mid-twentieth century. The MAP suggested to Gloster in the same year that the new engine might be used as the power plant for the E.1/44 and a possible installation drawing was prepared under Specification E.23/46. However, the redesign work necessary to produce an Avon-powered E.23/46 was considered too great, and the proposal was eventually dropped.

The Final Ignominy

On 2 November 1950, TX145 had a flameout while being flown by an RAE pilot who brought it down for a crash-landing, from which it sustained slight damage, which was repaired within two months. Then on 10 January 1951, the aircraft suffered a powerful shimmy of the nose-wheel assembly and this more or less proved the end so far as the RAE's use for the two aircraft was concerned.

Both aircraft were consigned to the Proof and Experimental Establishment at Shoeburyness on 24 September 1951. There they joined several other distinguished airframes that together represented tens of thousands of hours of technical endeavour, to become targets, proving the efficiency of armaments of the time. So ended a programme that commenced eight years earlier, in the summer of 1942, for which high hopes were anticipated by the MAP and the RAF, but they remained just hopes.

The Third of the Trio

Although the two GA.2s were destined for the RAE, Gloster was getting the third prototype/fourth airframe, TX150, near to completion. Designated the GA.3, it was planned to have this aircraft powered by a de Havilland Ghost DGt.3, which by this time was also producing 5,000lb (2,300kg) thrust. But in November 1949, before TX145 departed to Farnborough, work on TX150 was terminated and the airframe, in an advanced state of construction, was used for structural testing.

Technical Data – Gloster E.1/44	
Dimensions:	Span 36ft (10.97m); length (TX145) 38ft (11.58m), (TX148) 38ft 11in (11.87m); height (TX145) 11ft 8in (3.55m), (TX148) 12ft 1in (3.68m)
Powerplant:	One Rolls-Royce Nene RN.2 turbojet, producing 5,000lb (2,300kg) thrust
Weights:	Empty 8,260lb (3,746kg); loaded 11,470lb (5,202kg)
Performance:	Maximum speed at sea level 620mph (1,000km/h); normal service ceiling 44,000ft (13,400m); maximum range 650 miles (1,050km)
Production:	Three aircraft partially built to Specification E.5/42 with serial numbers NN648, NN651 and NN655. Three aircraft built to Specification E.1/44 with serial numbers SM801, SM805 and SM809. Following write-off of SM801, SM805 and SM809 completed as TX145 and TX148 respectively, plus TX150, not completed.

CHAPTER SEVEN

Supermarine E.41/46

Swift Evolution

When the mantle of Chief Designer for the Supermarine Aviation Works Ltd (later the Supermarine Division of Vickers-Armstrongs (Aircraft) Ltd) descended upon Joseph 'Joe' Smith, through the death of Reginald J. Mitchell on 11 June 1937, he became responsible for developing the Spitfire into one of the great aircraft of World War Two. It progressed through the laminar-flow wing stage into the Spiteful/Seafang, which was stalled by the ending of the war. But before this, Smith had turned his attention to the new source of power that had been born in Britain through the endeavours of Frank Whittle.

Rolls-Royce started the design for their RB.40 centrifugal-flow engine in March 1944, which initially showed promise of producing over 4,000lb (1,800kg) thrust. Supermarine were asked to design a new fighter around the engine to Specification E.1/44, drawing on their experience with laminar-flow wings. The RB.40 was a large engine and Joe Smith approached Rolls-Royce to see if a reduction in size could be made. They obliged and the RB.41, later named the Nene, came into existence. Supermarine's fighter, built to revised Specification E.10/44, first flew in prototype form on 27 July 1946, and materialized as the Royal Navy's first turbojet-powered aircraft, produced to Specification E.1/45 and named the Attacker F.1, in June 1947.

The Wake-up Call

The volumes of research data gleaned from the defeated German aircraft industry in 1945 were eagerly grasped by both the United States and the USSR. The principle of swept-wing flying surfaces was seized upon by the two powers so enthusiastically that the Soviet Mikoyan-Gurevich design bureau – taking advantage of Britain's gift of a quantity of Nene engines – had a prototype MiG-15 airborne by 2 July 1947,

followed that October by North American Aviation's XP-86, the prototype Sabre.

By the end of 1946, the British Air Staff started to realize that the UK was lagging behind in experience with high-speed turbojet aircraft, at an ever-increasing and alarming rate. They saw the adaptation of existing straight-wing designs as their quickest option, and Hawker Aircraft was given Specification E.38/46 to produce a fighter with wing-sweep, based on their P.1040, which emerged as the P.1052 described in detail in Chapter Four; while Supermarine received E.41/46 to cover the

When rolled out as the first prototype Type 510, VV109 had a sharply pointed nose-cone, which it still had at the 1949 SBAC Display. It showed, when landing, its large flap area. *Aeroplane*

ABOVE: The 'Attacker with all flying surfaces swept' description is easily confirmed as the first Type 510 flies over the coast, minus the original pointed nose-cone. *Aeroplane*

RIGHT: The early horn-balanced tailplane is visible in this shot, as is the sloping jet-pipe orifice. Author's collection

development of a swept-wing aircraft from the Attacker. The E.10/44 prototype's maiden flight on 27 July 1946 was around the time that Specification E.41/46 was issued, and over a year later, on 2 September 1947, Hawker got their P.1040 airborne. Both companies received contracts to cover the building of two prototypes of their respective swept-wing designs, with Supermarine's offerings being allocated serial numbers VV106 and VV119.

The Start

Hursley Park, outside Winchester, was the company's experimental establishment and the foundations of both prototypes had been laid down there by the end of 1946. Type number 510 was given to the project but, although half the design was in existence as the Attacker, work already

in hand at Supermarine meant that progress on the swept-wing prototypes was a little on the slow side, to say the least – in stark contrast to their American and Russian counterparts.

Two years elapsed before VV106 was rolled out and, following basic system checks, it was dismantled for transportation by road to the A&AEE at Boscombe Down, a distance of some 30 miles. Supermarine's long-serving Chief Test Pilot Jeffrey Quill lost his medical category in 1948 and handed the reins over to Lt Cdr Mike Lithgow RN. On 29 December 1948, Lithgow made his first prototype maiden flight when he lifted VV106 off Boscombe Down's vast runway.

In appearance, the Type 510 was an Attacker with all the flying surfaces swept back. The 10 per cent thickness/chord-ratio wing, with its 44-degree leading-edge sweep, was attached to the fuselage at the

same pick-up points as on the Attacker, as was the 45-degree swept tailplane. A leading-edge sweep angle of 45 degrees was employed on the fin/rudder assembly and the undercarriage, including a twin-wheel tailwheel, was straight off the Attacker production line. Only the main wheels' oleo pivot angle was altered to compensate for the wing sweep. An anti-spin parachute was carried in a blister fairing on the upper rear fuselage, aft of the rudder. The finish was overall natural metal and only the national markings produced any comment, as the fuselage carried the wartime C-Type roundels and fin flash, while on the wings post-war D-Type roundels, reintroduced around 1947–48, were applied. A possible explanation could be that the fuselage, together with the tail unit, came straight off the Attacker line and had already received its markings, whereas the wings were specially constructed items.

Trials, Problems and a Nose Job

From an early stage in the test programme, poor handling at both low and high speeds became apparent. While the Type 510 showed a considerable superiority in maximum speed over the Attacker, gradual lateral trim changes as the speed increased culminated in the port wing dropping to such an extent that the control-column needed full movement to starboard in order to counteract this. Together with a tip-stall tendency at low speeds, it confirmed that the aircraft was in need of a fully powered control system.

On 16 March 1949, Lithgow made a wheels-up forced landing at Boscombe Down and the trials programme was temporarily suspended until 10 May, when the repairs had been completed. Also early in the programme, the cockpit canopy became detached in flight and modifications were made to the hood jettison mechanism. A pointed nose-cone containing a pitot head was fitted for part of the high-speed testing and the aircraft was painted in an overall silver finish, with D-Type markings all round.

In its demonstration routine at the 1949 SBAC Display VV106, performing at speeds in excess of 600mph (970km/h), proved to be the fastest aircraft at that year's Display and Lithgow executed some very tight-radius turns.

But by October 1949, the vibrations that occurred when the engine was throttled back became severe enough for the A&AEE to return the aircraft to Supermarine for modifications. These involved the fitting of an Attacker's front engine mounting, plus a redesigning of the boundary layer bleed louvres above and below the intakes, while the cockpit ventilation system was removed just in case this too affected the intake airflow. Boscombe Down pilots also disliked the tail-wheel undercarriage and voiced their opinion that the aircraft needed a tricycle undercarriage, as well as improved elevator control.

Deck-landing Trials

During the late summer of 1950, VV106 was modified for deck-landing trials and evaluation requested by the Admiralty, to assess swept-wing aircraft as potential Fleet Air Arm (FAA) fighters. A standard A-frame arrester hook was installed, the undercarriage main-wheel doors were removed and provision made for four Rocket Assisted Take-Off (RATO) units at the wing-root trailing edge, one above and below on each side. The increase of 613lb (278kg) in all-up-weight was not considered enough to affect the take-off performance. The cockpit hood was also changed from the Attacker-type blown canopy to a heavily-framed unit, and the pointed nose-cone was removed.

Mike Lithgow first flew VV106 in its naval configuration on 14 September and fellow Supermarine test pilot L. R. Colquhoun delivered it to RAE Farnborough six days later to begin a three-month trials programme. This included simulated

For the deck-landing trials on HMS _Illustrious_ in November 1950, VV106 had its undercarriage doors removed and an A-frame arrester hook installed, as well as provision for a Rocket Assisted Take-Off unit to be fitted on each side, aft of the wing root. _Aeroplane_

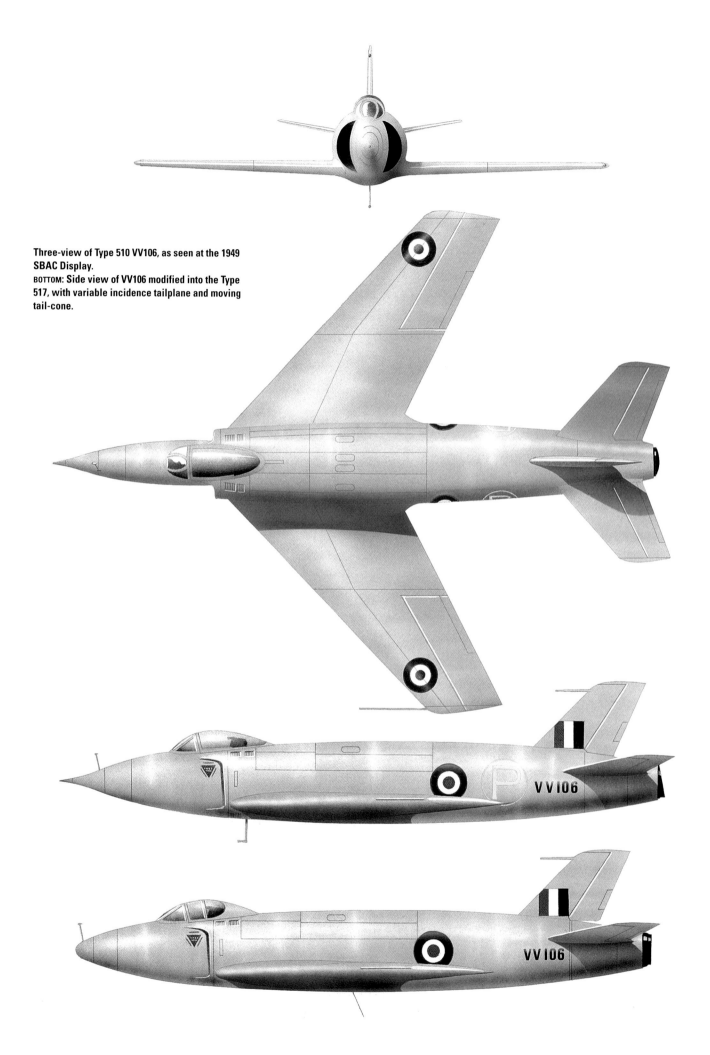

Three-view of Type 510 VV106, as seen at the 1949 SBAC Display.
BOTTOM: Side view of VV106 modified into the Type 517, with variable incidence tailplane and moving tail-cone.

VV106

VV106

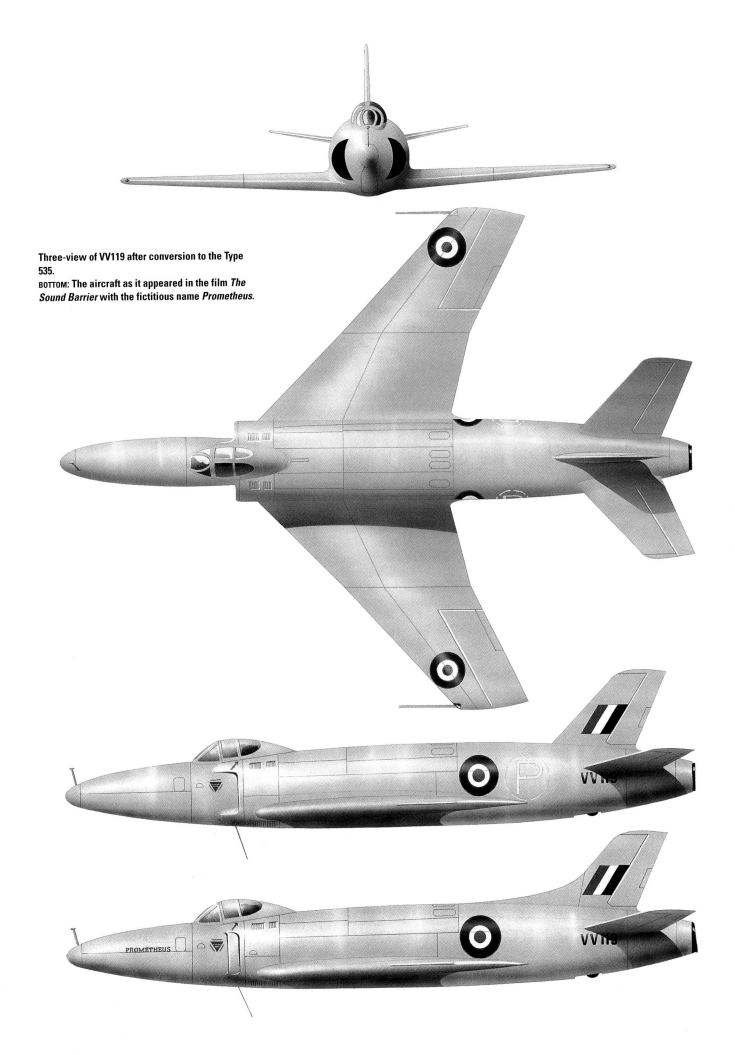

Three-view of VV119 after conversion to the Type 535.
BOTTOM: The aircraft as it appeared in the film *The Sound Barrier* with the fictitious name *Prometheus*.

deck landings, plus take-offs with and without RATO assistance. The aircraft was cleared for operations using the four rocket units and on 8 November, Lt J. Elliott RN approached HMS *Illustrious* to make the world's first landing of an aircraft with swept-back flying surfaces onto a carrier. A dozen take-offs and landings were made during the day by Lt Elliott, together with Mike Lithgow and A&AEE pilot Lt Cdr D. G. Parker, who went on to become Rear-Admiral Parker before retiring from the Royal Navy.

Take-offs were achieved using only two rockets and the following day the naval trials were completed with drama, as Lt Cdr Parker encountered asymmetric thrust when the RATO unit on one side failed to provide full power and VV106 swung violently, so that a wingtip struck the top of one of the vessel's gun turrets. The flying skills that had gained the pilot admission into the ranks of A&AEE aircrew enabled the take-off to be satisfactorily completed.

The Second Prototype

Eight months before VV106's naval excursion, the second E.41/46 prototype, VV119, was ready to fly and although visually similar to its stablemate, it received a new company designation, the Type 528. In anticipation of an afterburner being installed – though this never came to fruition – the tail-cone outer skin was cut back by over 12in (30cm), which had the Nene's jet-pipe protruding aft more noticeably than on the first aircraft. It went by road to Boscombe Down for Lithgow to take it into the air for the first time, on 27 March, but within six weeks it was back at Hursley Park to start a

3½-month metamorphosis to become the Type 535, and the name Swift was announced for the forthcoming operational fighter for which the two E.41/46 aircraft were providing data.

In its Type 535 form, VV119 followed the A&AEE's assessment made on VV106 that a tricycle undercarriage would greatly benefit the aircraft, and an entirely new nose section to accommodate the forward-retracting nose-wheel increased the aircraft's overall length by nearly 3ft (0.9m). Supermarine stood their ground, however, and a retractable twin-tailwheel unit was retained, to act as a bumper during high-angle-of-attack take-offs and landings. A Rolls-Royce Nene RN.3 giving 5,100lb (2,300kg) thrust and with provision for afterburning was installed, which required 20 per cent larger and re-contoured intakes sited further forward, as well as the fitting of a new tail-cone to allow for an afterburner to be added at a later date. (When this was eventually installed, it created an unacceptable weight penalty and proved to be unreliable, so it was soon discarded.)

VV119 retained the original fin/rudder assembly from its short Type 528 life, but was fitted with a new wing whose planform, with reduced-span ailerons and increased chord at the centre-section, conformed to the proposed Swift wing, with a larger fuel capacity and a wing-mounted cannon armament, for which dummy fairings were fitted. The cannon installation was not, however, carried forward to the production fighter. While supplementary perforated airbrakes were mounted on the wing's upper surfaces for evaluation, the scheme was abandoned as it was found that the new wing flaps

required virtually no trim changes or buffet when lowered, so they were strengthened to be used as airbrakes as well as conventional flaps. The heavily framed cockpit hood as fitted on VV106 was applied to the Type 535 and in this form, with a natural-metal finish, VV119 made its second maiden flight from Boscombe Down on 23 August 1950. Thirteen days later, it was flown to Farnborough to participate in the SBAC Display flying programme, alongside Hawker's all-swept flying surfaces representative, the P.1081.

Further Development and Stardom

Post-Farnborough, VV119 flew for a period with wing fences, to investigate their effect during speed checks conducted at various altitudes up to 35,000ft (11,000m), but they were removed following the completion of the trials. In October 1951, Supermarine production test pilot Sqn Ldr David Morgan took over responsibility for VV119's further development. An original directional instability problem was traced to the fin/rudder assembly, which had not been altered despite the nose length being increased. A long dorsal fairing that increased its effective area was fitted to run from the fin leading edge

For the film *The Sound Barrier*, in which Dave Morgan did the flying, VV119 assumed the fictitious name 'Prometheus'; by this time it had acquired a dorsal extension to its fin. Author's collection

Technical Data – Supermarine E.41/46		
Dimensions:	*VV106* Span 31ft 8½in (9.65m); length without pointed nose-cone 39ft 6in (12m), with pointed nose-cone 39ft 10in (12.13m); height 8ft 9in (12.5m)	*VV119* Span 31ft 8½in (9.65); length as Type 528, 39ft 10in (12.13m), as Type 535, 41ft 1in (12.5m); height 12ft 7in (3.8m)
Powerplants:	VV106, one Rolls-Royce Nene RN.2 turbojet, producing 5,000lb (2,270kg) thrust; VV119, one Rolls-Royce Nene RN.3 turbojet, producing 5,100lb (2,310kg) thrust	
Weights:	VV106, loaded 12,177lb (5,522kg), loaded with RATO 12,790lb (5,800kg); VV119, loaded 14,390lb (6,526kg)	
Performance:	Maximum speed (VV106) 655mph (1,054km/h), operational ceiling 30,000ft (9,144m), (VV119) 698mph (1,123km/h), 35,000ft (11,000m)	
Production:	Two aircraft built to Specification E.41/46, with serial numbers VV106 (Types 510 and 517) and VV119 (Types 528 and 535)	

to blend into the fuselage at a point above the national roundel.

With its new fin, the aircraft found stardom in the autumn of 1951 as the fictitious 'Prometheus' in David Lean's *The Sound Barrier*. Flying was undertaken by Morgan, together with other company pilots, in the airborne sequences of the film, which was a serious attempt to portray flight at transonic speed before fully powered controls and variable-incidence tailplanes became standard. (However, the film's advocated pushing forward of the controls in order to pull out of a transonic dive did extend 'artistic licence' to its limits!)

A VI Tail at Last

VV106 spent a large part of 1952 at the RAE, following its HMS *Illustrious* trials, during which time the arrester hook was removed and the undercarriage main-wheel doors were restored. The North American F-86 had featured a variable incidence (VI) tailplane from the outset and Supermarine's design office were of the opinion that the Type 510's general handling could be improved by such a unit. Furthermore, it would be another step along the road to developing the Swift as a Service aircraft.

In July 1953 VV106 was returned to Supermarine, who had evolved an unconventional way of providing a VI installation on the existing airframe. A new hinged rear fuselage, capable of arcing through 4 degrees above and below the datum line, was installed, with the tailplane attached to the moveable tail-cone. The hinge point was on a line with the rudder hinge and, as the jet-pipe also moved with the rear end, a

cut-out was made at the base of the rudder to facilitate the movement. While being unorthodox, the arrangement worked successfully and was approved by all the pilots.

With this modification, VV106 became the Supermarine Type 517, to remain as such for the next eighteen months until, on 17 January 1955, it was grounded and, as Instructional Airframe 7175M, it went to RAF Halton as an engineering apprentice's airframe. There followed many years on display at the Aerospace Museum at Cosford (now the Royal Air Force Museum, Cosford), before being given on indefinite loan to the Fleet Air Arm Museum at Yeovilton, who currently hold it in storage.

Enter the Fireflash

Following its film debut, VV119 suffered a crash landing early in 1952, while engaged on airbrake trials. Being a robust airframe, repairs only took a few weeks and by mid-March it was back in the air. As already stated, upper wing-surface brakes originally incorporated in the Type 535 conversion were discarded in favour of reinforced main flaps, to operate in a dual capacity as airbrakes. This was a reasonable compromise for test-flying purposes but was not acceptable for an operational fighter.

The age of the air-to-air missile dawned in the early 1950s and on 28 May 1953, VV119 started trials to evaluate the aerodynamic effects of carrying the Fairey Fireflash. Developed under the codename *Blue Sky*, this was the first British air-to-air missile, but it was a rather cumbersome-looking weapon by today's standards and did

not in the end see operational service. The warhead carrier was situated between a pair of solid-fuel booster motors situated above and below its body. These were jettisoned on burning out, to leave the missile to ride on a pencil-thin radar beam projected by the carrying aircraft towards its target; this was considered superior to anything else that came into service for several years.

Various combinations of the dummy missiles were tried, to obtain data on the aircraft's general handling and manoeuvrability while carrying them on short underwing pylons. Flight tests were carried out up to Mach 0.95 with two dummies and Mach 0.90 with four, which proved that either configuration had only a marginal effect on performance.

The actual evaluation of the Fireflash as an operational weapon and the Swift as its carrier was made by the first production prototype WJ960, which made a great contribution to the Swift programme as a whole. This aircraft, however, was built to Specification F.105 and consequently goes beyond the parameters of the E.41/46.

Test flying with VV119 ended in 1955. WJ960 had been flying since 1 August 1951 and was more representative of the Swift, with the wing armament abandoned in favour of a lower-nose installation. VV119 was given Instructional Airframe number 7285M before going to Halton, where its historical trail goes cold.

In preparation for the 1950 SBAC Display, the aircraft was fitted with a dummy cannon installation on its wings. The jet intake warning sign was a little more obvious in those days and VV119 was unique in having the yellow circle around the prototype 'P' as a broken line. Author's collection

CHAPTER EIGHT

Avro 707 Series

En route to the Vulcan

When Roy Chadwick, Chief Designer for A. V. Roe & Co Ltd, sketched out an idea for a delta-wing airliner on a scrap of paper in 1945, nearly six years of war had just finished and thoughts of advanced military aircraft were not very high on the nation's agenda.

By 1947, things had changed. The aspirations of Communism had become apparent and Britain was developing a nuclear weapon, for whose delivery a modern bomber would be required. Specification B.35/46 had been placed with the aircraft industry and various designs were submitted, from which the offerings of Avro and Handley Page were short-listed. Chadwick plumped for his delta-wing concept, given the designation Type 698, while Handley Page indulged in a crescent-wing format for their H.P.80, and contracts for two prototypes were placed with each company in March 1947.

Expediency

In view of the fact that they were dipping their toes in an unknown pond, Avro considered it would be expedient to build a glider modelled on the configuration, in order to obtain some experience of delta-wing aerodynamics. However, to its credit, the MoS were of the opinion that a powered, one-third scaled-down trials aircraft would provide better research data. They issued Specification E.15/48 to cover the design and construction of the trials aircraft, which was allocated the company designation Type 707.

Avro also produced drawings for a projected twin-engined, high-speed, scaled-down research aircraft under the Type number 710, to investigate a flight envelope up to an altitude of 60,000ft (18,000m) and a speed of Mach 0.95. On further consideration, however, they agreed that the additional data this aircraft would yield did not merit the time and expenditure

involved in its construction, so the Type 710 was dropped while still on the drawing board.

To replace it, the company received contract 6/ACFT/2205/CB(6)b to build one high-speed and two low-speed variants of the Type 707. Each aircraft was to be powered by a Rolls-Royce Derwent 5 turbojet producing 3,500lb (1,600kg) thrust, and metal was cut for the first aircraft in September 1948.

First British Delta-Wing

The first Type 707, allotted serial number VX784, was to provide data for the Type 698 bomber, rather than investigate the

from the Avro Athena trainer which had started being produced, while the nose-wheel assembly and cockpit canopy came from Gloster's Meteor F.8 line.

Construction of VX784 was completed by mid-August 1949. The aircraft was small, with the Derwent 5 mounted in the rear fuselage and fed via a dorsal air intake that was dissected by an extension of the fin leading edge mounted above the intake duct. The aircraft was of all-metal stressed-skin construction, with its short nose section ahead of the delta-wing's leading edge and the cockpit, which was not provided with an ejector seat, positioned well forward on the section, from which a nose-tip yaw-meter boom projected. The wing leading and trailing edges were straight,

The only Type 707 stands on its Athena main wheels, with a Meteor nose-wheel and cockpit canopy, for its first photo session. Author's collection

behaviour and handling of delta-wings in general. It was to be a low-performance research aircraft and, in the interests of economy and speed of construction, elements from aircraft already in production at fellow Hawker Siddeley Group companies were to be used. Consequently, the main undercarriage units were supplied

meeting at pointed tips, while a spin-recovery parachute was carried in a tubular housing at the base of the rudder.

Control was to be provided by four surfaces hinged on the rear wing spar, in conjunction with the rudder. Of these, the outboard pair of surfaces were ailerons, with the inboard pair acting as elevators,

while two retractable airbrakes were situated either side of the rear fuselage cone below the fin/rudder assembly and two more in an underwing position forward of the main-wheel bays.

Maiden British Delta-Wing Flight

When rolled out from Woodford's assembly shop, painted an overall silver, VX784 carried a national colour fin flash and a large yellow prototype 'P' on the nose, but no roundels. Preliminary systems checks were made, together with initial taxiing trials, before the aircraft was dismantled for transportation to Boscombe Down on 26 August 1949, where it was prepared for the start of flight trials.

These did not start as scheduled, because a strong cross-wind over the A&AEE's runway was considered to be too hazardous for the first flight of an aircraft with a configuration of virtually unknown aerodynamic properties. More than twenty-four hours of frustration followed, until by 19.30hr on 4 September the wind had abated and Avro's Assistant Chief Test Pilot, Flt Lt Eric 'Red' Esler, took the little delta-winged prototype into the Wiltshire air for a 35-minute maiden flight.

Over the next two days, a further two and a half hours of test flying increased Esler's confidence in the aircraft, which he found handled in a similar fashion to conventional-winged turbojet-powered aeroplanes, but required a much longer take-off run. By 6 September, Avro were keen to show their new trials aircraft and Esler flew VX784 across-country to Farnborough,

where that year's SBAC Display was being held. Parked in the static enclosure, it certainly generated great attention amongst the aeronautical fraternity.

Twenty-six Days

After attending the SBAC's annual event, VX784 was flown back to Boscombe Down where further data-measuring equipment was installed, prior to test-flying being resumed during the last week of the month.

The delta-winged aircraft handled perfectly and provided no cause for concern during its twenty-six days of flying. Therefore its crashing near Blackbushe on 30 September came as a great shock to Avro

VX784 here shows its underwing and, just discernable, rear fuselage airbrakes, deployed in the extended position. *Aeroplane*

and the A&AEE, made all the more disastrous by 'Red' Esler being killed in the accident. While the cause of the crash has never been fully established, the prime suspect was a failure of the airbrake control system, which locked the airbrakes in a fully extended position while the aircraft was flying a low-speed, low-altitude test programme. The ensuing stall would have occurred at too low an altitude for recovery, and had VX784 been fitted with an ejector seat, it is doubtful if Esler would have

Eric Esler lifts VX784 off for the first time on 4 September 1949, only twenty-six days before its fatal crash. *Aeroplane*

survived, as the safe operating parameters of 1949-vintage ejector seats were a lot smaller than those of today's sophisticated seats.

Type 707B

While VX784 was the Type 707 without any suffix letter, the second aircraft, also covered by contract 6/ACFT/2205/CB(6)b, was designated the 707B. With the serial number VX790, it was well on the way to completion when VX784 crashed. However, the loss of the first aircraft took Avro by surprise and their reassessment of what was required for the second 707 came to the conclusion that a Martin-Baker Mk 1 ejector seat was top of the priorities list. Further lessons learned from VX784's short span of flying were incorporated in VX790, with the net result being that, to accommodate them, together with the ejector seat, a completely new, longer front fuselage needed to be designed and it required a revised cockpit canopy. An extension was added to the fin, but the Derwent had a dorsal air-intake similar to the Type 707's.

In view of the suspected reason for VX784's demise, the whole airbrake system was revised. The rear fuselage installation was discarded and a new unit was fitted, consisting of an airbrake positioned on the top surface of each wing that retracted flat with the outer skin, to work in conjunction with the retained underwing unit, while modifications were also made to the elevators. The same speed/economy factor in construction was adhered to where possible, and this time the nose-wheel unit was taken off the Hawker Sea Hawk production line. All in all, the revisions in the 707B led to an aerodynamically improved aircraft, with a better centre of gravity than its predecessor's.

Data Provider to Several Masters

The basic requirement of the 707B was to evaluate the low-speed handling characteristics of the delta-wing as an entity, not necessarily related just to the Type 698.

With an overall blue colour scheme and, as the nose section was considerably longer than that of VX784, the D-Type roundel, VZ790 went by road to Boscombe Down during the last week of August 1950. Once there, comprehensive systems checks were made; and taxiing trials, during which the aircraft lifted off the tarmac on at least one occasion, culminated in it having a maiden flight on 6 September with Avro's CTP, Wg Cdr R. J. 'Roly' Falk OBE AFC at the controls. During a distinguished career in the RAF, Falk made test flights in several captured Luftwaffe aircraft in his position as CTP to the Experimental Flying

The first Type 707B had a longer nose and revised cockpit canopy compared with VX784, covering a Martin-Baker Mk 1 ejector seat, but it had the same air-intake profile. It carries a Hawker Siddeley Group logo ahead of the roundel, ready for attending the static park at the 1950 SBAC Display. Author's collection

ABOVE: On the Type 707B, the airbrake's profiles were changed, with the Type 707 rear fuselage unit deleted in favour of an upper-wing-surface location. Author's collection

BELOW: VX790 acquired prototype markings while fitted with the original air intake, but by 1951 turbulence from the new canopy had necessitated a change to the intake geometry. *Aeroplane*

Department that evaluated enemy aircraft. Prior to World War Two he had flown for the British press corps during the Abyssinian and Spanish civil wars, so when he joined Avro in 1950 the company received a very experienced pilot.

His responsibility was very considerable, with the future of the company's whole delta-wing programme being, to a large extent, dependent on his findings with the 707B. Consequently, a great sigh of relief echoed over the whole north-west of Britain when he brought VX790 in for landing after the fifteen-minute flight, to report that everything worked and the aircraft handled well. This galvanized the company's Managing Director, Sir Roy Dobson, together with Air Marshal Boothman, Controller of Supplies (Air), into requesting the aircraft be included in the static section at the SBAC Display, which had opened the previous day. With permission granted, Falk flew the same course to Farnborough as Esler the year before, for it to be on view for the remainder of the week.

With the public relations exercise completed, VX790 left Farnborough to begin a concentrated programme of test flying, and on 24 October it was flown to the A&AEE for their general assessment. This was the first time that the Establishment had been able to undertake such an exercise, as VX748 had not lasted long enough.

The considered opinion of A&AEE pilots was favourable, with the delta-wing geometry not presenting any unpleasant surprises. However, when Falk flew the aircraft over a speed range of 95–410mph (153–660km/h), he found that at the higher speeds, air starvation to the dorsal intake was occurring. Rolls-Royce assisted by making their wind tunnel available for tests, and it was found that the cockpit canopy generated turbulence between itself and the intake, such that a smooth airflow to the engine could not be maintained. This was remedied during February 1951 by increasing the depth of the intake, together with the fitting of an airflow guide channel between it and the canopy.

The length of the take-off run was similar to the first prototype's, as was the fact that the elevators were virtually inactive until the aircraft was on the point of lift-off. The angle of incidence needed to be adjusted and this was accomplished by the relatively simple expedient of increasing the nose-wheel oleo's length by 9in (23cm), thereby reducing the take-off run by a considerable margin.

In the course of 1951, VX790 logged over 100 hours of test flying, plus its first demonstration flight slot at a SBAC Display. During the year, trials were made using the anti-spin parachute as a retardant on landing, which was carried forward to all Type 698 operations. Experiments with jet-pipe angles also revealed that the bomber would benefit in longitudinal stability from attention to this area, rather than just letting the jet efflux exhaust parallel to the line of flight.

By September, with the 698 now taking shape at Woodford, VX790 was transferred to the A&AEE at Boscombe Down for a programme of delta-wing stability trials, but these were delayed due to an accident shortly after the aircraft's arrival. Repairs were completed for the trials to resume on 16 May 1952, and they added another thirty hours to the aircraft's flying time.

The A&AEE trials completed, operations of the 707B were again transferred, this time to RAE Farnborough who, in turn, passed it back to Boscombe Down on 26 January 1956, but this time to the Empire Test Pilots' School (ETPS) who shared the Wiltshire base with the A&AEE. However, this opportunity does not appear to have been taken too seriously by the School for, following a landing accident on 29 September that year, it was not considered a viable proposition to have the aircraft repaired and it was put into

The third aircraft built, WB280, was the first of two Type 707As, which had air intakes in the wing-root leading edge. These were used to obtain data on this configuration for the Type 698 Vulcan programme. Aeroplane

storage at No.71 MU at Bicester for a year. On 22 October 1957 VX790, still in its damaged state from the ETPS landing accident, was passed to the other RAE complex on the former USAAF's 306th Bomb Group base at Thurleigh, which post-war was generally known as RAE Bedford. At this Establishment it became a source of spares for the third aircraft in the Type 707 series, before finally being scrapped.

Third Type 707

As already stated, construction of the Type 698 was under way by 1951 and a continuation of the Type 707 series was considered unnecessary: the bomber's design had benefited from data already supplied by VX790. However, a full-size model tested in the wind tunnel had shown that wing-root air-intakes for its four engines, together

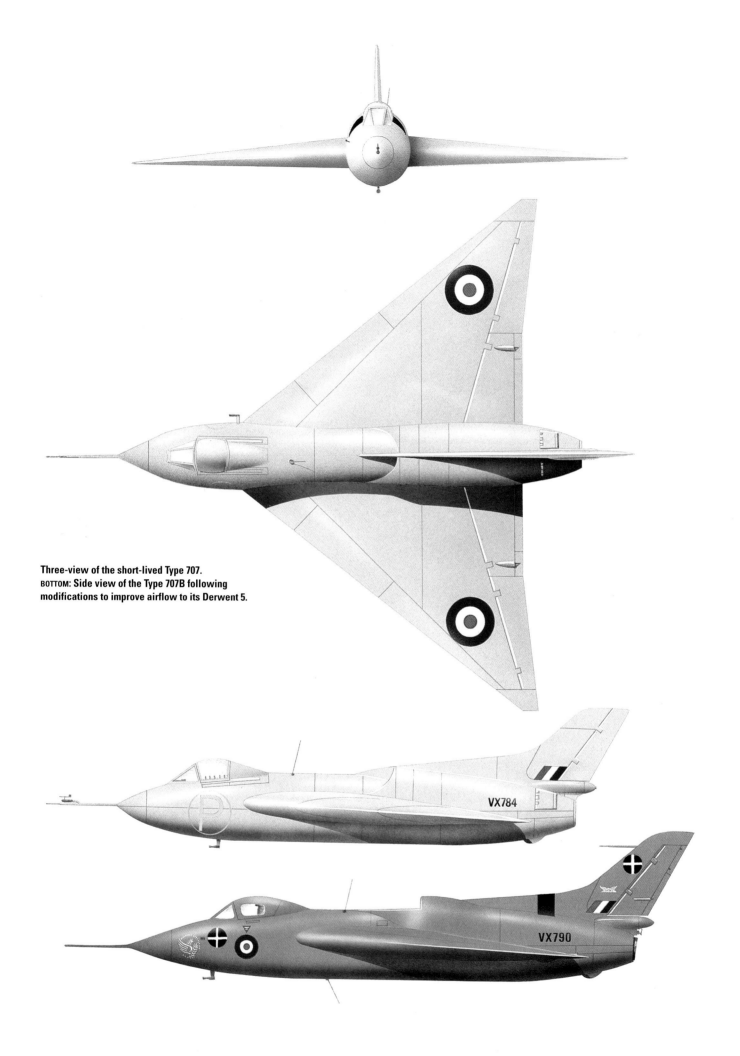

Three-view of the short-lived Type 707.
BOTTOM: Side view of the Type 707B following
modifications to improve airflow to its Derwent 5.

VX784

VX790

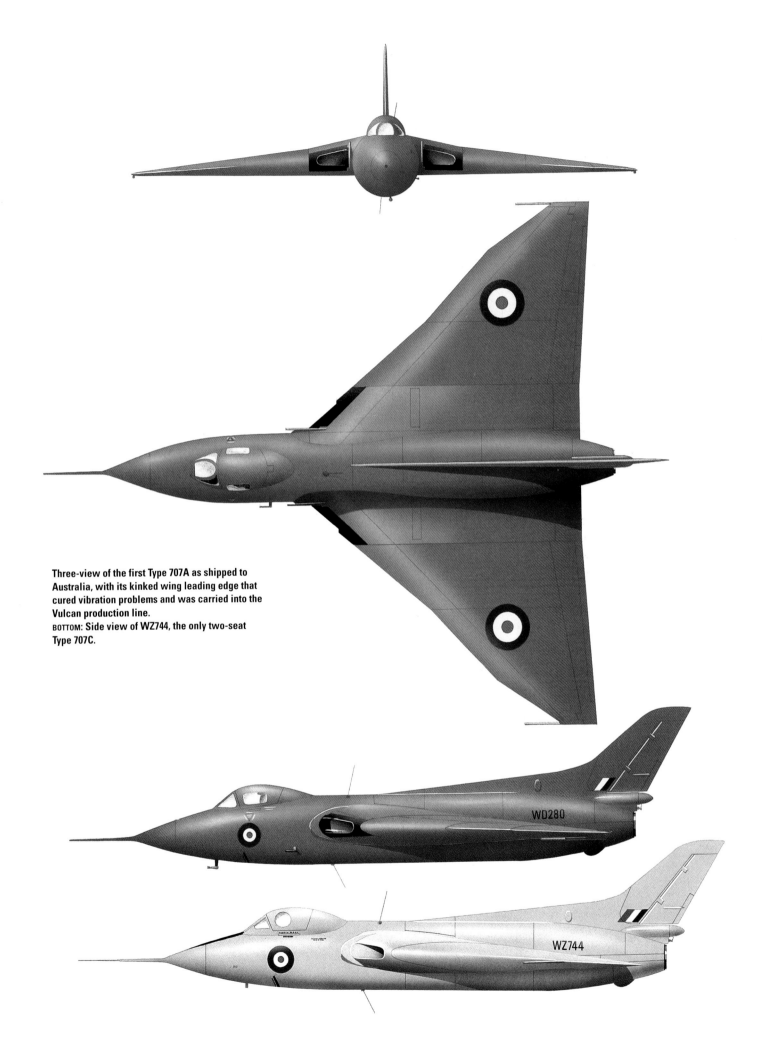

Three-view of the first Type 707A as shipped to
Australia, with its kinked wing leading edge that
cured vibration problems and was carried into the
Vulcan production line.
BOTTOM: Side view of WZ744, the only two-seat
Type 707C.

WD280

WZ744

ABOVE AND RIGHT: **Seen on its way to the 1953 SBAC Display, WD280 carries the Hawker Siddeley Group logo on its nose and an Avro logo on the fin, whereas the second Type 707A, WZ736, seen landing at the display, is devoid of any company publicity.** *Aeroplane* and author's collection

BELOW: **The second Type 707A stands alongside Shackleton MR.2 WG531 at Woodford, with a Lancaster and an Ashton in the background.** Harry Holmes

Type 707 Number Four

Irrespective of the MoS's initial thought that maybe a third Type 707 was unnecessary, Avro's ideas were entirely the opposite and, besides WD280, they decided to build another Type 707A. Given the serial WZ736, the second 707A was covered by contract 6/ACFT/7470/CB(6)b, to be built at the company's repair and overhaul establishment at Bracebridge Heath, south of Lincoln. This site dated back to World War One, when Maurice Farman Longhorns were produced and various Sopwith fighters were test-flown from the small airfield. By 1920 it was closed, but Avro reopened the site shortly before the start of World War Two, for it to become a major maintenance and salvage base for Lancasters in squadron service.

On completion, WZ736, finished in the same colours as WD280, took a different path for its first flight. RAF Waddington was just 2 miles down the A15 trunk road from Bracebridge Heath, so the aircraft was towed there on its own undercarriage and, on 20 February 1953, twenty months after WD280 first flew, Avro test pilot J. C. Nelson took it into the air for the first time.

with a wingspan greater than the dimensions proposed, would greatly enhance its performance. Consequently, Specification E.10/49 was issued to Avro, who put in hand the construction of a third aircraft to contract 6/ACFT/3395/CB(6)b, featuring the wing-root intakes and a wing-span exactly one-third scale to the bomber.

To demonstrate the inconsistency of aircraft nomenclature, this third aircraft was designated the Type 707A. Serial WD280 was allocated to the aircraft which, while having a slightly larger wingspan, had a

fuselage length identical to VX790. A Derwent 8 producing 3,600lb (1,630kg) thrust was installed, and the whole aircraft had a closer relationship to the Type 698, in so far as the dorsal intake of the earlier 707s was replaced by wing-root apertures.

WD280 was completed in summer 1951 and followed the route of its stablemates in being transported by road to Boscombe Down, where 'Roly' Falk took it for its maiden flight on 14 July. Painted an overall vermilion, apart from a black surround to the intakes, it made a colourful sight.

ABOVE: **When displayed at the 1968 Finningley Air Show, VX736 was bedecked in a new colour scheme and without main-wheel covers.** Dennis Robinson via *Aeroplane*

LEFT AND BELOW: **WZ744 was the only Type 707C built; the cramped side-by-side seating in the standard Type 707 front section is very evident.** Harry Holmes and *Aeroplane*

With airbrakes out and elevons raised, WZ744 holds formation with the photographer's aircraft. Author's collection

The 707As are Justified

The Type 698's first prototype, VX770, had its maiden flight six months before WZ736. WD280 had been flying for a year by then, and besides having confirmed the shape of the wing-root intakes it was destined, with WZ736, to have a greater input on the production 698 than any of their companions.

With both aircraft's wings being a true one-third scale of the bomber, they replicated its wing geometry more accurately. During their flight-test programme it was perceived that a slight vibration occurred in the wings, which had not been noticed in earlier, slower-speed sorties. The vibration became more acute as speed was increased and, furthermore, increased at higher altitudes. Once again the Type 698 was facing a crisis, not for financial or doubtful aerodynamic reasons, but because now the first prototype was flying, the second (VX771) was in an advanced state of construction and sub-assemblies for several production aircraft had already been manufactured.

Exhaustive tests by the 707As confirmed that the vibration was caused by the airflow over the wing tips. An early attempt to rectify matters involved WZ736 being fitted

with wing fences at about three-quarters span: these went some way in slowing down the airflow, but they were far from providing a satisfactory remedy to the phenomenon. The design and drawing offices pulled out all the stops, with the result that a reshaping of the wing's leading edge appeared to be the solution. This was verified by wind-tunnel tests, but would have to be confirmed in test flights.

The new wing, to be known as the Phase 2 wing in 698 production, involved a reduction of the leading-edge sweep on the inner section of the outer wing to a point approximately three-quarters across the span. The sweep was then increased to the tip, which featured a greater curve rearwards than on the original planform.

WD280 had a scaled-down pair of the new wings fitted at Bracebridge Heath for flight testing, and to everyone's great relief the remedy proved to be entirely successful across the whole speed/altitude envelope. The building of 698 sub-assemblies had gone on unabated during the time taken in finding a cure to the problem and sixteen sets of wing leading edges produced to the original configuration had to be scrapped; this included some already

installed on production aircraft. In retrospect it was obvious that a problem of this magnitude would have been picked up at an earlier stage, had the Type 707 programme been more co-ordinated with the 698's production schedules, but it is easy to be wise after the event. However, the validity of the delta-wing as an aerodynamic shape had proved to be capable of adapting to all that had been asked of it up to that date, and the continuation with the delta-wing bomber programme was fully justified.

A 707 Trainer

When Avro received contract 6/ACFT/7470/CB(6)b, giving the go-ahead to produce a second 707A, the order included the design and building of four two-seater trainer variants, to which the company designation Type 707C was applied. They were to have side-by-side seating with dual controls, the object being to initiate Service pilots into the handling of delta-wing aircraft. However, by August 1952 the first prototype 698 was flying and the second was well down the line at Woodford, so the question of requiring four 707Cs was raised. The MoS saw that they would not now be necessary, so three were cancelled and the one remaining trainer was constructed at Bracebridge Heath, as Woodford was now swamped with bombers.

Given the serial WZ744 and finished in an overall silver colour scheme, the trainer was completed in June 1953 and, like WD280, took the A15 to Waddington for a first flight to be made on 1 July, with company test pilot J. B. Wales at the controls.

The side-by-side seating arrangement, shoe-horned into the same fuselage width as the single-seater's and precluding the installation of ejector seats, proved to be very claustrophobic and you certainly had to be on good terms with your fellow pilot! The cockpit was covered by an all-metal canopy, with a circular window on either side being the only means of sidewards vision. Powered by a Derwent 8 like the two 707As, WZ744 was flown up to Woodford for its manufacturers trials but, with the whole 698 programme at an advanced stage of production, the 707C was unable to make any contribution to its development.

However, the field of modern aircraft controls benefited greatly, as the RAE flew the aircraft at Farnborough and Bedford for fourteen years. Its dual control system enabled manual controls to be retained on one side and electronic or powered controls on the other, thereby allowing constructive comparisons to be made. From these RAE trials, the modern 'fly-by-wire' control system evolved.

By 1967, the RAE had finished with WZ744 and, with the Instructional Airframe number 7932M, it went to RAF Finningley, where it joined WZ736. Today, having spent periods at both RAF Colerne and RAF Topcliffe, it is on display at Cosford's RAF Museum, restored to WZ744 markings.

Type 707A WZ736 was also employed by the RAE for many years, in automatic throttle development trials, relative to delta-winged aircraft controls. In particular, the high-incidence angle that deltas required on the landing approach needed to be compensated by throttle responses, which were made much easier to handle by automation. These trials also ended in 1967 and WZ736 received the Instructional Airframe number 7868M before going to Finningley, where it was refurbished. At the time of writing, carrying its original serial, the vermilion delta forms a part of the aviation collection at the Museum of Science and Industry in Manchester.

Farnborough 1953. BELOW: Family portrait reading from the front: WZ744, VX790, WZ736, WD280 ... BOTTOM: With Mum and Dad, VX777 and VX770. Harry Holmes and author's collection

WD280, with the production Vulcan wing leading-edge shape, moved to Australia in May 1956, aboard HMS *Sydney*. Author's collection

Technical Data

Avro Type 707

Dimensions:	Span 33ft (10m); length 30ft 6in (9.3m); height 10ft 7in (3.2m)
Powerplant:	One Rolls-Royce Derwent 5 turbojet, producing 3,500lb (1,1600kg) thrust
Weight:	Loaded 8,600lb (3,900kg)
Production:	One aircraft built to Specification E.15/48, with serial number VX784

Avro Type 707A

Dimensions:	Span 34ft 2in (10.4m); length 42ft 4in (12.9m); height 11ft 7in (3.53m)
Powerplant:	One Rolls-Royce Derwent 8 turbojet, producing 3,600lb (1,630kg) thrust
Weight:	Loaded 9,500lb (4,300kg)
Production:	Two aircraft built to Specification E.10/49, with serial numbers WD280 and WZ736

Avro Type 707B

Dimensions:	Span 33ft (10m); length 42ft 4in (12.9m); height 11ft 9in (3.58m)
Powerplant:	One Rolls-Royce Derwent 5 turbojet, producing 3,500lb (1,600kg) thrust
Weight:	Loaded 9,500lb (4,300kg)
Production:	One aircraft built to Specification E.15/48, with serial number VX790

Avro Type 707C

Dimensions:	Span 34ft 2in (10.4m); length 42ft 4in (12.9m); height 11ft 7in (3.53m)
Powerplant:	One Rolls-Royce Derwent 8 turbojet, producing 3,600lb (1,630kg) thrust
Weight:	10,000lb (4,500kg)
Production:	Four aircraft ordered to Specification E.10/4 but only one built, with serial number WZ744
Performance:	Type 707 aircraft flew with a minimum controllable airspeed of approximately 115mph (185km/h); maximum airspeed approximately 400mph (640km/h)

Antipodean Retirement

WD280 had an entirely different excursion after its great contribution to the Phase 2 wing development. On 12 March 1956, it was shipped aboard the Royal Australian Navy's carrier HMAS *Melbourne* at Glasgow, to arrive on 11 May in Sydney Harbour. At Sydney it was transferred onto HMAS *Sydney*, which sailed to Melbourne, where it arrived on 29 May. WD280 was off-loaded onto a transporter whose metal support collapsed under the weight, so that the aircraft needed relocating onto a sturdier vehicle for its journey to RAAF Laverton.

It was reassembled at Laverton and ground-tested before making its maiden Australian flight on 13 July 1956. Over the next seven years, WD280 was used in a great number of trials programmes, under the sponsorship of the RAAF's Aircraft Research and Development Unit (ARDU), until its last flight in 1963. It had flown 203 hours 30 minutes 'down under', and the same year the aircraft was sold at auction by the Department of Supply, on behalf of the Air Ministry in London.

The highest bidder was a Geoffrey Mallett, who paid A$1,000 and the aircraft was removed to his home in the Melbourne suburb of Williamstown on 12 June. In 1999, WD280 moved to the RAAF Museum at Point Cook, Victoria. It was repainted several times and Mr Mallett, being a maintenance engineer, was able to give the aircraft countless hours of 'TLC'.

In a lifetime associated with its larger stablemate, the Type 698, one of the lasting impressions of the Type 707 held by the very many thousands who attended the 1953 SBAC Display at Farnborough is the sight of the two white bomber prototypes, by now named Vulcan, flying in line astern, flanked by four Type 707s. The silver 707C, blue 707B and two vermilion 707As contributed to the highlight in that year's Display, in what was a most exciting era for British aviation development.

CHAPTER NINE

Avro Type 706 Ashton

Woodford's Flying Laboratory

Following World War Two and into the 1950s, a very large percentage of British turbojet engine development was handled by Avro aircraft converted to the test-bed role. The new generation of axial-flow engines that were emerging were test flown by Lancasters, Lancastrians and Lincolns, who between them test-flew some twenty-three basic engines, plus several upgraded variants. Several Gloster Meteors were pressed into service for the same purpose, and some became trials vehicles to advance the field of airborne radar systems.

However, these aircraft were only able to operate at the altitudes for which they had been originally designed, while their interior space was really quite inadequate for engineers and observers to monitor tests to the standards that were required.

The Tudor 8

Avro's venture into the world of post-war, long-distance, pressurized passenger airliners was the Tudor, but the combination of never-ending customer changes and political interference, plus the normal aerodynamic problems associated with getting a new aircraft into service, brought about a production curtailment that eventually led to the aircraft's demise.

At the request of the Ministry of Supply, Vickers-Armstrongs had equipped a Viking airliner with a pair of Rolls-Royce turbojets and Avro considered that a similar exercise with a Tudor merited investigation. The second prototype Tudor 1, GAGST/TT181, was surplus to requirements by 1947, so the airframe was modified to be fitted with four Nene 5 engines, each delivering 5,000lb (2,300kg) thrust, in paired nacelles, to be designated the Avro Type 688 Tudor 8. (It was quite common practice in those days for new civil aircraft to have civil registration and a military serial at the same time, in case a par-

ticular aircraft was used for military trials purposes. In the case of the Tudor, a batch of forty-six serials in the range TS866 to TS912 was allocated, as well as TT176 and TT181, but none of them were taken up by any of the production airliners.)

When its metamorphosis in the Tudor 8 was complete, the new serial VX195 was allocated to TT181 and it was first flown in its new guise on 6 September 1948, by the company's Chief Test Pilot J. H. 'Jimmy' Orrell. Following demonstrations at the SBAC Display in the same month, the aircraft was handed to the A&AEE at Boscombe Down who operated it for various research programmes for two years, before transferring it to the RAE at Farnborough. VX195 was scrapped in 1951, though the fuselage survived to be presented to Teddington Controls for use as a test rig.

Purpose-Built Aircraft Required

Being a modified piston-engined aircraft, the Tudor 8 had its limitations, not the least being its tail-wheel undercarriage layout, so Avro drew up plans for the Type 706 Tudor 9 with a tricycle undercarriage. This did not progress beyond the drawing board, but it did arouse interest at the MoS, who considered that a requirement existed for a limited-production, high-altitude research aeroplane, for flight-testing engines, weapons and the larger avionic equipment that was then being developed.

The Ministry invited Avro to submit proposals for such an aircraft and, as they had a number of Tudor 2 airframes surplus to requirements, they used the type as the basis for their design, with turbojet engines and a new fin/rudder outline being the major changes from the airliner. With an 11ft-diameter (3.35m) fuselage, there was ample interior space for the larger pieces of avionic equipment, together

with the engineers, and the company proposed that the existing fuselages should be altered to the shorter Tudor 1 length, clad in a heavier-gauge skin.

The Bold Step

Given the designation Type 706 and the name Ashton, the project was presented to the Ministry, who placed an order for six aircraft to be built in four different Marks. This was quite a courageous step for them, as aircraft designed specifically for research purposes were usually only ordered as single items, or at the most in pairs.

The Ashton was the first British turbojet aircraft built solely as a general research vehicle, not associated with any other project or design. Of the six aircraft, one was to be a Mark 1, allocated serial number WB490, one a Mark 2, WB491, three Mark 3s, WB492, WB493 and WE670, together with a Mark 4, WB494. The question of why there was the anomaly of a 'WE' serial, when all six aircraft were covered by the one order, remains unanswered. With all six aircraft being built around the same basic Tudor 2 airframe, with the reduced size already mentioned, they had a great similarity in appearance. The variations between Marks were mainly internal, according to the particular research role for which each was earmarked.

The Mark 1 and Mark 2 were to have a longer pressurized section installed, placing the rear pressure bulkhead well aft of the rear entrance on the port side. The remaining four were destined to have an approximately 50 per cent shorter pressurized section, where the entrance door was behind the rear bulkhead. The Ashton was a large aeroplane, with a normal crew of a pilot, co-pilot, flight engineer, navigator and radio officer. The fuselage was pressurized to a differential of 8.25lb/sq in, which provided an 8,000ft (2,400m) pressure equivalent at 40,000ft (12,000m). This differential, which came into operation above 7,000ft (2,000m), originated from two-stage supercharging.

The Ashton's Importance

Power was provided by four Rolls-Royce Nene 5 or 6 turbojet engines, which had the same output of 5,000lb (2,300kg) thrust, mounted as pairs in a single nacelle on each wing with a common air intake, positioned low on each mainplane.

Avro was proud of its new aircraft. Sir Roy Dobson CBE, the company's Managing Director at the time, put out a statement that read:

> Hitherto, high-altitude research has been confined mainly within small aircraft of fighter size, in which it was impossible to install and inspect all the complicated flight reporting instruments. Free movement was hindered by the necessity of wearing oxygen masks. The Ashton is a Flying Laboratory, big enough to hold all the instruments we require, and the pressurized cabin makes it possible for engineers to stay aloft for long periods in comfort. It is most important that we have an aeroplane like the Ashton, to seek out the problems which will determine future design trends.

Mark 1, WB490

The first aircraft, and only Ashton Mk 1, was unique in being the only one fitted with an instrument boom, protruding from a pointed nose-cone, which remained for nearly all its life. The aircraft's basis was the Tudor 2 airframe G-AJJV/TS896. The tricycle undercarriage had Electro-Hydraulics-designed main wheel units obtained from the Handley Page Hastings/Hermes production line, which retracted forwards into bays situated between each pair of Nenes. The nose-wheel unit retracted forwards into a bay in the nose, ahead of the forward pressure bulkhead. A 3,200gal (14,400ltr) fuel load was carried in four flexible tanks within each wing, with the system having an electrically operated cross-feed cock to supply all four engines if necessary. This enabled the aircraft to have an endurance of approximately two and a quarter hours after it had reached its normal operating altitude of 40,000ft (12,000m).

WB490's assembly was completed at Woodford during August 1950 and, with an

WB490, the first of the six Ashtons, flies on its way to the 1950 SBAC Display, where it carried out low passes along the flightline, for all to see it was a product of the Hawker Siddeley Group. *Aeroplane*

overall silver finish and the obligatory prototype marking, together with Hawker Siddeley logos on both sides of the nose, 'Jimmy' Orrell piloted it for an hour-long maiden flight on 1 September, that terminated at the A&AEE. Avro were anxious to have their first Ashton at that year's SBAC Display, which started on 5 September, so nine hours' flying was put in from Boscombe Down during the next four days, in order that the aircraft had flown the ten-

hour minimum flying required to qualify for a demonstration slot. Orrell gave an impressive demonstration each day, at low levels that can only be dreamed of today. Then on 10 September, his deputy Johnny Baker flew the prototype up to Woodford, to begin a thirteen-month manufacturer's proving flight programme, which finished in October 1951.

From Woodford, WB490 returned to Boscombe Down for the Civil Aircraft

Test Section (CATS) of the A&AEE to give it a handling assessment. This lasted until 20 December and the Establishment considered the aircraft to be suitable for the roles that were intended, if flown by experienced test pilots. The controls were described as 'not excessively heavy' at its operating altitude, where Mach 0.6 was attained with ease. However, at Mach 0.66 buffeting was encountered and it was found that the blower access panels on the nacelle top surfaces required special sealing, in order to give a smooth flight at the higher speeds. The A&AEE pilots suggested that speeds in excess of Mach 0.65 should be approached with caution.

Several individual elements were criticized, such as the autopilot, the layout of some cockpit items and the de-icing system for the windscreen. Again, however, they considered that experienced test pilots would be able to cope with what the Establishment rated as shortcomings that did not justify the making of alterations.

At the beginning of 1952, WB490 returned to Woodford, where the windscreen de-icing system and the sealing of the blower access panels were attended to during a routine service, that for good measure also included revisions being made to the autopilot. A further set of manufacturer's trials were conducted to clear the modifications before the aircraft went back to Boscombe Down once more, to join the A&AEE's fleet of aircraft. The Establishment's CATS flew WB490 on radio and navigation equipment trials for a considerable time, during which an additional fuel tank was installed on a pylon under each outer wing section, in order to increase flight-testing duration, before it was replaced by Vickers Valiant WP200, which was also used by the Radar Research Establishment for NBS proving flights (see the section on Ashton Mk 3 WB492 later in this chapter). The Ashton was kept busy on an assortment of other research programmes until December 1956. In the spring of 1957, WB490 went back to Woodford again, but this time it was dismantled and the fuselage was used as an internal pressure test rig. Since then, it is believed that this, together with the remainder of the airframe, have been destroyed.

WB490, the only Ashton to be fitted with a nose probe, looked a very sorry sight when photographed at Woodford in May 1959 with underwing fuel tanks, the rear cone of the starboard unit having been removed. *Harry Holmes*

Mark 2, WB491

Although WB491 was the next Ashton chronologically, it was the third of the six to fly. Production test pilot J. C. Nelson flew the aircraft from Woodford on 2 August 1951 to keep the Mark 2 airborne for an hour and five minutes for its maiden flight. The following month, it had a flying demonstration slot at the Farnborough SBAC Display, where the piloting was shared by Nelson and Jimmy Orrell.

The Ashton Mk 2 was derived from Tudor 2 G-AJJW/TS897 and had the longer pressurized working section but was without the nose-mounted instrument boom of its predecessor. Following its week at the Farnborough display, the aircraft returned to Woodford for manufacturer's trials, and on their completion went back to Farnborough, but this time to join the

The Mk 2, WB491, flies low between crowded spectator and aircraft parking lines at the 1951 SBAC Display. In the background, from left to right, are Sperrin VX158, Wyvern TF.2 VW870, Hawker P.1067 WB188, Firefly AS.7 WJ216, Avro 707B VX790, Valiant WB210, Hawker P.1052 VX272, Meteor G-7-1, Venom VV612, Sealand G-AKLV and Heron G-ALZL. *Aeroplane*

In 1955, WB491 was again at an SBAC Display, but this time as a Rolls-Royce Conway flying test bed. *Aeroplane and author's collection*

RAE's fleet of research aircraft. For three years it was employed on a series of trials associated with cabin pressurization, temperature control, instrumentation and air conditioning, all conducted at the high altitudes for which it was designed.

In the list of requirements for the Ashton, when it was first drawn up, the MoS demanded the capability of flight-testing the forthcoming generation of axial-flow turbojet engines at high altitudes. To further this aim, WB491 departed from Farnborough in the early winter of 1954 to go to N. D. Napier and Son's Luton works, to be converted for an engine test-bed role. The National Gas Turbine Establishment (NGTE) at Pystock, adjacent to the RAE, had need of a universal flying engine-test facility. Napier manufactured a ventral cradle under the Ashton's centre-section,

which could be adapted to take any engine for its testing programme.

In January 1955, a Rolls-Royce Avon RA.28 series axial-flow turbojet was installed in its own nacelle on the Ashton's cradle, before WB491 returned to Farnborough for the RAE's evaluation of the engine. By September these trials had been completed and a nacelle, tailored to the Rolls-Royce Conway 505 engine's installation on the Boeing 707-420, replaced the Avon. This in turn was superseded by a 17,500lb (8,000kg) thrust Conway 508. With this engine in place, an icing rig was installed a few feet ahead of the under-slung nacelle to create icing conditions, and the build-up of ice within the nacelle was monitored on instrumentation in the aircraft's pressurized working section. This was a typical

example of just why the Ashton was required, for no other aircraft then extant could have been adapted for such high-altitude tests.

Together with its Conway test engine, but minus the icing rig, WB491 flew at the 1955 SBAC Display to show-off the Rolls-Royce engine and then returned to the trials programme, during which time a flap control rod failed, but the aircraft was successfully landed. In 1956, Armstrong Siddeley took over the aircraft for flight-testing its Sapphire ASSa.7, rated at 10,500lb (4,800kg) thrust, and for these tests the icing rig was restored.

In 1960, WB491's test-flying days ended and it languished at Farnborough for over a year before being broken up. However, a major section of the fuselage escaped the cutters and went to Hawker Aircraft's airfield at Dunsfold, before going to the Wales Aircraft Museum at Rhoose, where it had to endure an outdoor existence. Today, the fuselage section is displayed at the Newark Air Museum.

Mark 3, WB492

The first of the three Ashton Mk 3s became airborne for the first time on 6 July 1951, a month before the Mk 2. Flown by Orrell from Woodford, the aircraft's maiden flight lasted thirty-five minutes. It was the first Ashton to have the shorter pressurized section and was built from the basis of Tudor 2 G-AJJX/TS898.

WB482's principal difference from the two earlier aircraft was that it was fitted with wing-mounted bomb-carrying nacelles. Lying flush under the mainplanes, each nacelle was 15ft 6in (4.72m) in length and protruded ahead of the wing leading edge by 5ft 7in (1.7m). Each nacelle could carry two 1,000lb (450kg) bombs, which were released via a pair of 11ft-long (3.35m), outward-opening doors.

From its constructor's trials conducted at Woodford, WB492 went to the future RRE at Defford on 4 March 1952. Defford had been a satellite for No. 230 OTU at Pershore in the early days of World War Two, before being taken over by the MAP in May 1942 to house the Flying Unit of the Telecommunications Research Establishment (TRE) – upwards of 150 aircraft were based at Defford in 1944–45.

At Defford, the first Ashton Mk 3 was tasked with the continuation of the centrimetric H_2S development, aimed at

ABOVE AND RIGHT: WB492 was the first of three Ashton Mk 3s. It was the first to have bomb-carrying nacelles under its wings and was used by the RRE for Mk IX H$_2$S radar trials, with an X-band scanner housed in the ventral radome under the fuselage centre section. Author's collection and Harry Holmes

BELOW: Close-up views of an underwing bomb-carrying nacelle on WB492, which was capable of carrying two 1,000lb (4,500kg) bombs, and its X-band H$_2$S scanner housing. Harry Holmes

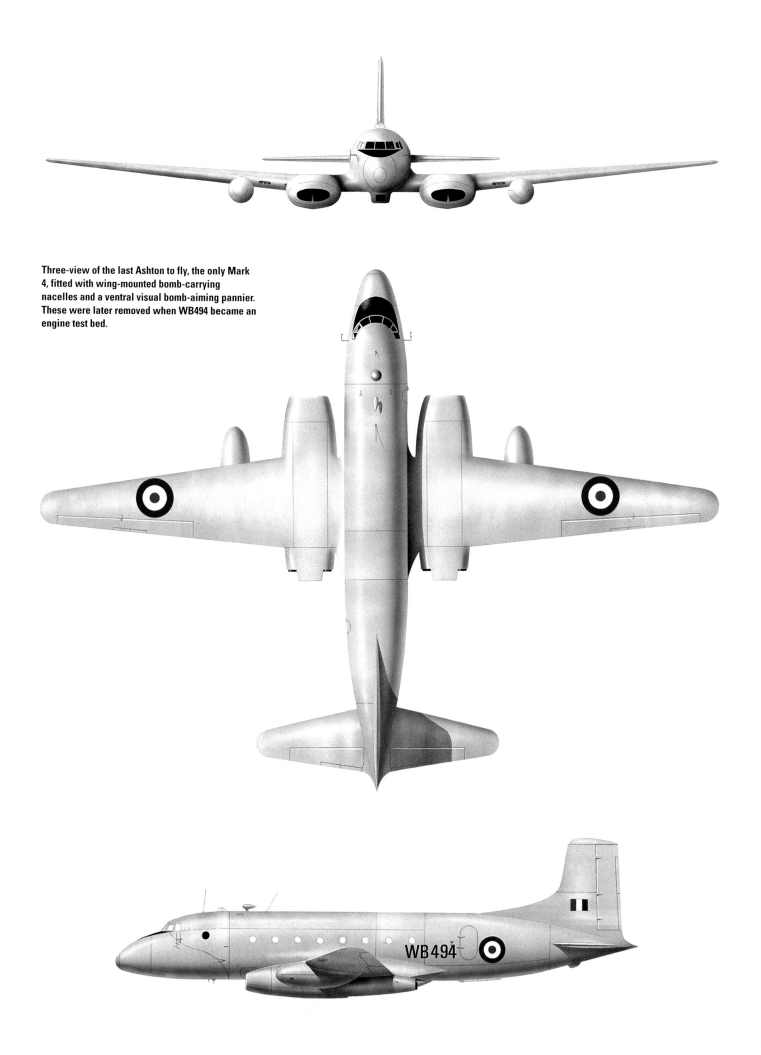

Three-view of the last Ashton to fly, the only Mark 4, fitted with wing-mounted bomb-carrying nacelles and a ventral visual bomb-aiming pannier. These were later removed when WB494 became an engine test bed.

ABOVE: The Mark 1, as fitted with under-wing fuel tanks in later years.
BELOW: The first Mark 3 as used by the RRE Telecommunications Flying Unit (TFU) in March 1952.

ABOVE: The last Mark 3 after its conversion into an engine test-bed.
BELOW: The second Mark 3, WB493, as painted to represent an airliner in the film *Cone of Silence*, while still carrying outboard test engines for the Bristol Engine Division.

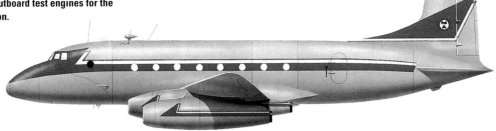

Technical Data – Avro Type 706 Ashton	
Dimensions:	Span 120ft (36.5m); length 89ft 6in (27.27m) (WB490 was slightly longer due to the nose boom); height 31ft 3in (9.5m)
Powerplants:	Four Rolls-Royce Nene 5 or 6 turbojets, each producing 5,000lb (2,300kg) thrust
Weights:	Basic all-up-weight 72,000lb (32,650kg), but many variations depending on test engines or equipment installed
Performance:	Maximum speed 440mph (700km/h); maximum altitude (WE670) 82,000ft (25,000m)
Production:	Six aircraft built, with serial numbers WB490, WB491, WB492, WB493, WB494 and WE670

The second Mk 3, WB493, takes off from Filton on its maiden flight as an Olympus flying test bed. *Aeroplane*

supplying the forthcoming V-bomber force with a ground mapping/target location radar called the Navigation Bombing System (NBS). The aircraft had a radome installed under the centre fuselage to house the Mk IX H_2S scanner. This operated with an X-band system, integrated with the existing Doppler navigation radar, bombing altitude measuring and ballistics data, a G4B gyro compass for heading orientation, together with an operator's Plan Position Indicator (PPI).

These trials occupied WB492 for three years, during which time it operated from Pershore as well as Defford, but in 1955 the second production Valiant, WP200, took over and later events saw the end of the Ashton.

The Ashton's projected bomb load of two 1,000lb bombs in each nacelle had not met with universal success. With the two nacelles being wide apart on the outer wing sections, an aerodynamic imbalance occurred if the bombs were not released at the same time from each nacelle and any release malfunction leading to a bomb

'hang-up' created real problems. Consequently it became common practice to carry four 100lb (45kg) weapons in each nacelle, rather than the pair of larger bombs.

Shortly after the Valiant took over the NBS trials, WB492 suffered fire damage that was considered uneconomic to repair, and the aircraft was struck off charge on 4 August 1955. In May 1956, the fuselage compartment went to RAE Farnborough for static test use, until it was finally scrapped.

Mark 3, WB493

Tudor 2 G-AJJY/TS899 was the starting point for the second Ashton Mk 3. Its first flight, in the hands of J. C. Nelson, took place on 18 December 1951, with the aircraft only remaining airborne for fifteen minutes – Avro were becoming blasé about their research laboratory! RAE Farnborough was its recipient following the usual constructor's trials, but on 8 May

1952 WB493 was transferred to the Engine Division of the Bristol Aeroplane Company at Filton, to serve as a flying test bed for uprated variants of several of the company's turbojet engines.

When Lancasters, Lancastrians and Lincolns were used in this capacity, the outer piston engines were replaced by the turbojet to be tested. However, with the Ashton's engines being in enclosed pairs within tailor-made nacelles, it was not possible to substitute any of the Nenes with a trials engine. Therefore, whereas the engines tested on WB491 were carried on a cradle structure under the centre-section, Bristol engines were flight tested in single-engine nacelles, mounted on wide pylons under the outer wing sections in the position where the bomb-carrying nacelles were sited on WB492.

The first Bristol units tested on the second Mk 3 were a pair of Olympus engines, rated at 11,000lb (5,000kg) static thrust, with one of them fitted with a reheat system. This flight testing continued until 1956, when the aircraft went into the Engine Division workshops at Patchway, on the opposite side of Filton's airfield from the aircraft assembly lines, where the port Olympus was replaced by a 4,850lb (2,200kg) thrust Orpheus BOr.3. Reheat was installed on this engine at various times, and uprated variants replaced it, until the whole test programme was terminated in June 1962, after which WB493 was grounded.

As the various trials programmes involved spells when the aircraft was not

The Mk 3 Ashton taxis along the perimeter track on a windy day, during its ten-year tenure at Filton on Olympus flight trials. Author's collection

engaged on flying duty, WB493 was used in a film staring Michael Craig and Peter Cushing, entitled *Cone of Silence*, which was released in 1960. For this, the aircraft was painted in the red/white livery of a fictitious civil airline and the film contained some excellent air-to-air footage of the six-engined 'airliner'. But as already stated, its employment in the engine test-bed role finished in June 1962 and the aircraft was scrapped.

Mark 3, WE670

The third of the Ashton Mk 3s carried the out-of-sequence serial WE670 and was constructed from the last of the surplus Tudor 2 airframes, G-AJKA/TS901. J. C. Nelson was again the pilot who took it for its first flight, which took place at Woodford on 9 April 1952 and lasted twenty-five minutes. After its maker's trials, it was fitted with wing-mounted bomb nacelles like WB492's, and went to Boscombe Down for comparison with the handling trials of WB490.

The Mk 3 differed from the Mk 1 in several ways, which included having a camera under the fuselage, as well as the bomb nacelles. The A&AEE's testing found that WE670's general handling characteristics were very similar to the earlier aircraft, although the weapon nacelles produced some buffeting at speeds above approximately 170mph (270km/h). When the bomb-doors were opened, these characteristics took a sharp turn for the worse, and above 230mph (370km/h) the buffeting became decidedly unpleasant. The Establishment disagreed with Avro's assessment that the aircraft could be dived up to Mach 0.7 and considered that such a manoeuvre should not be attempted above Mach 0.61. They recommended that a notice to this effect should be placed in the cockpit and were of the opinion that bombing accuracy was affected by the aircraft's behaviour at high Mach numbers. One final comment by the A&AEE pilots was that the Ashton needed airbrakes.

WE670 went to the Armament and Instrument Experimental Unit (AIEU) at Martlesham Heath after its Boscombe

During the mid-1950s, WB493 was repainted to perform as an airliner of the fictitious Monarch Airways in the film *Cone of Silence*. *Aeroplane*

Down assessment. It had been intended for AIEU service from the start and was employed on bombing trials at RAE Orfordness until July 1953, when the Ashton's excellence as an engine test-bed was again called for. WE670 went to Napier for the same modifications to the centre-section underside as had been performed on WB491, before joining Rolls-Royce's experimental unit at Hucknall. Among a variety of engines test-flown were an Avon RA.14, producing 9,500lb (4,300kg) thrust and for which a water-spray installation

The last of the Ashton Mk 3s was WE670, which was fitted with underwing bomb carriers when photographed at Woodford in October 1952. The combination received a good report as a bomb ballistic research aircraft, when tested by the A&AEE. *Harry Holmes*

In July 1953, WE670 was modified for engine test-bed flying and is seen here carrying an Avon RA.14 in the ventral nacelle, with the shadow of the water-spray unit – used for icing trials – projected onto the starboard engine nacelle. Harry Holmes

was positioned ahead of the engine's pod, to evaluate its operating capabilities under icing conditions.

In 1962, WE670's engine test-bed employment came to an end and it was retired at Hucknall, where it is believed to have been scrapped.

Mark 4, WB494

The sole Ashton Mk 4 was built with parts of Tudor 2 G-AJJZ/TS900 and was completed at Woodford by late October 1952. This meant that all six of these very large and sophisticated trials aircraft had been produced in just over two years. Once again J. C. Nelson was the pilot when it had a first flight, lasting fifty-five minutes, on 18 November. Like two earlier Ashtons it had bomb-carrying nacelles, but it differed from them in having a pressurized ventral pannier to accommodate a bomb aimer.

With company trials completed, WB494 went to RAE Farnborough on 17 July 1953

for over a year's flying on visual bombing research, before being nominated for engine test-bed service. It went to Luton for D. Napier and Son to undertake the necessary conversion, which was more complicated than on the earlier aircraft, as it involved the removal of the bomb-aimer's pannier and the bomb-carrying nacelles. A centreline pod was fitted to take an Armstrong Siddeley Sapphire for

further de-icing trials, for which the water-spray rig was installed.

The Sapphire trials occupied the aircraft for a year, following which, in 1955, WB494 was transferred to the de Havilland Engine Company who used it for development work, operating out of Hatfield. These kept the aircraft occupied for nearly eight years, but in 1962, like three earlier Ashtons, WB494 was retired and broken up.

Justification

The Ashton was one of those cases where everyone benefited. Avro had surplus Tudor 2 airframes, produced in anticipation of airline orders that did not materialize. Therefore the MoS order was most fortuitous. All the major Establishments had an aircraft to call upon for high-altitude research work for nearly twelve years. All three leading engine manufacturers were able to have their new generation of axial-flow engines tested at altitudes above the capabilities of previous bomber conversions, particularly in the research of individual types of engine's behaviour in icing conditions. Many of the operational capabilities of the V-bomber force were forged on trials conducted with Ashtons and, all-in-all, Sir Roy Dobson's comments made on the announcement of the Ashton order in 1949 were fully justified.

A senior engineer involved with research in the 1950s and 1960s told me that, before the Ashton, many of Britain's aviation research establishments had conducted trials using 'yesterday' aircraft to further the project work for the transonic era of 'tomorrow'. The six Ashtons enabled these researches to be extended much further, faster and higher than had previously been possible.

Like WB492, the Ashton Mk 4, WB494, also had underwing bomb-carrying nacelles, before it was converted into a Sapphire engine test bed. Philip Jarrett

Boulton Paul P.111, P.111a and P.120

Sensitive Triangles

From the Alpine-size mountain of data captured from the Germans by the Allied Technical Intelligence Mission in 1945, it became disturbingly obvious that German aerodynamicists had entered fields well in advance of British, American or Soviet thinking. In Britain, much of this was greeted with a large amount of scepticism, despite a display of captured Luftwaffe aircraft put on at Farnborough proving some of the points. One well-respected Chief Designer was utterly dismissive of all that was put before him. Hadn't his designs helped to defeat the Luftwaffe?

However, for some unknown reason, one aspect of German research that did generate interest in Great Britain was that conducted in delta-wing technology, and while Avro's Roy Chadwick has opted for this configuration for the Type 698, it was felt that there was some justification for an aircraft to evaluate the delta-wing planform's aerodynamic stability as a whole, particularly at transonic speeds, in conjunction with a programme being initiated by the RAE at Farnborough in the same field. Specification E.27/46 was raised and handed to Boulton Paul Aircraft Limited, based at Pendeford, on the north-west outskirts of Wolverhampton.

A Company of Variety

Boulton and Paul Ltd was formed in Rose Lane, Norwich, as woodworkers and construction engineers before World War One. Their major concern turned to aviation in 1915 and their first indigenous design, the P.3 Bobolink, emerged in 1917. Of great financial benefit to the company was the production of over 300 F.E.2bs under licence from the Royal Aircraft Factory. In 1919 the company moved on from wooden construction to concentrate on metal

aircraft, and their first really successful model was the twin-engined Sidestrand bomber, produced in 1926. This was developed into the Overstrand of 1933, which was unique in being the first bomber to have a power-operated, enclosed gun turret.

On 30 June 1934, a new public company, Boulton Paul Aircraft Limited, was formed and two years later, to meet Specification F.9/35, their Defiant fighter emerged as the first fighter to have a four-gun power-operated turret as its offensive armament. However, the weight and drag of this installation proved its undoing. The Defiant went into RAF service in 1939 and had its moment of glory over France in 1940, when Luftwaffe pilots attacked from the rear in the belief that the aircraft were Hurricanes. Their error and aircraft recognition was soon amended, leading to heavy Defiant losses during the Battle of Britain, and the Defiant was transferred to night-fighter service in the early days of the Blitz, where its success was slightly longer-lived.

With a World War Two centred on the development and manufacture of gun turrets for Bomber and Coastal Commands, the company only returned to aircraft

design with the P.108 Balliol, to meet Specification T.7/45 for a three-seat advanced trainer. The prototype, VL892, was powered by a Bristol Mercury 30 radial engine but the second, VL917, fitted with an Armstrong Siddeley Mamba, became the world's first single turboprop aircraft to fly. However, a change in Air Ministry policy resulted in the Balliol going into service powered by a Rolls-Royce Merlin 35 piston engine.

The P.111 Research Aeroplane

As already stated, the RAE wanted to run a programme of experiments into the properties of a delta-winged aircraft at transonic speeds, and Boulton Paul set about designing such a vehicle in 1947. As the research was purely concerned with the wing planform, the aircraft's size was determined by the smallest amount of airframe necessary to contain a pilot in a Martin-Baker ejector seat, a Rolls-Royce Nene RN.3 engine and sufficient fuel to get the whole package airborne and provide the RAE with the data that it required.

When the prototype P.111 started taxiing trials at Seighford in September 1950, the cockpit canopy had not been fitted, nor had it received any paint finish. *Aeroplane*

Boulton Paul were certainly successful in this, for the nose section, including the cockpit, protruded barely 5ft (1.5m) ahead of the wing leading edge; and the rear fuselage section, including nearly 12in (30cm) of Nene jet-pipe sticking out from the airframe skinning, extended just over 4ft (1.2m) aft of the trailing edge. In the cockpit, the pilot's feet fitted into the nose intake centre-splitter body, which

span, acted as both elevators and ailerons, with the rudder on the tall triangular fin also being power-operated.

A large bulged fairing on the left-hand side of the rear fuselage housed a 7ft-diameter (2.1m) anti-spin parachute, that also served as a brake during landing. The fuel load of 230gal (1,035ltr), carried in four tanks within the wings, was found to give the aircraft approximately twenty minutes

The company had use of an adjacent airfield, which was opened on 24 June 1938 as Wolverhampton Airport, but its grass runway was totally unsuitable for test-flying an aircraft of the P.111's abilities, so after preliminary taxiing, VT935 was transported by road to Boscombe Down. The original predicted date for the P.111 to be ready for flight was March 1948 and Capt Eric Brown RN, the Commanding

By 10 October 1950, the P.111 had become VT935 and was finished in overall silver with a black anti-glare panel around the cockpit, together with national and prototype markings. Author's collection

diverted the air around the cockpit and nose-wheel bay.

The delta mainplane was manufactured with a leading-edge sweep angle of 45 degrees and its basic structure ended in a squared-off wing tip measuring approximately one third of the root chord. Two pairs of fibreglass extensions were designed, one with a square tip about one sixth of the root chord and a longer one that created a virtually pointed tip. It was a thin wing, with a thickness/chord ratio of 10:1 held throughout its span. Power-controlled elevons, the full length of the shortest

of trials flying, plus climb to operating altitude and let-down for approach.

The wings also accepted the inward-retracting main wheels of the undercarriage, while the nose-wheel assembly retracted rearwards to fit into a small bay under the cockpit. With a generous 14ft 3in (4.34m) track, the P.111 was very stable during ground manoeuvring.

Finished in an overall natural metal state, with D-Type national markings, the obligatory prototype 'P' and serial number VT935, the aircraft came out from the Pendeford assembly bay in September 1950.

Officer of the Aerodynamic Flight at RAE Farnborough, was assigned as the pilot to make the maiden flight. However, delays in the aircraft's construction put the date back beyond Capt Brown's departure in August 1949. His successor, Sqn Ldr J. S. R. Muller-Rowland DSO, DFC, was to take over, but he was killed in D.H.108 VW120's crash on 15 February 1950. Comprehensive taxi trials were conducted before, on 10 October, A&AEE test pilot Sqn Ldr Bob Smythe took the little delta-winged VT935 into the air for the first time.

Aero Flight Management

The development and flight trials of the P.111 were handled entirely by the RAE's Aero Flight for the first fifteen months, with fellow Establishment pilots Lt 'Jock' Elliott and Jim Harrison joining the programme. At the 1951 SBAC Display, the aircraft was resplendent in a fresh overall silver paint scheme, with a dark blue flash extending down the fuselage from the black anti-glare panel. Smythe and Elliott shared the flying, which was noted for the demonstration of the aircraft's manoeuvrability in the air before a distinctly 'hairy' landing, with the roll-out seeming to go on down the runway for ever.

Following the Display, Boulton Paul's Chief Test Pilot, Alexander 'Ben' Gunn entered the test flying programme, although it was still under RAE control, to make a total of two and a half hours' flight time during December 1951. Either side of Gunn's flights, VT935 suffered two landing mishaps. In the first, the nose-wheel parted company with its leg, while Jim Harrison was landing in a turbulent crosswind, with the resultant damage being repaired comparatively quickly. However, in January 1952, after a series of problems with the landing gear, Harrison was forced to make a wheels-up landing, in which the aircraft was damaged enough for it to be returned to Pendeford for repair.

On the whole, the test-flying programme had been rather pedestrian and longitudinal oscillation had occurred from very small movements of the control column. Ben Gunn is on record as stating that the aeroplane was 'touchy' and piloting it was 'like flying a razor's edge'. The principal reason for the high landing speeds had been the fact that the Nene required 7,000rpm to keep the generators functioning: the thrust generated by the high engine revolutions meant that a long, flat approach had to be made, not taking advantage of the delta-wing's natural high angle of attack to induce drag from the large wing area. This meant a protracted roll down the runway was necessary, in order to lose velocity before the turn-off.

The 'Yellow Peril'

From the fifteen months' flying that VT935 had accumulated, it had become very noticeable that, while the P.111 was

VT935 had been repainted in silver with a dark blue flash incorporating the anti-glare panel to take part in the 1951 SBAC Display. *Aeroplane*

pleasant to fly, as speed was increased it became rather a handful to control, due to its very sensitive system of controls. Therefore, its return to Pendeford for repairs following the belly landing was an ideal opportunity to incorporate modifications.

A gear-change mechanism was positioned between the control column and the power unit, which had an 8:1 ratio that gave the pilot the ability to vary the control's sensitivity. Trim was enabled through a datum shift that adjusted the

position of the elevons without affecting the position of the column. A nose probe was built into the air intake splitter, which contained a pressure head that gave readings nearly 5ft (1.5m) ahead of the aircraft's position.

To reduce the landing speed which, as explained, was always a source of uneasiness for whoever was flying it, a quartet of rectangular airbrakes was installed on the fuselage sides, one above and one below each wing, in a position level with the Nene's

In 1953, VT935 was converted into the P.111a and received a new bright yellow finish, with a black flash on each side, that ran into the wing-root leading edge. Author's collection

At the 1953 SBAC Display, the P.111a uses the new airbrakes that were part of the conversion, as was the long nose probe. It runs on with its braking parachute deployed, past the Viscount 708 in Air France markings and Shackleton MR.2 WG796 parked in the background. Author's collection

ABOVE: **When parked at Farnborough, prior to its flying display at the 1953 event, its braking parachute housing is seen to advantage and it has interested more spectators than in 1951. In the background are a Bristol Freighter and a Canberra to the left, with a Shackleton MR.2 on the right.** *Aeroplane*

impeller intake. Their movement was fully variable on three slim arms, through an 80-degree arc, from their retracted position flush with the fuselage outer skin.

Together with various amendments to instruments, the modifications were considered extensive enough to justify a change of designation, so in the late spring of 1953, VT935 became the P.111a. As if to accentuate the difference from its former P.111 status, it was painted an overall vivid yellow, with a thin black line on each side, running down the front fuselage section from the nose air intake and along the wing leading edges, to taper out at approximately half-span.

The P.111a had preliminary taxiing trials at Pendeford before being transported

Today, the P.111a is parked under the shadow of Argosy G-APRL and behind Vulcan B.2 XL360 at the Midland Air Museum. Author's collection

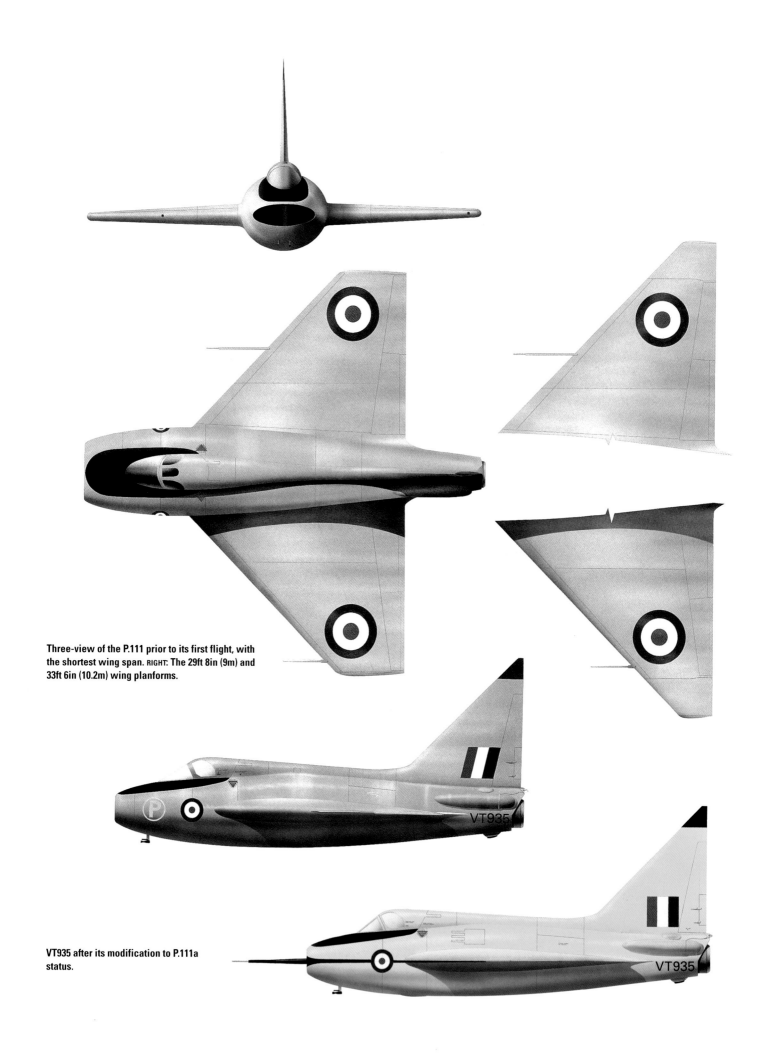

Three-view of the P.111 prior to its first flight, with the shortest wing span. RIGHT: The 29ft 8in (9m) and 33ft 6in (10.2m) wing planforms.

VT935 after its modification to P.111a status.

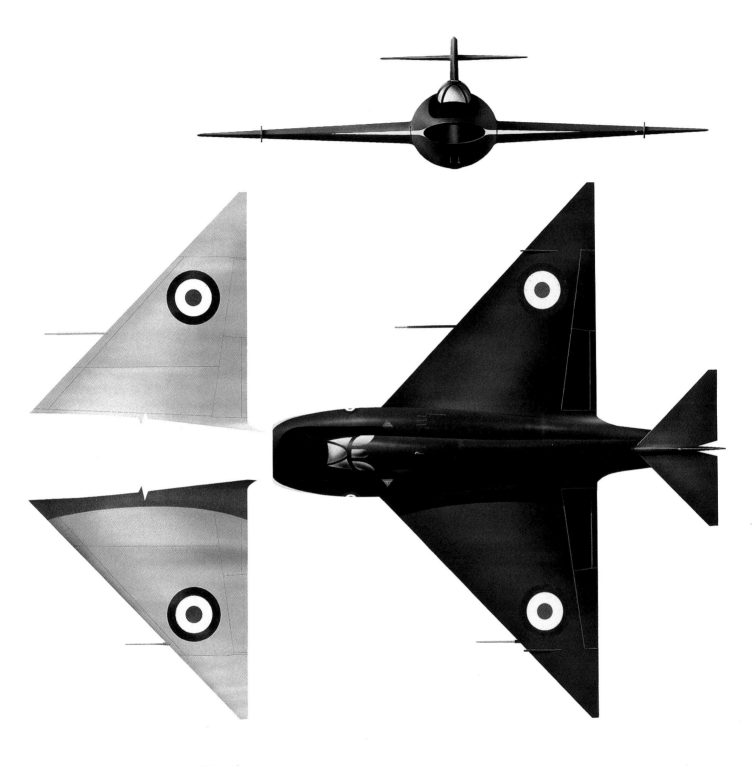

Three-view of the P.120 VT951, in the striking colour scheme that it carried when it crashed on 29 August 1952.

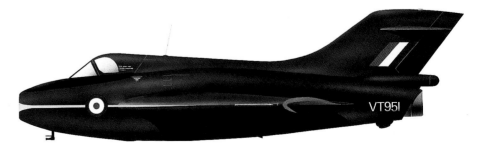

once again to Boscombe Down, which was not as straightforward as it sounds. Because the wings could not be dismantled from the fuselage, VT935 had always been difficult to take by road, for even in its basic wing configuration it was over 25ft (7.9m) wide, which was not easy on British roads back in the early 1950s. There was not a profusion of motorways at that time – in fact, there were none at all.

VT935's second maiden flight, which lasted ten minutes, was made on 2 July 1953 with Ben Gunn at the controls and twenty-two further flights, totalling ten and a quarter hours, were made before the aircraft flew to Farnborough for that year's SBAC Display. All the flights had been made from Boscombe Down, whose ATC was often heard to tell other Establishment aircraft in the vicinity to 'Clear the circuit, the Yellow Peril is airborne'. Gunn gave a ten-minute

conducted as a Boulton Paul programme, with Ben Gunn flying the aeroplane for sixteen hours and thirty-three minutes. Following its last flight in this status, on 14 January, it was delivered to the RAE's Aero Flight at Bedford in February, where it spent another four years' testing with RAE Farnborough. Their joint programmes concentrated on delta-wing stability and behaviour under all flight conditions, which was precisely what Specification E.27/46 called for. During this time, VT935 was flown with all three wing-tip variables, but its appearance at the RAE's Jubilee Display in 1955 is believed to be the only occasion when it appeared in public with the full wingspan. Its flight envelope was quite broad, ranging from a minimum of 124mph (200km/h) in level flight, to a recorded Mach 0.98 in a dive, when it is arguable as to whether the pilot or the aircraft was in

instructional airframe for the College's students for over sixteen years. Not being an ex-RAF aircraft, it was not allocated an Instructional Airframe number with an 'M' suffix. On 13 July 1975, eighteen months of negotiations with the Midland Aircraft Preservation Society came to fruition and the aircraft was once again on the road, this time to Baginton, to form the nucleus of the Midland Air Museum. Today it stands beneath the shelter provided by the wings of an Armstrong Whitworth Argosy, in a very imposing collection of aircraft held by the museum.

The P.120

In order to widen the knowledge on delta-wing behaviour, it was considered necessary to investigate the planform's reactions

The P.120, VT951, stands resplendent in a glossy black finish, with a yellow flash in the same style as the black one on VT935 – in fact, the colours have been transposed for VT951. Author's collection

demonstration on each day of the Display, after which the P.111a returned to the A&AEE's airfield to resume flight testing. On 23 October 1953 the power controls locked at 30,000ft (9,000m), but they unlocked during the descent.

A Busy Aeroplane

All the P.111a's flying since the maiden flight and up to January 1954 had been

control! At sea level, the speed of 648mph (1,043km/h) attained was quite an achievement for an aeroplane powered by an engine developing 5,100lb (2,300kg) thrust at best, and it speaks volumes for the original design. The modifications from P.111 to P.111a had made a vast difference to its all-round aerodynamic efficiency.

The RAE made the last flight with VT935 on 20 June 1958, after which it was passed to the College of Aeronautics at Cranfield, where it became a research and

when flown in conjunction with a horizontal tailplane. One prime reason for this was the fact that Gloster Aircraft proposed such a layout for its forthcoming all-weather fighter, the GA.5 Javelin. The fitting of a tailplane on VT935 was considered, but with the very active research programmes on which it was engaged and needed to complete, it was decided that a new aircraft was required.

Specification E.27/49 was issued to cover Boulton Paul's work in designing and constructing the new aircraft, to which the designation P.120 and serial number VT951 were allocated. The P.111 conversion to P.111a was in hand at Pendeford and its design formed the basis for the new aircraft, with the fuselage forward of the engine mounting bulkhead being identical to VT935. A new rear section was designed, embodying a broad, swept fin/rudder with a small delta-shaped horizontal tailplane installed near its top. In reality, this was just a trimming surface controlled by a press-button system in the cockpit, because the power-operated wing elevons were retained, as were the airbrakes as fitted to the P.111a. A braking parachute was carried in a neat circular-sectioned housing between the tail assembly and the Nene's jet outlet.

A New Wing

The delta-wing was almost identical to the P.111a's at full span, except for one fundamental difference: the wing tips were designed to be all-moving trimming surfaces, hinging on the P.111a's short-span wing-tip frame members; and a wing fence was positioned on each side, just forward of the pivot point. So far as is known, the system was locked and never brought into operation in the life of the aircraft. The Rolls-Royce Nene RN.3 was again used to power the new aircraft, which was first rolled out at Pendeford in an unpainted condition during July 1952. A few days after its first photocall, VT951 was taken to Boscombe Down, from where its maiden flight was to be performed in the hands of Ben Gunn.

An Eventful Take-Off

In the evening of 5 August 1952, Ben Gunn made a few high-speed taxi runs, but with the amount of runway available at the time, together with the aircraft's obvious high take-off speed, it was not possible to make the provisional hops that many pilots make, prior to a first flight.

Therefore, the following morning Gunn prepared for the maiden flight, which was full of uncertainties, and twenty seconds after releasing the brakes on line-up, these uncertainties became a major crisis: VT951 did not want to leave the ground. About three-quarters of Boscombe Down's runway had been used up and, with just over

200mph (320km/h) registered on the clock, there was no chance of closing the throttle, without becoming the centre of a serious accident. It was 'Hobson's choice' and the pilot had no alternative other than to pull back on the control column,

VT951 only flew for 11hr 15min before the port elevon became detached and the pilot, Ben Gunn, had to eject. It is possible that it only had one air-to-air photographic outing, and these shots were taken during that session. *Aeroplane*

trusting to luck that the aircraft would respond. A strong smell of burning rubber permeated into the cockpit and the runway threshold was approaching at an alarming rate as Gunn gave one final haul on the column, which forced the little delta off the ground in what he describes

as a staggering, wallowing, dipping flight, with the slowest rate of climb that he had ever experienced.

Once the aircraft had settled down to as normal a flight attitude as was possible, the pilot, realizing that the cause of the

protracted take-off must lie in the neutral angle of the tailplane's setting, started experimenting with the settings on a trial-and-error basis, through the press-button control. Response was positive, so that a final trim setting was made for the approach and landing, which was also entered with a certain amount of trepidation, as the cause of the burning rubber smell was unknown. A touchdown at some 40mph (65km/h) less than the take-off speed was safely accomplished and the air brakes, together with the braking parachute, brought the aircraft to a standstill before it ran out of runway. A subsequent inspection showed that the nose-wheel tyre was badly damaged but still inflated.

Black Colour-Scheme and Day

Over the next twenty-three days, eleven and a quarter hours' flying was made by VT951, with Gunn the only pilot. During this time, general handling and trim investigations were carried out, with a vibragraph being installed on 28 August in order to register rudder vibrations. On the same flight, Shell BP carried out an air-to-air photographic session. By this time, a very smart colour scheme had been applied, with an overall glossy black, broken only by a yellow line, similar to the black line on the yellow P.111a – in fact, it was a transposition of the colours between the two aircraft. VT951's new appearance was in preparation for its demonstration at the forthcoming SBAC Display.

The aircraft behaved very well now that the correct take-off trim had been determined and the P.120 was proving to have

much better flying characteristics than VT935's. It was therefore all the more alarming when the events of Flight No. 20, on 29 August 1952, occurred. Ben Gunn was flying at 5,000ft (1,500m) above the English south coast when a sudden high-pitched buzz preceded a series of extremely rapid rolls to the left, in which the pilot became disorientated but instinctively pushed the control column hard against the right-hand side of the cockpit. With full right rudder applied, the aircraft stopped rolling and Gunn took stock of the situation. The positions of the control column and rudder bar confirmed that something serious had occurred, particularly as the aircraft was now in a diving attitude. He dared not alter the main control settings, so made several pressings of the button controlling the all-moving tailplane and the P.120 responded sufficiently to regain level flight. He radioed Boscombe Down's ATC to explain the situation but, after putting out a general direction for RT silence to be observed by other aircraft in the vicinity, the ATC just shut down.

Using the throttle control gingerly, a descent was made in the general direction of the A&AEE's airfield, but at 3,000ft (900m) the aircraft again became unmanageable and Gunn decided that an exit, courtesy of Martin-Baker, was the best course of action. While reaching for the ejector blind and pulling it down hard,

VT951 had become inverted again and Ben departed from the aircraft in a downwards trajectory. He managed to release himself from the seat and deploy his parachute, but at too low an altitude for comfort, and his rapid descent was arrested by a substantial coniferous tree, working in conjunction with his parachute.

A Rapid Solution

His return to Boscombe Down was efficiently made within the hour and an immediate de-briefing could not come to a conclusion as to what had happened. As VT951 was in small pieces over a large part of Salisbury Plain, it could not provide an answer either. However, a telephone call was received from the ATC of No. 781 Naval Air Squadron at Lee-on-Solent, who described seeing the aircraft partially break up while passing over the base. He collected various bits of debris from around the airfield and immediately sent them to the A&AEE.

Only three hours after the accident, full proof was presented in the form of the complete left-hand elevon, a bit battered but in one piece. This had parted company with the aircraft, due to intense flutter that had fractured all its hinges, and it was considered that the stresses involved could not have been successfully simulated with a ground rig. The RAE Technical Report (Structures) 165 on the accident, concluded as follows:

> The results of the investigation reported here suggest very strongly that the accident to the P.120, in which the aircraft was lost while flying in level flight at 440kt, was caused by a flutter of the powered elevon-tab system in the wing. A 41cps symmetric wing mode provided a major contribution to a flutter at about 40 to 50cps, which was made possible by resonance of the elevon mass balance weights on their too-flexible attachments.

The Establishment added that the P.111 was free from this instability because of the stiffer attachments of the elevon mass balance weights. The P.120 had attained only twenty-three days' flying, so the research into the behaviour of a delta-wing in unison with a tailplane had to be handled by Gloster, through their GA.5 prototypes, and they proved that the configuration did not present so many problems as had originally been anticipated.

Technical Data

Boulton Paul P.111 and P.111a

Dimensions:	Span (short) 25ft 8in (8.71m), (intermediate) 29ft 9in (9.06m), (full) 33ft 6in (10.21m); length 26ft 1in (7.94m) without nose probe, 31ft 6in (9.60m) with nose probe; height 12ft 6in (3.81m)
Powerplant:	One Rolls-Royce Nene RN.3 turbojet, producing 5,100lb (2,300kg) thrust
Weights:	Empty 7,517lb (3,409kg); loaded 10,127lb (4,592kg)
Performance:	Maximum speed at sea level 648mph (1,043km/h); normal service ceiling 35,000ft (11,000m)
Production:	One aircraft for P.111 and P.111a built to Specification E.27/46, with serial number VT935

Boulton Paul P.120

Dimensions:	Span 33ft 5in (10.20m); length 29ft 7in (9m); height 9ft 6½in (2.91m)
Powerplant:	One Rolls-Royce Nene RN.3 turbojet producing 5,100lb (2,300kg) thrust
Weights:	Empty 10,656lb (4,832kg); loaded 12,580lb (5,705kg)
Performance:	No accurate performance figures were obtained in the twenty-three days that the aircraft existed.
Production:	One aircraft built to Specification E.27/49, with serial number VT951

CHAPTER ELEVEN

Fairey FD.1

Delta One

By 1944, the heavy Allied bombing campaign against German industrial targets, together with a growing shortage of raw materials, induced the Germans to experiment with many ambitious and innovative projects. In mid-summer, the German air ministry, the *Reichsluftfahrtministerium* (RLM) ordered studies into the feasibility of a semi-expendable rocket-powered interceptor. In view of its basic requirement to defend specific target areas, the aircraft would only require a short range, but it was considered mandatory that it carried a rocket projectile armament.

The Bachem Natter

Heinkel, Junkers and Messerschmitt all put forward designs of varying practicality, but it was the offering of Dr Erich Bachem that interested the RLM to such an extent that, on 1 August 1944, his small company received authorization to proceed further with its project, which was given the official designation of Bachem Ba 349A Natter. This little aircraft was to be powered by a Walter HWK109-509A-2 rocket engine, which produced 3,740lb (1,700kg) thrust, and its armament was to consist of twenty-four unguided Hs 217 Fohn or thirty-three R4M 55mm folding-fin, rocket projectiles.

The aircraft was to be ramp-launched vertically up to a preset, radar-detected altitude above a raiding bomber formation, in less than a minute. The launch would be assisted by a pair of 1,100lb (500kg) Schmidding 109-535 solid-fuel booster rocket motors, mounted externally on each side of the rear fuselage, that

fell away from the airframe once they had burned out. The pilot would then assume control, glide down among the bombers, release the nose-cone and fire a barrage of rocket projectiles from their bay in the nose. He would then eject the empty nose section, leaving himself exposed to the elements. This ejection sequence triggered a parachute attached to the rear fuselage and the resulting deceleration would propel the pilot forward from his seating area, to descend under his own parachute.

The rear fuselage, complete with the Walter rocket, returned to earth under its parachute, to be refuelled and attached to another nose section and set of wings, ready for a further launch, with a fresh pilot. Once the original pilot had landed, he was briefed to return to the launching site as soon as possible for another sortie.

Development of the project was in its infancy when World War Two ended. Several test flights, using dummies, had been successful, but in view of the impending arrival of Allied ground forces onto German soil, further unmanned trials were considered too time-consuming, so on 28 February 1945, test pilot Oblt Lothar Siebert volunteered to make the first manned flight. His upwards trajectory was fine up to 1,500ft (450m), but while the aircraft was still accelerating the canopy parted company with the rest of the airframe, which then made a graceful curve before plummeting into the Black Forest with Siebert still strapped in his seat.

The loss of the first pilot did not deter others from wishing to fly the radical aircraft and in April 1945 an operational site of ten launching frames was set up east of Stuttgart. Aircraft and pilots stood ready to intercept the next Allied bomber formations, but American armoured units

arrived before the bombers, to bring the whole project to an abrupt halt.

Fairey Interest

Though the Allied Technical Intelligence Mission knew that the Natter had not been properly developed, as it had been urgently needed to defend vulnerable German industrial targets, the Fairey Aviation Company Ltd took an interest in the project.

In the spring of 1946, they started an examination of the advantages and disadvantages of the vertically launched fighter. With their history of producing aeroplanes for the Royal Navy, their approach to vertical take-off (VTO) was heavily loaded in favour of it being ship-borne, though an RAF variant could be designed at that Service's request.

The Model Programme

Fairey had the outlines of a piloted aircraft to research VTO applications ready to submit to the Ministry of Supply (MoS) by July, but their timing was decidedly inappropriate. On 13 March of that year the Miles M.52 supersonic project had been cancelled (*see* Chapter Twenty-Three), and there still lingered within the Ministry a reluctance to proceed with radical piloted projects. Consequently Fairey's approach had to be amended and the official go-ahead was given to a programme of radio-controlled, pilotless models to be used for VTO research. These models were scaled-down variants of the piloted aircraft's configuration, with delta wings of 10ft (3m) span and powered by a Beta rocket motor, fuelled by

The cluttered rear end of VX350, originating from the initial idea of a vertical take-off interceptor with four rocket motors, is seen to advantage in this view. The top and side rocket housings have been faired-off to pointed ends, with the bottom one turned into an anti-spin/braking parachute housing. The fixed leading-edge slats on the outer wing sections were deleted early in its test flight programme. *Aeroplane*

a mixture of hydrogen peroxide and methanol hydrazine, that the company had developed from an original RAE design. It had two combustion chambers that each produced 900lb (400kg) thrust, and was augmented by two 600lb (270kg) thrust cordite booster rockets.

Pitch and yaw was effected by a pair of automatically controlled swivelling nozzles on the Beta motor, with in-flight data telemetered to a ground master station. Elevons provided roll control, working in conjunction with a rudder attached to a delta-shaped fin; the fin's base was cut away to clear blast from the Beta motor.

The design and production of more than forty of these models, handled by Fairey's Research and Armament Development Division at Heston in Middlesex, lasted over a period of five years. The RAE rocket range at Aberporth, in the former Welsh county of Cardiganshire, was the first test-firing site, but two potentially serious accidents caused the company to transfer operations onto HMS *Sulva*, a former tank-landing craft moored in Cardigan Bay. However, a combination of inclement

weather that prevented shore-based cine cameras from making records of trials for days and even weeks, together with the need to declare a portion of the bay a danger area to all shipping whenever test firing was to be carried out, made the location impractical. Therefore, in the spring of 1951 the whole operation was transferred to the Long-Range Weapons Establishment at Woomera, in South Australia.

While not having the low cloud, rain and high winds of Wales, Woomera had its own drawbacks. The heat was intense, while dust and millions of bush-flies that enjoyed a twenty-four-hour operating schedule encouraged the Fairey VTO team to keep their test firing to a minimum, principally carried out at night. The conditions took their toll of the delicate instrumentation as well as the operators, so the fact that the programme was eventually cancelled in 1953 came as no great surprise, but great relief. The surviving models were handed to the Australian Department of Supply for exhibition, but with the proviso that any captioning should not make any mention of the orig-

inal VTO aspect – which does beg the question as to what exhibition visitors were meant to consider was the reason for their being built in the first place!

Piloted, at Last

During 1947, before the whole Beta-powered model programme had got under way, the MoS asked Fairey whether the trials could be expanded to include transonic speeds, but the company expressed their reservations about such a plan. Their original piloted aircraft design still existed and the company's persistence concerning the obvious benefits of such a trials aircraft eventually overcame official reticence, so that on 19 September, Specification E.10/47 was raised to cover the Fairey Type R delta-wing project and the model-firing programme, although it was carried out, became somewhat academic. The official wording of the Specification stated that the aircraft was required 'for important research work with revolutionary possibilities in the design and operation of fighter aircraft'. One could make out what one liked from that!

In April 1948, the company was awarded contract 6/ACFT/1534/CB.7(b) to build three Type R prototypes, with constructor's numbering F.8466 to F.8468. Serial numbers VX350, VX357 and VX364 were allocated to the aircraft, for which metal was first cut in August 1948 at Fairey's Heaton Chapel factory, outside Stockport. The Type R designation, while still being officially recognized, was unofficially superseded by Delta One, or FD.1, and the aircraft became known as such throughout its life.

The vertical-launching aspect was still embodied in the project, but it was decided that early flight-testing would be conducted in a more orthodox mode and VX350 was amended to centre around a Rolls-Royce Derwent 5 centrifugal-flow turbojet. Using such a large-diameter engine meant that, if the aircraft's length was to be kept to a minimum, then it was going to be dumpy. A tricycle undercarriage was specified for VX350, which would be jettisoned once the aircraft was airborne, and landing would be accomplished on a ventral skid. With the delta wings being mounted in a mid-set position on the rotund fuselage, it is assumed that some form of wing-tip outriggers was going to be installed for the landings.

Whitehall's Change

As so often happened in the early post-war years – and has been perpetuated throughout the second half of the twentieth century – officialdom then had a rethink. The net result of this one was the abandonment of the whole vertically launched interceptor programme by the Air Ministry. Mixed power plants, of a turbojet augmented by a rocket motor to boost take-off and interception, became 'flavour of the month', but this, too, was cast aside at a later date. So far as Fairey was concerned, VX350 was retained, as it was in an advanced state of construction – which was not always a constraint in such matters – but the two other FD.1s were cancelled. It is believed that enough of VX357 had existed for a Derwent 8 to be installed and VX364 was also taking shape, but this has not been substantiated. The fate of these two airframes is unknown, but it is assumed that they were cut up on site.

Amazing as it may seem, even at this juncture Fairey was being asked to undertake another programme of model test-flying, with the transonic speed region still being its aim. However, strong repudiation by the company eventually won through, and as the FD.2 had been drafted as a high-speed delta-winged design (*see* Chapter Sixteen), the continuation of the FD.1 was justified in official eyes as a delta-wing research vehicle to further the FD.2 programme. For once, the official decision proved to be correct.

The FD.1 Emerges

In the first half of 1950, VX350 was rolled out from the Heaton Chapel assembly sheds and 'rolled out' is a very appropriate term: it was like a small barrel with delta wings, attached to an enormous delta-shaped fin/rudder assembly. A conventional retractable tricycle undercarriage was fitted, whose main wheels lay horizontal within the fuselage sides when retracted, enclosed by three doors. On lowering, the main doors opened and then closed behind the lowered undercarriage units, which were held locked down by the two smaller doors. The nose-wheel was hinged under the circular air intake, for a rewards retraction into a two-door bay, the main door of which also closed when the unit was in the landing position.

A pair of short-span delta wings were attached in a central position on each side of the circular-sectioned fuselage, with their tips squared off by anti-spin parachute housings and fixed leading-edge slats were installed on the outboard sections. The large fin/rudder assembly, which had a combined area of 43.63sq ft (4.05sq m) was topped by a small triangular-shaped fixed tailplane, which had no elevator. It was inclined at a 5-degree angle to the flight line and plans existed for its removal at a later date, when high-speed trials were scheduled. Powered elevons took up nearly 80 per cent of each wing trailing edge, with the remaining inboard sections carrying split airbrakes.

The rear end of VX350 can only be described as a confusion of shapes, which resulted from the cancellation of the VTO requirement after the rear fuselage had been constructed. With the Derwent's orifice in the middle, four circular-sectioned housings surrounded it, protruding aft at 90-degrees to each other; these were to have been for the rocket motors, before the VTO programme was abandoned. The bottom one was adapted to hold a braking parachute, but the remaining three were just faired over into circular points, to satisfy aerodynamic requirements.

Finished in natural metal with Type D service markings only on the fuselage and fin, the aircraft had a large black anti-glare panel ahead of the wrap-around windscreen, that was extended as a flash halfway along either side of the fuselage. It was transported to Ringway (now Manchester International Airport) for several months of taxiing trials, conducted by Fairey's Chief Test Pilot, Gp Capt R. Gordon Slade, and his deputy, Peter Twiss.

Flying and Problems

In February 1951, the little aircraft was dismantled and taken to Boscombe Down for a maiden flight, undertaken by Slade on 12 March and lasting seventeen minutes. One fact was immediately made apparent: when flying at low speed, which required an abnormally high angle of attack, there was a natural tendency to oscillate laterally. In the early 1950s, the reasons for this phenomenon were not fully understood, until it was discovered that delta-winged aircraft needed to have a substantially increased approach speed.

With the fuselage consisting of cockpit and Derwent, the fuel tanks had to be located in the wing leading edges, forward of the main spar; this meant that, with its small wingspan, the FD.1 had a very short flight endurance. This was exacerbated by a major problem in the fuel system that prevented an alarming percentage of what fuel there was from reaching the engine. This fuel-flow problem, coupled with the lack of understanding of the undesirable low-speed instability, led to a marked

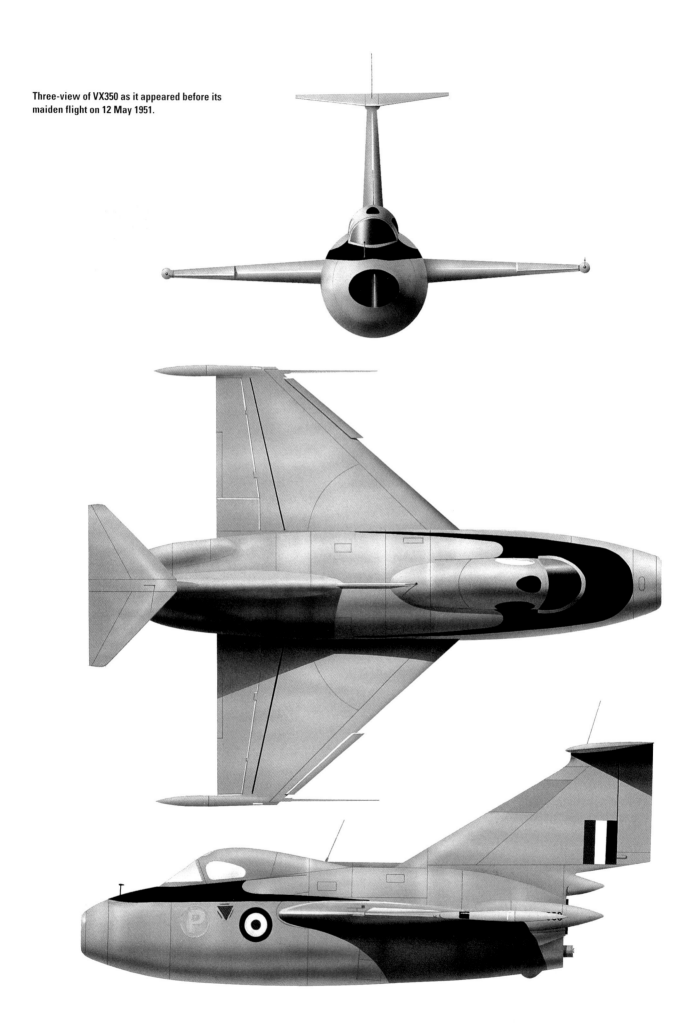

Three-view of VX350 as it appeared before its maiden flight on 12 May 1951.

ABOVE LEFT: The Bachem Ba349A Natter local defence interceptor fostered Fairey's interest in the vertical-take-off concept.

ABOVE: One of the forty or so Beta-powered research models built by Fairey, test flown in Wales and at Woomera, to explore VTO behaviours.

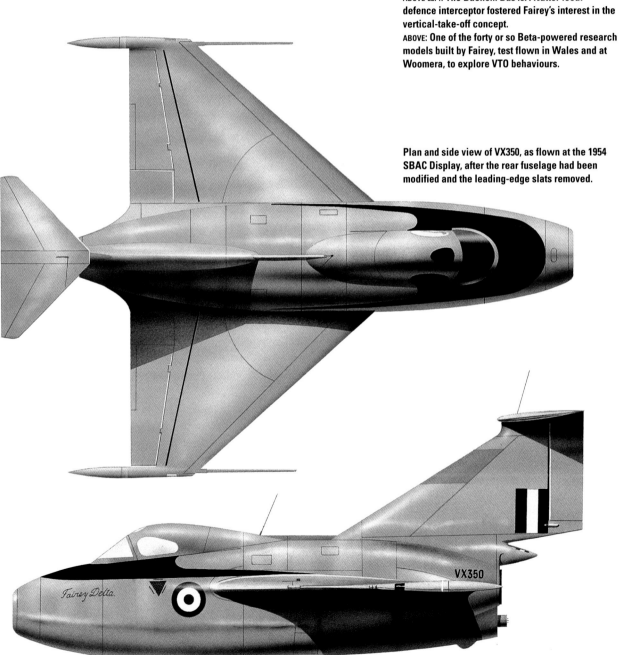

Plan and side view of VX350, as flown at the 1954 SBAC Display, after the rear fuselage had been modified and the leading-edge slats removed.

Fairey Delta.

VX350

reluctance on the part of the company's pilots to fly the aircraft: VX350 was considered a dangerous aeroplane.

It did not fly again for eighteen months, while the fuel-flow system was investigated and a contractual dispute between Fairey and the MoS was sorted out. In the matter of the fuel flow, it was found that a considerable proportion remained trapped in the wings: the installation of additional flow channels helped to reduce the problem. The contractual disagreement, however, presented a greater complication. The Ministry's final payment for the FD.1 to the company depended on the aircraft logging ten flying hours, which had not been achieved due to the instability and fuel-flow problems. The whole business became very protracted but eventually the stalemate was broken, once the necessary flying techniques had been understood and the fuel flow was improved.

An Aerodynamic Clean-up

While VX350 was grounded, and in view of this looking likely to last a considerable time, Fairey decided to implement aerodynamic improvements to the airframe. As the whole VTO project had now been abandoned, the rocket housings on either side of the wing trailing edge/fuselage joint were removed, and the wing was faired into the rear fuselage by a clean extension of the trailing edges. The housing between the jet orifice and the fin was an integral part of the tail assembly's structure, so it was retained, as was the lower housing containing the braking parachute. The leading-edge slats were removed and, on the resumption of flying in the summer of 1953, the FD.1 was considered purely a research tool to evaluate the stability of delta-wing planforms.

This programme had its limitations however, as the fixed tailplane imposed a

maximum speed of 345mph (555km/h) on the airframe. As has already been stated, there were plans to remove the tailplane and a theoretical speed of 620mph at 10,000ft (1,000km/h at 3,000m) was calculated. But this remained theoretical, as the necessary modifications were never made and the FD.2 (*see* Chapter Sixteen) was flying by August 1954.

Functional and Farnborough

The modifications that had been implemented now made the aircraft a useful research tool into general delta-wing planform behaviour, and the data obtained helped the FD.2 programme. The stability problems were explored with confidence, as was the configuration's rolling potential, but the endurance, although better than originally experienced, still remained on

Prior to its flying display, the aircraft attracts a good crowd as it stands beside Gannet AS.1 WN360, with Varsity T.1 VX835, a Canberra and Vulcan prototype VX770 on the other side of the taxi-way. The reflections in the overall natural metal reveal the undulations in its shiny surface. Although the streamlined wing-tip housings were originally intended for anti-spin parachutes, they were used to carry various instruments. The rear-protruding aerial is seen to be well protected against inquisitive fingers. Author's collection

The FD.1 was not a very elegant spectacle as it came in to land, and the narrow-track main wheels indicate that it required steady handling to accomplish a good touchdown. *Aeroplane*

the short side, and the aircraft was definitely happier in calm weather conditions.

The large flying-control surfaces imparted a very fast rate of roll and this was well demonstrated at Farnborough's 1954 SBAC Display, for which the little aircraft had been polished to a mirror-like exterior finish. The very fast landing speed also generated a certain amount of gasping from the gathered assembly. VX350's involvement with Farnborough was not restricted to the Display, for it spent a time in the RAE's blower tunnel, to investigate the jettisoning of its canopy in relation to the height of its fin; it also spent time with the Establishment's flying department.

Final Days

The majority of the FD.1's flying was undertaken at Boscombe Down and Farnborough, by pilots of both Establishments. On 6 February 1956, an RAF pilot had to make an emergency landing, which resulted in a detour off the runway that removed the undercarriage. A contributory factor to this is thought to have been a failure of the complicated main-wheel locking mechanism.

Whatever the cause, the damage sustained put VX350 into Farnborough's Mechanical Engineering Department for seven months; in retrospect this seems rather strange, for on completion of the repairs, on 9 October, the aircraft was conveyed to the Proof and Experimental Establishment at Shoeburyness to become another expensive armament target.

In hindsight, the whole vertical launching of an interceptor can be seen as fraught with problems, but it seemed a good idea at the time, although the 'time' was of short duration due to being abandoned before the FD.1 ever took to the air. In the United States, the concept was taken further by both Lockheed with their XFV-1 and Convair with their XFY-1, but they, too, only served to prove that the idea was not really practical. Dr Bachem's original idea, although bold in concept, was born of desperation rather than sound aerodynamic reasoning.

As it banks to port on its way to Farnborough, the tubby little delta looks far more photogenic. The streamlined fairing forward of the wing's main spar, with a similar housing on the port side, covered the flying control hydraulic actuators. *Aeroplane*

Technical Data – Fairey Type R/FD.1	
Dimensions:	Span 19ft 6in (5.94m); length 26ft 3in (8.0m); height 11ft 5in (3.5m)
Powerplant:	One Rolls-Royce Derwent 5 turbojet, producing 3,500lb (1,600kg) thrust
Weight:	Loaded, approximately 8,000lb (3,600kg)
Performance:	Maximum speed 345mph (555km/h)
Production:	One aircraft built to Specification E.10/47 with serial number VX350. Two additional aircraft, VX357 and VX364, not completed

CHAPTER TWELVE

Handley Page H.P.88

Crescent-Wing Crusader

In order to secure a contract to build the first of the V-bombers, the Valiant, Vickers-Armstrongs' Chief Designer in 1945, George (later Sir George) Edwards, guaranteed a production schedule that many believed would be impossible to meet. The fact that three prototypes and 104 production aircraft were all delivered on time, without requiring any aerodynamic modifications, speaks volumes about the man, his company and the correctness of the design in the first place. Some will say that the other two V-bombers were more complex aeroplanes than the Valiant, but Vickers-Armstrongs had to pioneer new production technologies, from which both Avro and Handley Page benefited.

One luxury that George Edwards' timetable excluded was the testing of his new design's aerodynamic qualities before it was built. Avro, on the other hand, were able to produce the Type 707 to test the delta-wing aircraft planform of the Vulcan, as related in Chapter Eight, and the crescent-wing planform chosen by Handley Page for the Victor was also considered radical enough to warrant flight-testing in a scaled-down form.

Crescent-Wing Evolution

One of the 'characters' in British aviation was the Cheltenham-born engineer Frederick (later Sir Frederick) Handley Page. From his founding of Handley Page Ltd on 17 June 1909, his name was associated with aeronautical pioneering on a large scale. On the night of 16–17 March 1917, he opened his account with British services, when H.P.11 0/100 aircraft bombed the Metz railway junction, and by the Armistice on 11 November 1918, forty-two 0/100 aircraft were serving with four RNAS squadrons. From the 0/100 emerged the H.P.12 0/400 and within a year, 554 of these large bombers had been built to serve with a dozen RAF units, among them being

No. 216 Squadron, who flew the aircraft in the Middle East until 1921. The largest bomber of the era was the H.P.15 V/1500, and in the post-war generation of civil airliners, the giant H.P.42 biplane kept the company name in the forefront of aviation.

In collaboration with Dr Gustav Victor Lachmann, the company's engineering consultant, the Handley Page Automatic Slat was perfected. This was an operating slat on a wing leading edge, fitted to obviate the problem of stalling, and today is a fundamental element of high-speed aircraft design. During Handley Page's building of, successively, Heyford, Hampden, Hereford and Halifax bombers for the RAF, Dr Lachmann suggested in 1936 that the company should investigate the stability of tailless aircraft. A small research aeroplane with the unofficial designation 'Manx' was designed, and its construction subcontracted to Dart Aircraft Ltd. A combination of Dart's financial problems, the internment of Dr Lachmann in 1939 as a German citizen and priority within Handley Page given to Halifax production meant that the aircraft did not fly until 25 June 1943. The RAE's Tailless Aircraft Committee were not terribly enamoured and on 2 April 1946, by which time the aircraft had been officially designated the H.P.75, it made its last flight. The degree of interest in the Manx is exemplified by the fact that it hung around at the company's factory at Radlett until 1952, when it was finally scrapped and incinerated.

The company's Research Engineer, Godfrey Lee, was a member of the Allied Technical Intelligence Mission in 1945, and he expressed great interest in the research that had been carried out by Arado Flugzeugwerke GmbH into the field of multi-angled sweep or 'crescent'-shaped wings, designed to maintain a constant Mach number from root to tip. When Handley Page received the invitation to tender for a four-turbojet bomber to meet Specification B.35/46, they vied with designs from Armstrong Whitworth, English Electric, A. V. Roe, Short Brothers

and Vickers-Armstrongs. Two designs, one from A. V. Roe and one from Handley Page, were considered to justify the ordering of prototypes, subject to satisfactory wind-tunnel test results.

While A. V. Roe's offering, which emerged as the Vulcan, was designed around a delta-wing format, Handley Page centred on the crescent-wing configuration, with leading-edge sweep varying from 50 degrees on the inboard third of the wing to 40 degrees on the middle third and 30 degrees on the outboard third. Trailing-edge sweep was a constant 25 degrees over the inboard and middle thirds, changing to 12 degrees on the outboard section. Under the company designation H.P.80, the original concept had the wing tips blended into vertical fin/rudder assemblies and a tailplane atop a stubby mount at the rear of the fuselage, but further research convinced the company that a more conventional tail unit would be preferable, and the shape of the H.P.8. Victor was more or less established.

A Trials Aircraft

The company, together with the MoS and the RAE, considered that as the wings were entering an area where no previous research had been undertaken in Britain, it would be advisable to build a scaled-down set of wings, which could be flight-tested and evaluated. With the research being purely aimed at the planform, it was not considered necessary to incur the time or expense of designing and building a complete aircraft, so the suggestion proffered by Vickers-Armstrongs' Supermarine Division, that an Attacker fuselage would be suitable to get the new wings into the air, was readily accepted by all concerned. Specification E.6/48 was issued on 12 March 1948 to cover the necessary construction, the company designation H.P.88 was given to the aircraft and serial number VX330 was allocated. Serial number VX337 was put on hold, in case a second aircraft was required,

ABOVE: When it was rolled out at Brough in June 1951 the H.P.88's fuselage displayed its Supermarine Type 510 origins, but the very noticeable long mass-balances on each aileron are pure Handley Page. *Handley Page Association*

BELOW: The large external airbrakes on either side of the rear fuselage are quite evident, as is the fact that the Martin-Baker Mk 1A ejector seat had yet to be installed when this photograph was taken. The enormous area-ruled bullet fairing at the fin/tailplane junction has a long boom in the front, on which a yaw vane will be mounted, while the rear end housed an anti-spin parachute. *Handley Page Association*

but as this did not materialize, that number was cancelled, never to be reissued.

A Profusion of Titles

Four weeks after agreeing to use an Attacker fuselage, Handley Page had a rethink and came to the conclusion that a Supermarine Type 510 fuselage would be more suitable, as this was already an Attacker that had been adapted at the

take the detail design required to develop a 40 per cent scale flying wing, together with the necessary tail assembly. Consequently, the work was subcontracted to General Aircraft Ltd at Feltham in Middlesex, where it was entered into that company's design numbering system as the GAL 63.

Yet another designation came about through General Aircraft Ltd's merger, on 1 January 1949, with Blackburn Aircraft Ltd, to become the Blackburn and General Aircraft Ltd. With this merger, the

In this rare flying photograph, possibly a ground-to-air shot, the crescent-wing planform and the four long covers for the Fowler flap actuators are well displayed.
Handley Page Association

wing root station to take a 45-degree sweep. Supermarine were in agreement, and they set about putting in hand a considerable modification programme to meet Handley Page's requirements to create the H.P.88. Within Supermarine there was a policy whereby a different type number was allocated to every variant that it produced and, in order to fall in line with this system, Handley Page's modified Type 510 became the Supermarine Type 521.

As the drawing office at Handley Page Ltd was already overstretched meeting H.P.80 work, it was in no position to under-

Feltham design office moved up to Blackburn's complex at Brough in Yorkshire and the H.P.88/GAL 63 work went with it, to be reallocated a Blackburn design office number, the Y.B.2. So even before it left the drawing board, the aircraft had received four different titles! The newly-formed company took over contract number 6/ACFT/2243/CB.6(b), which had been issued to Handley Page on 5 April 1948, to manufacture the trials aircraft and in which there was provision to build a second aircraft, though as already stated, this did not become necessary.

An Academic Exercise

On 25 November 1950, the Supermarine Type 521 fuselage was taken by road from the company's experimental works at Hursley Park to Brough, where it was promptly damaged during offloading from the transporter, but this was repaired on site – its history thus far really does show portents of problems for its future. Construction of the wings and tail assembly was well advanced when Handley Page's calculations showed that, in order to meet the Air Ministry's desire for the critical Mach number to be raised from 0.83 to 0.86, the H.P.80 wing root section needed modifying to a thickness/chord ratio of 16 per cent. However, this would reduce stability and in order to restore the status quo, the trailing edge sweep-change point had to be moved inboard. Therefore, before it was completed, VX330 was not a true test vehicle for the H.P.80's wings. Furthermore, the bomber design had originally featured an all-moving tailplane, but this was amended to a conventional unit with elevators and again, the H.P.88's construction had progressed beyond the point where a change could be implemented: it therefore had to have a non-representational tail assembly as well. Handley Page engineers agreed that at best, the H.P.88 could provide data on how the H.P.80 was likely to handle.

By the end of December 1950, the trials aircraft was virtually complete, but it was June 1951 before VX330 received an overall Royal Blue gloss finish and an official photographic session was held – although even then, the Martin-Baker Mk 1A ejector seat had not been installed. Each wing had a pair of prominent fairings protruding aft of the trailing edge, which covered the actuators for a large Fowler flap, while each aileron carried a 2ft 6in-long (0.76m) mass balance arm, set at 40 degrees above and below its surface.

The all-moving tailplane was sited high on the fin, with a large bullet fairing covering the intersection. Forward from this, a long boom pointed forwards to carry a yaw-vane, and the rear of the fairing housed a dual-purpose braking/anti-spin parachute. The need for a parachute for landing is questionable, in view of the very substantial airbrakes that were mounted on the outer skin on either side of the fuselage, behind the wing joint, with large fairings fore and aft. They had the ability to operate at 20, 45 and 80 degrees to the flight-line, with their movement being

controlled by three separate buttons within the cockpit.

The undercarriage was basically Supermarine 510, with adjustments made to facilitate inwards retraction into the new wings. The Type 510's Rolls-Royce Nene 2, delivering 5,000lb (2,300kg) thrust, was retained, together with the four fuselage fuel tanks containing 236.5gal (1,064ltr); the wing, being purely a trials installation, was not designed to be fitted with tanks. In this configuration, it was calculated that the H.P.88 was capable of reaching Mach 0.90.

miles north-east of Brough and as the runway, despite being non-operational, was still in good condition, it was ideal for hosting the H.P.88's first flight.

VX330 was dismantled to be taken by road from Brough to Carnaby on 14 June 1951, where, following reassembly, systems were checked and serious taxiing trials occupied the next seven days. On the 21st, 'Sailor' Parker took off for a five-minute maiden flight, following which several adjustments, lasting over a fortnight, were carried out. The next two flights, undertaken on 7 July, showed that

An angle bracket strip fixed to the tailplane's trailing edge helped to alleviate the problem and 310mph (500km/h) was attained with reasonable smoothness. As this modification proved that the remedial action was on the right track, the strip was lengthened on both the upper and lower surfaces of the tailplane so that, on 5 August, when Parker was making the seventeenth flight, he reported that a comparatively smooth flight was made up to 520mph (840km/h), Mach 0.82. Subsequent flights confirmed that, by employing a gentle backward pressure on the control

During the H.P.88's total of fourteen flying hours there was not too much time for air-to-air photographic sessions, and this shot was taken during what is believed to have been the only occasion. Handley Page Association.

Porpoising to Disaster

Some taxiing was carried out by Blackburn's Chief Test Pilot, Gartell 'Sailor' Parker, at Brough, but the 1,430yd (1,310m) long runway precluded any flight testing.

During 1944, three Bomber Command Emergency Landing Grounds (ELGs) were built on the east side of the British mainland: Manston in Kent, Woodbridge in Suffolk and Carnaby, outside Bridlington in Yorkshire. Each had a 3,000yd (2,740m) runway, with long under- and overshoot extensions. As Carnaby was only about 30

the H.P.88 had marked over-sensitivity in the tailplane, with the aircraft pitching at the slightest atmospheric pressure change. The natural reaction to correct this movement only increased the pitching, as low-amplitude porpoising set in, which could only be damped-out by the pilot adopting a fixed hold on the control column. Two further flights established that the cut-in speed for the pitching was 265mph (426km/h) and during the fifth flight, carried out on 25 July, things became decidedly dangerous at just over 290mph (467km/h).

column, the pitching was damped out after a couple of cycles, but pursuing the porpoising should not be advocated.

Handley Page's Deputy Chief Test Pilot, 'Duggie' Broomfield DFM, joined Parker and, after an extensive test flight, confirmed all that had been said about the aircraft, together with the remedial actions taken so far. On 23 August Broomfield, having assumed responsibility for H.P.88 test-flying, ferried it to Stansted, where a series of airspeed calibration flights was scheduled. The aircraft had been cleared up to 630mph (1,010km/h), with 0.85 set

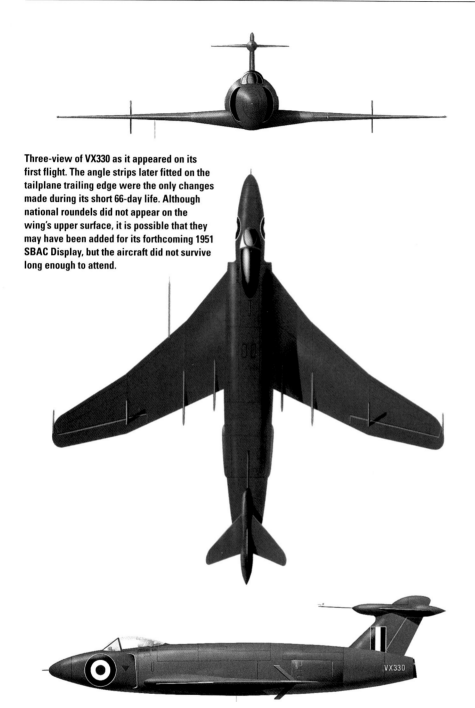

Three-view of VX330 as it appeared on its first flight. The angle strips later fitted on the tailplane trailing edge were the only changes made during its short 66-day life. Although national roundels did not appear on the wing's upper surface, it is possible that they may have been added for its forthcoming 1951 SBAC Display, but the aircraft did not survive long enough to attend.

as the limiting Mach number, in readiness for displaying at the year's SBAC Display.

Broomfield took off from Stansted on 26 August, to make several runs at low altitude. Fifteen minutes into the programme, he received permission from ATC to start the first run and positioned himself for a high-speed run down the main runway at an altitude of approximately 300ft (100m). Halfway through the run, VX330 broke up without any warning. Broomfield was too low for a successful ejection and his body was found still in the seat, clear of the wreckage.

Inquest

On 30 August, Mr B. A. Morris, senior investigating officer to the Accident Investigation Branch of the Ministry of Civil Aviation, stated at an inquest that he found structural failure to have caused the crash. He was satisfied that the H.P.88 was airworthy prior to the crash and concluded that the fuselage had failed aft of the wing's trailing edge, after which the pilot's seat had become detached from the cockpit.

This theory was strongly contested by William MacRostie, Handley Page's works foreman, who advanced his own belief that very high accelerations could have arisen from instability within the hydraulic flying control system. A local farmer, Mr George Brown, had witnessed the event and gave evidence that the nose had gone up before the aircraft levelled off, then rose again steeply. He stated that the starboard wing came off, the aircraft turned and the port wing then broke away.

Detailed examination of the wreckage and flight recorder indicated very high oscillations on a trace showing just over 600mph (965km/h), which meant that this was the fastest that VX330 had flown at such a low altitude. The official conclusion was that an inertia coupling between the powered controls and the elevator, which produced a load greater than the aircraft could absorb, caused the structural failure.

The H.P.88 had lasted just over two months since its maiden flight and a total of fourteen flying hours had produced virtually nothing of relevance to the H.P.80 programme. In fact, the majority of the testing related to its own shortcomings, and whether 'Duggie' Broomfield's life was needlessly sacrificed is open to conjecture.

Technical Data – Handley Page H.P.88 (Supermarine Type 521, GAL 63 and Blackburn Y.B.2)	
Dimensions:	Span 40ft (12.2m); length 39ft 10in (12.14m); height 12ft 8in (3.87m)
Powerplant:	One Rolls-Royce Nene R.N.2 turbojet, producing 5,000lb (2,300kg) thrust
Weights:	Empty 10,841lb (4,916kg); loaded 13,197lb (5,985kg)
Performance:	No figures officially classified; maximum speed attained prior to crash 517mph (833km/h)
Production:	One aircraft built to Specification E.6/48, with serial number VX330. Second aircraft, VX337, included in order, but not built

CHAPTER THIRTEEN

Supermarine N.9/47

Forging the Scimitar

When the Type 508 prototype took off on 31 August 1951, it was Supermarine's first twin-engined aircraft to fly since the Stranraer flying boat, which had been built to Specification R.24/31 and first flew on 27 July 1934; although the Supermarine Type 327 six-cannon fighter project, to Specification F.18/37, was planned to be powered by two Rolls-Royce Merlins, it got no further than a partial mock-up stage. Furthermore, the Type 508 was the progenitor of the last type designed and produced entirely by the Supermarine Division of Vickers-Armstrongs (Aircraft) Ltd, the Scimitar. These two facts alone are not its only claim to aviation history as, when originally proposed, it was to meet a new Royal Navy concept of operating aircraft from a flexible carrier deck and dispensing with the conventional undercarriage.

Consideration of such a scheme within Admiralty House stemmed from information obtained in the autumn of 1944, about trials being conducted in Germany. Both the Messerschmitt Me 163B interceptor and the early versions of the Arado Ar 234B reconnaissance bomber employed a jettisonable wheel chassis for take-off, landing instead on ventral fuselage skids. Production was under way at the respective companies and by the end of World War Two they were both operational.

The Landing Options

Through RAE investigations into the most suitable format, by December 1944 a project had emerged for a turbojet-powered aircraft of up to 10,000lb (4,500kg) weight and without an undercarriage, to operate from a carrier. Three schemes were put forward: one involved spring-loaded wires fore and aft of a conventional carrier deck; and one a sponge-rubber carrier deck surface, with the final stopping of the landing aircraft being effected

No doubt many people have their favourite aircraft for one reason or another. This is one of the writer's. The first prototype Type 508, VX133, banks to display its top surface, together with the large butterfly tail assembly, during an early publicity display. Author's collection

by a flexible crash barrier. The third solution, which was preferred, featured a rubber or plastic-impregnated fabric, supported by inflatable rubber bags and standard arrester wires to operate as the retarding agents. The aircraft would be mounted on a dolly for deck handling, but take-off would be via a catapult accelerator built into the carrier and the landing on the flexible deck safely accomplished by the aircraft having a reinforced underside.

The Trials

Two flexible rubber deck mock-ups were constructed on grassed areas at Farnborough, complete with arrester wires. The surface's absorbing properties were assessed by

dropping a heavily ballasted General Aircraft Hotspur glider, BT752, complete with pilot, from a crane. In addition, Bell Airacobra AH574 was employed for trials of the catapult gear.

De Havilland Vampire F.1s TG285 and TG426, together with F.3s VG701, VT802, VT803 and VT805, were all modified for involvement in the trials. With the Vampire and Meteor being the only jet types in service at that time, the Vampire's shape was considered more suitable than the twin-engined Meteor's. The RAE Aero Flight's Commanding Officer, Lt Cdr Eric 'Winkle' Brown, was the designated pilot for the programme, which was extended by the conversion of the carrier HMS *Warrior* to take a flexible deck. Lt Cdr Brown's first landing on a Farnborough deck mock-up,

ABOVE AND RIGHT: VX133's only SBAC Display was in 1951 and it is here seen lifting-off to begin its flying routine during which it executed tight turns to prove its agility at low level. Cannon ports are in the underside of the front fuselage section, but as the guns themselves were never installed, ballast was carried in their place. *Aeroplane*

performed on 29 December 1947, resulted in an accident, but the trials continued and naturally, with such a new conception, further mishaps occurred, but none proved fatal. Trials were conducted on HMS *Warrior* from 8 December 1948 to 31 May 1949, but by that time the Admiralty had abandoned the whole project. It is believed that a Sea Hawk was catapulted off a Farnborough flexible deck in 1952, where a landing was made without the undercarriage being lowered, but the reason for this sortie seems to have been purely academic.

Supermarine's Involvement

Both de Havilland and Supermarine were invited to participate in the flexible deck project, although, apart from supplying the Vampires, de Havilland took no further part. But during 1945, the design team at Hursley Park, Supermarine's experimental establishment, started work on a twin-engined aircraft designated Type 505. As an undercarriage, together with its systems, constituted at least 7 per cent of the average aircraft's weight, it was envisaged that an aircraft without this encumbrance

would have a superior climb and speed performance. The absence of an undercarriage would also enable a very thin wing to be designed, and the Type 505 was drawn up with a 7 per cent thickness/chord ratio. Swept wings were initially considered, but at that time insufficient research had been carried out in this sphere, so a straight wing with a constant aerofoil section was proposed.

Rolls-Royce had made overtures throughout the aircraft industry as to the development potential of their AJ.65 axial-flow turbojet, and they convinced Supermarine that a pair of AJ.65s would satisfy all their requirements for the Type 505 project. Consequently the aircraft was designed around such an installation and, as the Attacker's intakes had become established, a similar layout was proposed for the twin-engined design. By having the AJ.65s mounted side-by-side in the fuselage centre-section, jet outlets could be sited just aft of the wing trailing edge joints, thereby keeping the jet-pipes short: this minimized thrust loss, and a considerable portion of the rear fuselage was available for internal fuel tanks. In order to clear the jet efflux from the jet outlets, a 'butterfly' tail was

adopted, with the two surfaces set at a 35-degree angle of dihedral.

The Type 505 was finalized and put forward to the Admiralty at about the same time as the flexible deck concept was cast aside, but the design was considered good enough to meet a new naval requirement for a twin-engined interceptor. Specification N.9/47 was written around the design, modified for it to be equipped with a tricycle undercarriage.

Type 508

In keeping with the company's numbering policy, the Type 505 modified to Specification N.9/47 requirements became the Supermarine Type 508. Two prototypes were ordered initially, on contract number 6/ACFT/1508/CB.7, with a third added to the same contract at a later date, and as each would have slightly different features, each had a different type number: the second prototype was designated Type 529 and the third Type 525. Serial numbers VX133, VX136 and VX138 were allocated, respectively.

A full-size Type 508 mock-up was constructed at Hursley Park and one immediately noticeable feature was the increase in wing thickness/chord ratio. In order to accommodate the main wheel oleos on retraction, the ratio had to be increased to

Supermarine had a penchant for fitting a horizon bead sight on the upper nose-cone of their prototypes in the early 1950s. Author's collection

9 per cent. The specification called for an armament of four of the new 30mm Aden cannon, and provision for this was made under the air intakes. When built, VX133 had gun-ports incorporated in the airframe, although the cannon themselves were simulated by ballast. By this time, Rolls-Royce had bestowed the name Avon on their AJ.65 turbojet and with two Avon RA.3s, each delivering 6,500lb (2,950kg) static thrust, the Type 508 was the most powerful single-seat naval fighter at that time.

One unusual feature involved the rear end of both the Types 508 and 529. The butterfly tailplane had two large flying surfaces, hinged to the units' rear spars, which acted in unison for rudder control and differentially when serving as elevators. In line with the tailplane's leading edge, the whole fuselage tail cone hinged to provide an all-flying tail unit, with the arc of movement being over a range of 9 degrees upwards and 3 degrees downwards, of the fuselage datum line. This type of installation had also been applied to the Type 517 adaptation of the Attacker, which was one of the stepping stones along the road to the Swift.

The Type 508 wings, too, had new features, in that they had full-span leading-edge flaps hinged to the forward spar, and dive-recovery brakes were fitted flush with the wing under-skin surface.

Maiden flight

VX133 was completed in the summer of 1951 and the necessary paperwork was prepared for it to go by road to Boscombe Down for its first flight. The dismantling for transportation and reassembly at the A&AEE's base occupied the best part of two months. On 31 August, Supermarine's Chief Test Pilot, M. J. 'Mike' Lithgow, lifted VX133 off for its maiden flight which, bearing in mind the problems that often occur during an aircraft's first venture into the sky, was quite uneventful.

The whole test-flying programme progressed very smoothly and the leading-edge flaps, operating in conjunction with the generous trailing-edge flaps, proved that despite having a high wing loading, the aircraft's landing speed could be maintained within the Royal Navy's carrier operating limits (which were stringent), without any trouble. In May 1952, VX133 was able to amply demonstrate the fact during carrier deck landing trials made on HMS Eagle.

ABOVE: The second aircraft, VX136, was designated Type 529. It did have the four Aden gun armament installed, together with a slightly longer rear fuselage with provision for rear-warning radar, as well as long, fixed strakes projecting forward from the Vee-tailplane junction with the fuselage. Just aft of the roundel can be seen the line of the hinging rear fuselage cone which provided the aircraft, like VX133, with a rather rudimentary but effective all-flying tail. *Aeroplane*

BELOW: From October to November 1953 VX136, which was fully equipped with folding wings, carried out carrier trials aboard HMS *Eagle*, during which time it made catapult-assisted take-offs where, as can be seen, the strop dropped away over the bow. *Aeroplane*

109

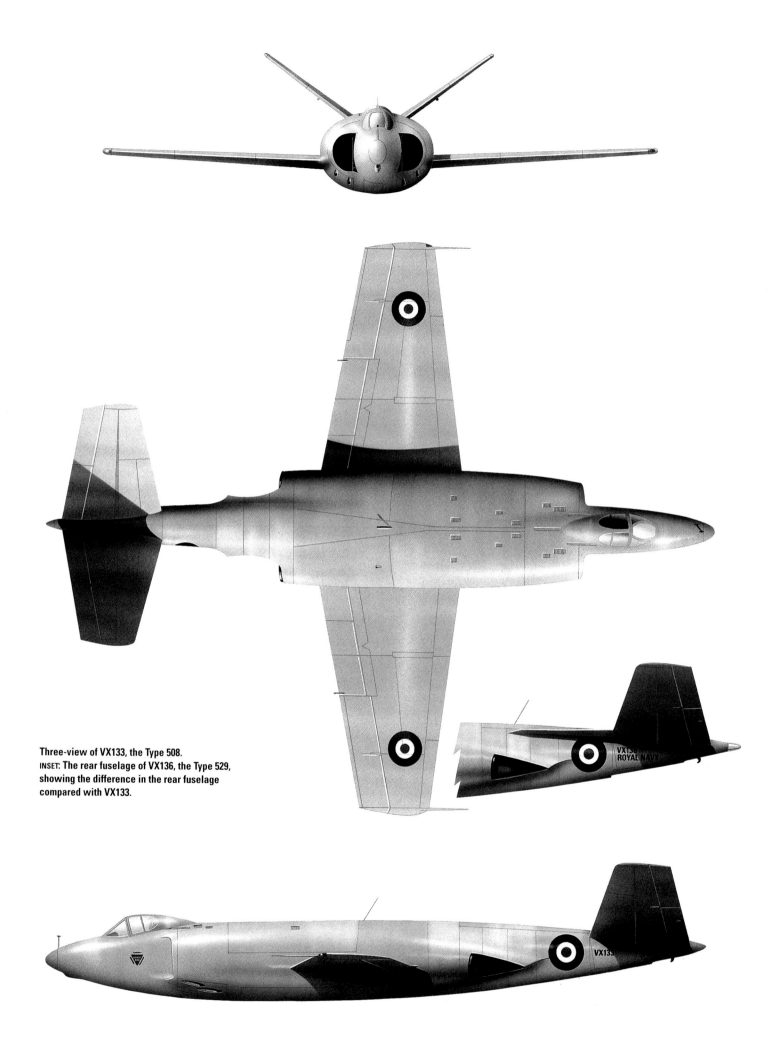

Three-view of VX133, the Type 508.
INSET: The rear fuselage of VX136, the Type 529, showing the difference in the rear fuselage compared with VX133.

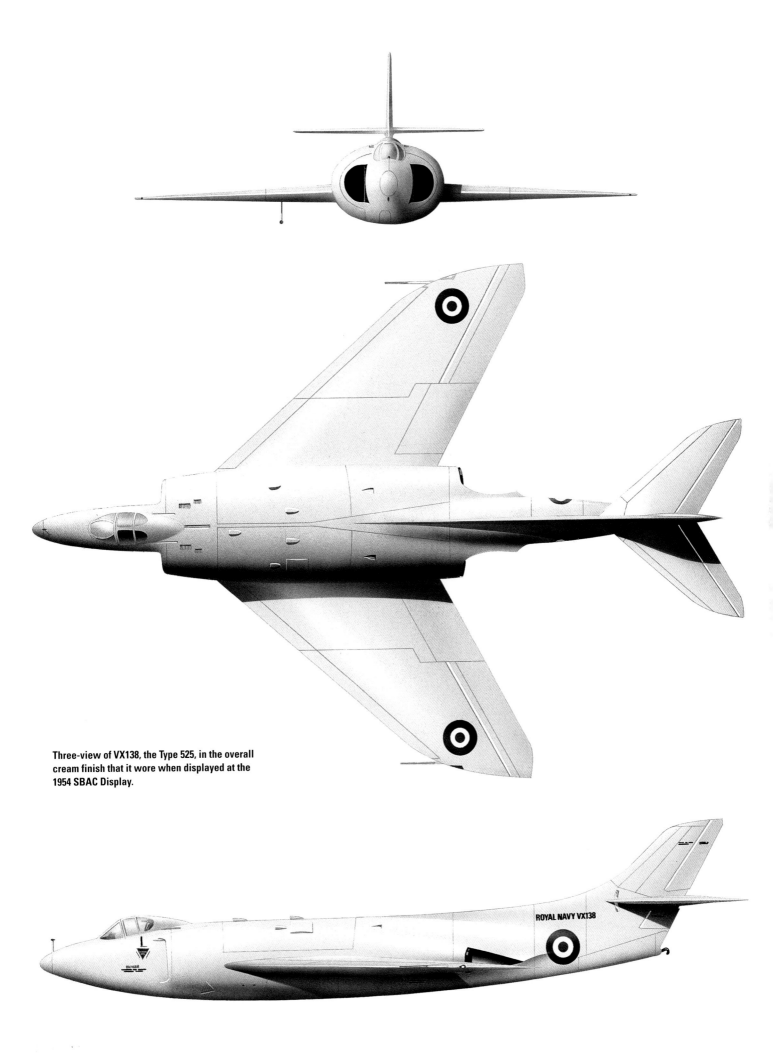

Three-view of VX138, the Type 525, in the overall cream finish that it wore when displayed at the 1954 SBAC Display.

ROYAL NAVY VX138

Type 529

Construction of the second prototype progressed well during 1952 with data obtained during VX133's testing incorporated in the airframe. The fuselage was 6in (15cm) longer that its predecessor by virtue of a new tail-cone housing an adaptation of *Orange* *Putter* rear warning radar. Some alteration to the profile of the air intakes took place and the arrester-hook retraction was simplified. Another variation from VX133 was the installation of 7ft (2.1m) fixed strakes in a dorsal position on the rear fuselage from the leading-edge of the tailplane. With the serial number VX136, the second N.9/47 emerged from Hursley Park nearly a year after VX133. To ensure nobody was in any doubt for whom the aircraft was intended, the wording 'Royal Navy' appeared under the serial on the rear fuselage. On 29 August 1952, it joined VX133 in the test-flight programme and the next year it was also involved in carrier trials on HMS *Eagle*.

ABOVE: The third aircraft, VX138, was the Type 525, which had a conventional fin/rudder assembly and all its flying surfaces swept, but no provision for armament was made on this prototype. Author's collection

RIGHT AND BELOW: Supermarine's Chief Test Pilot, Lt Cdr Lithgow, makes a flat approach in VX138 and deploys a braking parachute, consisting of three miniscule canopies, on touchdown. *Aeroplane*

Type 525

The flight trials of the first two N.9/47 prototypes had, on the whole, been satisfactory, but a wing-flutter tendency that sometimes occurred did foster doubts within the RN as to whether the design, in its existing form, could fully meet the operational role for which it was intended. Since 1945, when the Type 505 design was on the drawing board at Hursley Park, Supermarine had accumulated considerable experience in the technology and aerodynamics of swept wings. This had been gained through the adaptation of the basic Attacker into the Type 510 and the general progression that eventually led to the Type 541 Swift Mk 1.

Supermarine were therefore in a stronger position to propose that the third N.9/47 be redesigned to have wings swept at 50 degrees on the leading edge, a slightly longer fuselage and a swept conversion of the butterfly tail unit. Although the project was agreeable to Admiralty House, when the detailed design stage was put in hand it became rather obvious that there would be considerable structural problems with the swept butterfly tail. This generated a complete redesign of the rear fuselage, resulting in a more conventional cruciform, swept fin/rudder assembly, incorporating an all-flying tailplane, with a movement range of 10 degrees above and 5 degrees below the datum line.

Supermarine received the new contract 6/ACFT/5772/CB.7 for the new prototype; obviously a new type number had to be allocated, but just why the bypassed Type 525 was chosen has never been made clear.

Together with several other manufacturers, the company had conducted research into new methods of mastering boundary-

As VX138 is accompanied to Farnborough's 1954 SBAC Display by Swift F.3 WK247, it shows the numerous ventral intakes that have been fitted since its early flights. It has a slightly wider fin and is finished in an overall glossy cream colour scheme. *Aeroplane*

layer turbulence, and either sucking or blowing through slots in the aerofoil surface was proving to be successful. They had also accumulated considerable experience with laminar flow, through the Spiteful/Seafang range of Griffon-powered fighters, which was carried forward into the design of the Attacker's wings. In view of the large amount of air that could be tapped off the compressors of turbojet engines, a revised system of flap blowing, which at the time went under the term 'super circulation', was suggested by Supermarine as being beneficial to the Type 525. The fact that the aircraft was to have a pair of Avons meant that there was an abundance of air available from their combined compressors, so the project office drew up a system where a thin

jet of high-pressure air, bled from the Avons, was projected through a narrow slot in the wings, just forward of the flap hinges. This air followed the flap's contour when it was extended, to maintain the laminar-flow, which, it was calculated, would lower the landing speed by approximately 18mph (29km/h) and also improve the wings' stalling speed. Another advantage, especially for carrier-based aircraft, was that the angle of attack would be reduced, thereby improving a pilot's forward view on the landing approach.

On touchdown at Farnborough, the variable-incidence tailplane and full-span wing leading-edge slats are clearly visible. Author's collection

First Flight and Disappointment

On completion, with a natural metal finish, VX138 followed its two predecessors in going by road transport to Boscombe Down, where Mike Lithgow undertook the maiden flight on 27 April 1954. By this time, Rolls-Royce had proved that their original claims of the AJ.65's development potential were well founded and VX138 was powered by the RA.7 variant, producing 7,500lb (3,400kg) thrust at sea level, which meant that it had nearly 20 per cent more power available than the Type 508. Therefore, everyone was rather disappointed when it became apparent that, in spite of the increased power, together with the swept flying surfaces, the Type 525 was still essentially a subsonic design. Mach 1 was marginally exceeded in a shallow dive, but in level flight it was only slightly faster than its straight-wing predecessors, and it was actually inferior in the climb.

At certain attitudes instability presented problems, but these were redressed by an increase in fin area, obtained through a redesign of the leading edge. For the 1954 SBAC Display, VX138 was finished in an overall gloss cream scheme and by this time it had gathered a number of ventilation intakes protruding above the fuselage centre-section, which became more obvious in the new colour. A spirited demonstration was put up by the aircraft, with its size becoming more apparent when it was parked alongside a trio of Swifts.

Shortly after Farnborough, VX138 had another repaint, this time in the Royal Navy's dark sea grey/duck-egg green finish that was the current finish at that time. As it was the closest in shape to the proposed production aircraft, it provided considerable data towards this programme, with some of it being negative and no doubt it could have provided more, but in July 1955, it went to the A&AEE for evaluation. On the 5th, the first Establishment pilot to fly the aircraft got it into a spin at 10,000ft (3,000m) while investigating low-speed handling. He could not jettison the canopy, so had to eject through the reinforced metal framework, but by this time he was at too low an altitude for the ejector seat to fully function, and was killed.

The Type 529 suffered a couple of forced landings during its flying time and the second, in December 1953, resulted in damage that was considered too extensive for an economic repair. It was therefore put into storage and, nearly three years later, was finally scrapped. VX133, the first of the N.9/47 trio, was put to use at the Flight Deck Handling School at RNAS Culdrose once its flying days were finished; it stayed at the School for several years before being consigned to scrap.

Due to the rather disappointing performance of the Type 525, considerable modifications were made to the design of the wings and tail assembly, and the tailplane was set at a distinct angle of anhedral. The fuselage also incorporated considerable area ruling before, as the Type 544 and meeting production Specification N.113D, the aircraft was named Scimitar. Three prototypes and seventy-six production aircraft were built; the latter served with eight RN squadrons, aboard five different carriers, and were the largest fighters operated by the Fleet Air Arm until the McDonnell Phantom arrived.

In 1955, VX138 was repainted in the current Royal Navy colour scheme of that time, consisting of sea grey/duck-egg green, and it can be seen that the chord of the fin's top has been increased. *Aeroplane*

Technical Data

Supermarine Type 508 and 529

Dimensions:	Span 41ft (12.5m) extended, 20ft (6.09m) folded; length (Type 508) 50ft (15.24m), (Type 529) 50ft 6in (15.40m); height 12ft 4in (3.74m), 16ft 7in (5.04m) wings folded
Powerplants:	Two Rolls-Royce Avon RA.3 turbojets, each producing 6,500lb (3,000kg) thrust
Weight:	Loaded 18,850lb (8,548kg)
Armament:	Four 30mm Aden cannon proposed, but installed only in VX136
Performance:	Maximum speed 602mph (969km/h) at 30,000ft (9,000m); service ceiling 50,000ft (15,000m)
Production:	Two aircraft built to Specification N.9/47, with serial numbers VX133 (Type 508) and VX136 (Type 529)

Supermarine Type 525

Dimensions:	Span 37ft 2in (11.29m); length 53ft (16.15m); height 14ft 11in (4.55m)
Powerplants:	Two Rolls-Royce Avon RA.7 turbojets, each producing 7,500lb (3,400kg) thrust
Weight:	Loaded 19,910lb (9,030kg)
Performance:	Maximum speed 646mph (1,039km/h) at 30,000ft (9,000m); service ceiling 50,000ft (15,000m)
Production:	One aircraft built to Specification N.9/47, with serial number VX138

CHAPTER FOURTEEN

Short S.B.5

Wilbur Wright's flight at Kittyhawk on 17 December 1903 was one year after the three Short brothers, Eustace, Horace and Oswald, had flown their first balloon. By November 1908, however, they had become convinced that the aeroplane had more potential than the balloon; they registered their company, Short Brothers Ltd, that month, and henceforth the company became an integral part of the British aircraft industry.

With this long pedigree, it is understandable that, when the supersonic fighter began to emerge as an operational requirement, the company took an important participation in its development.

Experimental Requirement 103

The disastrous decision to cancel the Miles M.52 (see Chapter Twenty-Three) early in 1946 and at the same time abandon piloted supersonic flight, meant that for several years the British aircraft industry lagged behind the progress made in the United States, Russia and France. In 1948, discussions between the industry and the MoS started a slow, tentative renewal of the desire to design an aircraft capable of investigating the whole sphere of supersonics, with an obvious ultimate goal of equipping the RAF with a fighter capable of exceeding Mach 1 in a fully operational role.

Experimental Requirement (ER) 103 was issued to cover the requirements of such a programme, which was approached in many different ways by various companies. Of these, the Fairey Delta 2 appeared to offer the best design for an aircraft purely dedicated to research – this aircraft is described in detail in Chapter Sixteen. English Electric's contribution, given the company's designation P.1, had obvious potential to be developed into a supersonic fighter, and Specification F.23/49 was raised by the MoS to cover the design, plus its prototype and development.

In contrast to the Delta 2's delta-wing configuration, the English Electric Aircraft Division's Chief Engineer, W. E. W. 'Teddy' Petter, opted for a highly swept wing. The company built Europe's first supersonic wind tunnel at Warton and this was fully operational by 1950, to set their aim at providing an initial research aircraft, prior to any fighter development, with a maximum speed of Mach 1.5 at 36,000ft (11,000m). When Petter left English Electric in February 1950, the whole project was handed over to F. W. Page.

English Electric P.1

Petter tendered the first brochure for Project 1 (P.1) in November 1948, but by March 1949 discussions with the Rolls-Royce experimental department at Hucknall concerning the shape of the air intake had led to a considerable revision of the design. Wind-tunnel testing and the construction of a mock-up received MoS approval in early April, for what the company called the 'Transonic Fighter'.

It featured two fuselage-mounted axial-flow engines in a vertical stagger, with the upper engine aft and the lower engine forward. From any frontal view, it was dominated by a gaping mouth-like air intake and the whole fuselage was designed to keep the frontal area to a minimum, in order to reduce supersonic drag.

The wing's angle of sweep and the position of the tailplane became bones of contention between the company and RAE Farnborough. Petter advocated a mid-set wing with a leading edge sweep of 60 degrees and a tailplane sited low on the rear fuselage. Sixty degrees was a radical angle of sweep for a wing in the late 1940s, but the whole layout of the flying surfaces had been substantiated by results obtained in the company's wind tunnel. However, the RAE had strong reservations about the whole planform and considered that 50 degrees would be more suitable. Furthermore, the low-set position of the tailplane was dismissed out of hand, in favour of a T-tail assembly.

The MoS was between a rock and a hard place. They did not wish to be seen as disregarding Petter's concept, nor did they wish to be at odds with the RAE. They therefore took a middle course, in suggesting that a separate research aircraft should be constructed embodying the main P.1 features. This could investigate the low-speed handling characteristics of an aeroplane with such high angles of sweep and be capable of having its tailplane set in either of the proposed positions. This was quite a tall order, but ER.100 was raised towards the end of 1949 in conjunction with the RAE, and Short and Harland was considered capable of meeting its requirements.

Belfast's Chameleon

Short and Harland was registered as a Belfast-based company in June 1936, through the collaboration of the original Short Brothers Ltd, with Harland & Wolff, a well-established Belfast firm of shipbuilders. The company's aim was to manufacture both land and marine aircraft in the Northern Irish capital, which resulted in Short eventually leaving their long-established factory at Rochester in Kent.

As British experience at that time with aircraft having a 60-degree sweep was nil, it was decided that the design approach would be gradual and the RAE brought pressure to bear by dictating that the first configuration would be a wing having a leading edge sweep of 50 degrees. Furthermore, their predilection for the tailplane being mounted on top of the fin was enforced. Built to contract number 6/ACFT/5347/CB.7(a) and given the company designation S.B.5, the design could also have the tailplane set at the base of the rear fuselage, because English Electric's design team was adamant that this was the optimum location.

The fixed leading-edge droop of 20 degrees is shown to advantage as WG768, with the 50-degree swept wings and high tailplane, banks sharply to starboard. *Aeroplane*

As well as being able to reposition the tailplane, the S.B.5 was designed with mid-set wing attachment points that had the capacity of taking a wing of 50-, 60- and 69-degree sweep, with the latter requested to enable the aircraft to be used for general research directed at the stability of highly swept wing sections, after its use for the English Electric project had terminated. The leading edge of all three angles had to be capable of easy modification, in order to assess the results of various installations. To further this, while the basic wing was of a light-alloy construction, the leading and trailing edges were plywood-covered, to facilitate the changes incurred with the various wing configurations.

Serial number WG768 was allocated to the aircraft and it was stipulated that it should be a simple, inexpensive design, that had to be completed well before the first prototype P.1, which by this time had been redesignated the P.1A, so that test results could be channelled into the supersonic design prior to its undercarriage being finalized. However, things were not as simple as had been hoped. In order to be functional at three different wing-sweep angles, the main wheels of the S.B.5 had to be capable of castoring, in order to maintain a parallel line with the aircraft's cen-

treline. Also, their rake had to be capable of adjustment, to ensure a correct balance, no matter which wing was being tested.

The *Raison d'Etre*

WG768's principal function was to verify whether English Electric's or the RAE's calculations in relation to the wing-sweep angle and the position of the tailplane were correct, particularly regarding the supersonic aircraft's low-speed handling. Consequently, the shape of the fuselage had to have some affiliation with the P.1A's, and to this end, a none-too-pretty aircraft emerged from the Belfast assembly shop in the autumn of 1952. It had a 50-degree swept wing, with a full-span leading-edge drooped at 20 degrees. Dome-headed rivets were used throughout its construction. A delta-shaped tailplane, mounted on a short vertical post atop the swept fin/rudder assembly, had a variable incidence capability through a 20-degree arc, with the necessary controls and electrics routed within a dorsal spine that ran from behind the raised cockpit canopy to the fin/fuselage junction.

As the test programme would be confined to low-speed handling and as three different wings were to be fitted, the tri-

cycle undercarriage was fixed and, for the 50-degree wing, the main-wheel oleos were raked slightly forward. There were two 7ft (2.1m) protrusions forward from either side of the circular nose intake: the port side one carrying a yaw and pitch vane, while the starboard one was a pitot head, with its end angled 15 degrees downwards, in order to obtain more accurate readings at high angles of incidence.

The S.B.5's engine was a Rolls-Royce Derwent 8, which produced 3,500lb (1,600kg) static thrust at sea level. It was positioned central within the fuselage length, with its outlet at the extreme rear, above which braking and anti-spin parachutes were carried in separate housings.

Flights and Changes

WG768 was transported by sea and road to the A&AEE base at Boscombe Down during November 1952, where the company's Chief Test Pilot, Tom Brooke-Smith, started taxiing trials. This was his return to test flying after being involved in the crash of the Short S.B.1 aeroisoclinic-winged glider in October 1951, which had resulted in his being hospitalized for many months while several crushed vertebrae healed.

The S.B.5 was finished in a gloss silver and black colour scheme, and on 2 December 1952 Brooke-Smith was at the controls for its maiden flight. A take-off roll of nearly 2,000yd (1,830m) confirmed one thing before it even got airborne – it was grossly underpowered. A second problem soon presented itself: the lack of power resulted in the aircraft taking twenty minutes, with the Derwent at full power, to reach the 7,000ft (2,000m) optimum altitude for the test programmes. With a fuel capacity of only 300gal (1,350ltr), there was very little time left for the actual tests.

By the spring of 1953, the handling qualities of the S.B.5 had been assessed without too many incidents and the aircraft was returned to Belfast for the 60-degree swept wing to be installed. In this configuration the ailerons were at right angles to the line of flight and the wing, put in simple terms, was a delta planform with the inner rear section removed. To appease the RAE, the tailplane remained above the fin/rudder assembly and the external finish remained unchanged. For this wing, the main wheels were repositioned to an unraked attitude.

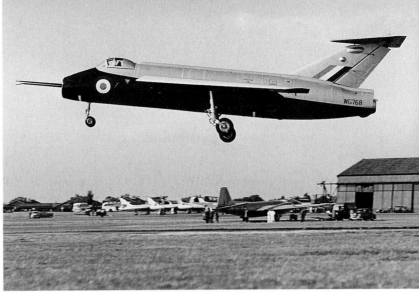

LEFT: WG768 on its way to the 1953 SBAC Display. The 50-degree swept wings had the drooped leading edge seen here for certain periods of its flight-testing life. *Aeroplane*

ABOVE: Just flaring out, WG768 shows that the undercarriage is raked to the rear for the 50-degree wing sweep. The clearance at the top of the fin, to allow for the tailplane's incidence arc of 20 degrees, is also clearly visible. The parked aircraft include Canberra B.2 WJ716, a trio of Hunters and, well to the rear, one of the Vulcan prototypes. Author's collection

The maiden flight with the new wing was made on 29 July 1953 and a month later English Electric's Chief Test Pilot, Roland Beamont, who was in charge of the company's P.1A programme, made his first flight in the aircraft. He was singularly unimpressed and subsequent flights confirmed that not only was the T-tail layout unsatisfactory, it was potentially dangerous. However, in this form WG768 had a flying demonstration slot at the 1953 SBAC Display, with Brooke-Smith at the controls.

The Third Configuration

In October, the aircraft returned to Belfast where the tailplane was removed from the top of the tail assembly and relocated, in a redesigned shape, at the base of the rear fuselage, which was where Teddy Petter had wanted it in the first place. The fin and rudder were modified to have the T-tail's mounting post removed and finished off with a smooth backwards-sloping top.

The P.1A wing design had hinged leading edge flaps at the wing root, which deflected 26 degrees downwards for take-off and landing. In order to be fully representative of the fighter's control aspect, these were incorporated in the S.B.5 wing as a fixed assembly, while the leading edge 20-degree droop was retained on the rest of the span. When the P.1A eventually flew, the hinged wing root leading edge

was used in the very early days of its test flying, but were found to be unnecessary and were locked in the 'up' position.

At the beginning of 1954, with the revised tailplane in position, WG768 was again transferred from Belfast to Boscombe Down, where it had another 'first flight' at the end of January. The RAE's involvement in the S.B.5 programme gave them the right to conduct its operations, even though these were aimed at evaluating the P.1A's low-speed performance, for the whole concept of the fighter was pretty radical and the Establishment wanted to gain as much experience for themselves, as did English Electric. Consequently, shortly after the latest maiden flight, RAE Bedford became another operating base, along with Boscombe Down. At Bedford, the fixed inboard 26-degree leading edge flaps were removed and the S.B.5 became as approximate to an 85 per cent flying model of the P.1A as it was ever going to be.

Roland Beamont renewed his acquaintance with the aircraft, in order to gain experience of the low-speed characteristics that he was likely to have with the supersonic fighter and is on record as saying that he found WG768 'an interesting aircraft to fly'. In particular he confirmed that the low position of the tailplane was correct, and said that the aircraft was proving to be a:

fascinating trainer for the low-speed handling of a highly swept wing. Its high-induced-drag

characteristics were so exaggerated by the low power/weight ratio that marked variations in speed could be produced at fixed power settings, generally at full throttle, merely by slightly increasing or decreasing the angle-of-attack with the stick.

He also commented on the fact that, like Brooke-Smith, he found the inordinately long take-off run took a bit of getting used to!

The RAE's feathers were still slightly ruffled over the issue of the tailplane's position, so when, in the spring of 1954, Short's CTP found a problem with a sharp wing-drop at about 165mph (265km/h), the Establishment immediately sought to impose their solution to the problem, in the form of wing fences. However, they were once more at odds with the English Electric design office, who confirmed that a small notch in the wing leading edge, about 60 per cent out from the root, would be more effective; this modification eradicated the problem so effectively that it was carried over to the P.1A.

More Changes and Operators

RAE Bedford and A&AEE Boscombe Down combined the test flying for over two years, as well as placing the aircraft in the static exhibits park at the 1954 SBAC Display. After the removal of the inboard

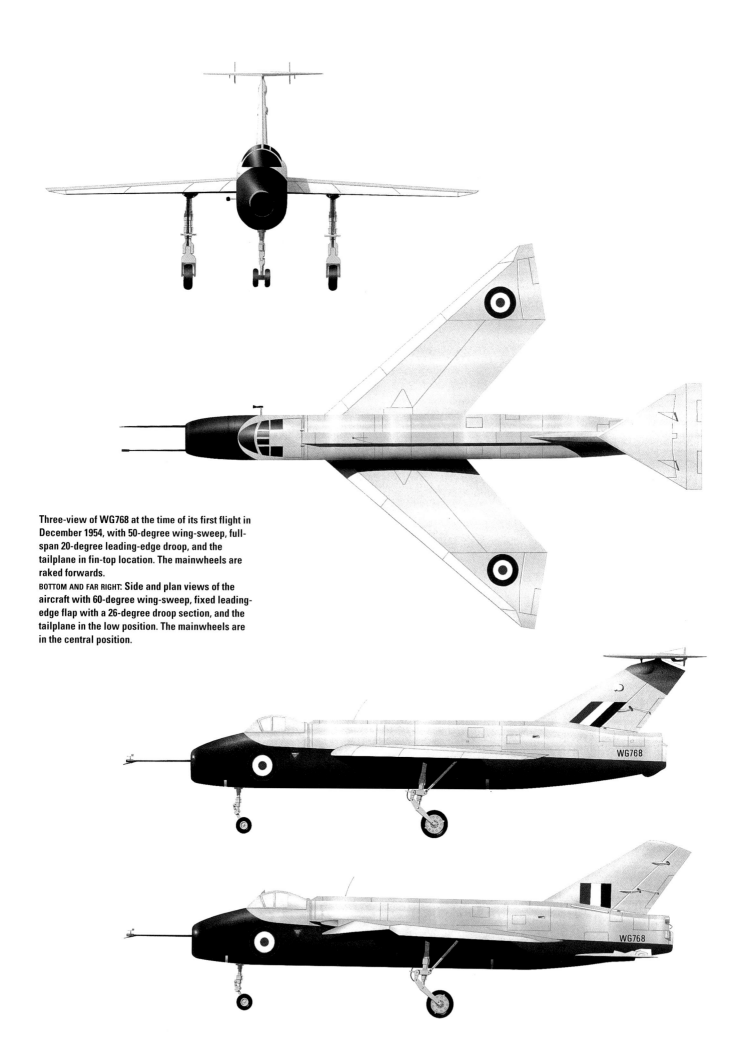

Three-view of WG768 at the time of its first flight in December 1954, with 50-degree wing-sweep, full-span 20-degree leading-edge droop, and the tailplane in fin-top location. The mainwheels are raked forwards.

BOTTOM AND FAR RIGHT: Side and plan views of the aircraft with 60-degree wing-sweep, fixed leading-edge flap with a 26-degree droop section, and the tailplane in the low position. The mainwheels are in the central position.

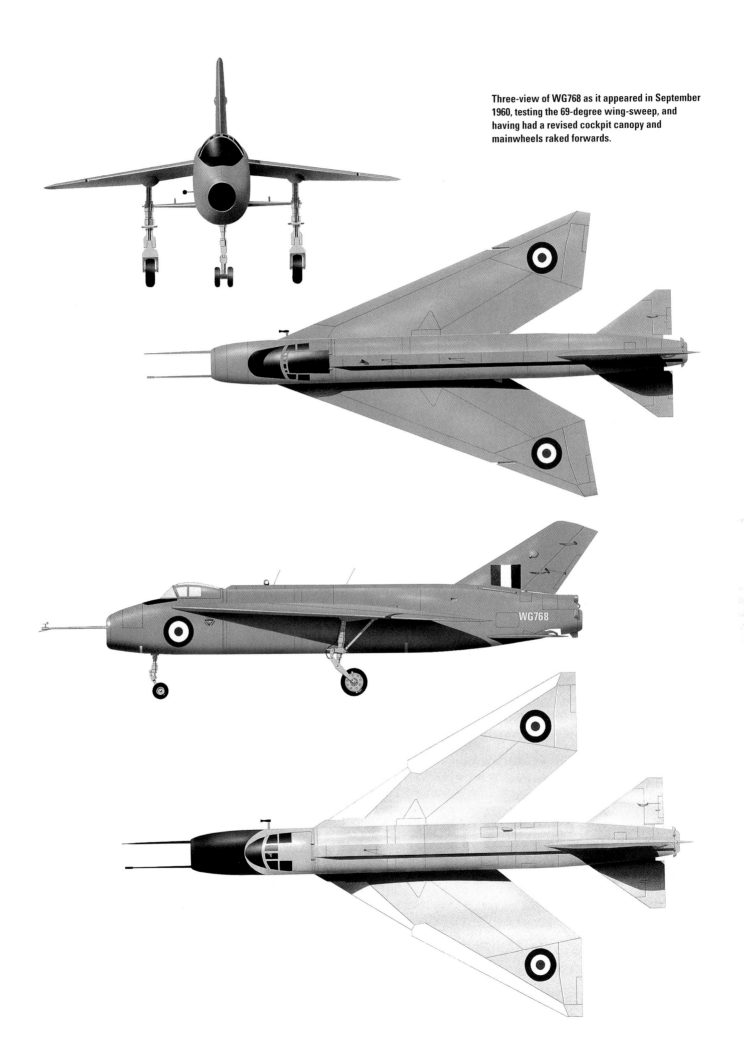

Three-view of WG768 as it appeared in September 1960, testing the 69-degree wing-sweep, and having had a revised cockpit canopy and mainwheels raked forwards.

In October 1953, the aircraft's tailplane was moved to the low position originally advocated by English Electric's design team. The 60-degree swept wings had a 26-degree fixed leading edge flap inboard, while retaining the earlier 20-degree droop on the rest of each wing. Derek James

leading edge flap, a full-span leading edge droop of 10 degrees was installed. The S.B.5 flew in this condition for some considerable time, before the whole wing leading edge was again revised, this time being entirely clean, without any flaps or droop.

English Electric's use for the S.B.5 was now ended and the RAE's desire to test the 69-degree swept wing took over. The aircraft's lack of power had been a persistent problem and thought was given to fitting an auxiliary turbojet at one time. When

WG768 once again returned to Belfast in 1958, in view of the amount of work to be undertaken it was considered a good time to install an entirely new engine.

What took place over the next two years was a virtual rebuild. The 69-degree wings were installed, a Martin-Baker 'zero-zero' ejector seat was fitted and the majority of the instrumentation was brought up to date, for a lot of changes had been made in this sphere since the original maiden flight in 1952. At last the Derwent 8 was discarded and a Bristol Siddeley B.E.26 Orpheus axial-flow turbojet was put in its place. Producing 4,850lb (2,200kg) static thrust at sea level, the Orpheus bestowed an increase in power of nearly 40 per cent on the aircraft.

The new ejector seat demanded a redesign of the cockpit canopy, with a clear section replacing the original heavily-framed cover, so that an ejection through

the canopy could be made in an emergency. The S.B.5's aesthetics were greatly enhanced by its first colour change. An overall glossy light blue finish was applied, with the serial picked out in white, and in this condition WG768 returned to Boscombe Down in September 1960.

Yet Another Maiden Flight

On 18 October, RAE Aero Flight test pilot Denis Tayler took the S.B.5 with its 69-degree wing into the air for the first time, and over the course of the next few years, the Establishment carried out a variety of trials programmes, which were all concentrated on the stability and general handling of an aircraft with highly swept wings. Various leading-edge changes were incorporated, the aircraft flying with and without a 20-degree full-span droop. The notch applied to the 60-degree wing was carried over to the higher-swept unit and when the droop was fitted, the notch was taped over.

Handley Page had flown their H.P.115 on 15 August 1961, with its prime object being to investigate the aerodynamics of the slender delta. This was based at Bedford, where it joined WG768 in a series of supersonic transport-related trials programmes. The port wing of the S.B.5 was tufted for some of these trials, with the airflow effects being captured on film by a small cine camera on the fin leading edge. (The H.P.115 is described in detail in Chapter Twenty.)

Roland Beamont flew WG768 again in 1964, for a series of test flights conducted from RAE Bedford. He found that the greater wing sweep and more powerful engine gave the aircraft 'a much more reasonable performance'. Its aerodynamic input to the Concorde programme proved to be more than had been expected, but eventually its useful days were expended.

Finis

In Australia, the Aeronautical Research Laboratory (ARL) operated along the lines of the RAE and WG768 was offered to the ARL as a full-scale experimental instrument, but they declined. Consequently, the aircraft was transferred to the inventory of the Empire Test Pilot's School (ETPS) in 1967. The School used it as a familiarization vehicle for the slow-speed handling of highly swept and slender-winged aircraft. Monochrome photographs show that during its time at the ETPS it was repainted in a very dark blue or black finish, with a white '28' painted on the nose. During November 1967, the aircraft was struck off charge at the School, when a major airframe inspection was due. However, this was considered an uneconomic exercise, so WG768 was grounded and went to RAF Finningley in March 1968 with the Instructional Airframe number 8005M.

By 1990, after having endured another respray, this time an overall matt silver with the '28' in black, it was handed to Royal Air Force Museum Cosford (known as the Aerospace Museum in those days) where, restored to its original black and silver finish, it resides today. It had provided nearly two decades of valuable research data and substantiated many design office calculations. The S.B.5

When the 69-degree swept wings were installed the undercarriage had to be raked forward in order to maintain balance, as the increased wing-sweep angle changed the aircraft's centre of gravity. *Aeroplane*

The modifications incorporated when the aircraft received the 69-degree swept wings included a new cockpit canopy and a blue overall colour scheme. It can be seen here – during a sortie made out from RAE Bedford in July 1962 – that the wings retain the full-span leading-edge droop and the port wing outer section carries numerous wool tufts. Author's collection

Technical Data – Short S.B.5	
Dimensions:	Span 35ft 2in (10.7m) with 50-degree sweep, 30ft 6in (9.30m) with 60-degree sweep, 26ft (7.92m) with 69-degree sweep; length 47ft 9in (14.55m) with high tailplane excluding booms, 45ft 9in (13.94m) with low tailplane excluding booms, 54ft 9in (16.68m) with high tailplane including booms, 52ft 9in (16.07m) with low tailplane including booms; height 17ft 4in (5.27m) with high tailplane, 16ft 3in (4.95m) with low tailplane
Powerplants:	Originally, one Rolls-Royce Derwent 8 turbojet, producing 3,500lb (1,600kg) thrust. Later, one Bristol Siddeley B.E.26 Orpheus turbojet producing 4,850lb (2,300kg) thrust
Weights:	Empty 9,196lb (4,170kg); loaded (maximum) 13,000lb (5,900kg)
Performance:	Maximum airframe speed 402mph (650km/h); service ceiling 10,000ft (3,000m); maximum duration 45 minutes
Production:	One aircraft built to Experimental Requirement 100, with serial number WG768

proved to be one of the British aircraft industry's best 'value-for-money' research aircraft and, despite the unknown aerodynamic territories in which it flew, did not suffer any major misfortunes during its entire working life.

CHAPTER FIFTEEN

Short S.B.1 and S.B.4 Sherpa

Tailless Aspirations

Back in 1910, John W. Dunne experiment-ed with tailless model gliders that employed sharply swept-back wings and I am sure that every reader has folded a sheet of paper to form a sharp delta-shaped aeroplane that cavorted around the classroom when the teacher was otherwise engaged. Dunne's health precluded him from carrying his ideas further, but Professor Geoffrey Hill, together with his brother Roderick, had also been pursuing similar lines and even went so far as to build an actual glider.

The 1914–18 war put the brothers' endeavours on hold, although Professor Hill was engaged on aircraft control research during the conflict, but his post-war thoughts turned back to John Dunne's original ideas. These hardened into a practical glider that was built in 1924, in which a 30hp Bristol Cherub III engine was later installed by the RAE at Farnbor-ough. This aeroplane had pivoting wing tips in place of the usual control surfaces, which could be used as elevators or as ailerons; such wing tips are referred to today as elevons. A first flight was made on 2 November 1925 and it was demon-strated to the Secretary of State for Air, Sir Samuel Hoare, as well as appearing at the 1926 Hendon Air Display. The air-craft was finally presented to the Science Museum at Kensington, London and can be seen on display there to this day.

Westland Involvement

Following a trials programme at Farnbor-ough, the Establishment placed an order with Westland Aircraft to build a larger version capable of carrying two people, and Geoffrey Hill was seconded to the Somerset-based aircraft manufacturer to oversee the development of the project.

This association led to the Pterodactyl family of 'flying wing' aircraft, which com-menced with the Westland-Hill Ptero-dactyl IA J9251 built to Specification

With the Short Sturgeon TT.2 VR363 yet to leave the runway, the S.B.1 glider G-14-5 takes off from Aldergrove on 30 July 1951 for its first towed flight. Short's Chief Test Pilot, Tom Brooke-Smith, is at the glider's controls, while the Sturgeon is piloted by 'Jock' Eassie. The second such flight, on 14 October, ended with G-14-5 crashing and Brooke-Smith suffering several crushed vertebrae. *Aeroplane*

23/26 and progressed to the Pterodactyl V fighter design, to meet Specification F.3/32. With serial number K2770, the Pterodactyl V eventually flew from Andover in May 1934. After modifications to cure several faults, K2770 went to RAE Farnborough for evaluation but, considering its radical design, the Establishment rather surprisingly thought it was not as advanced a design as contemporary projects in existence at the time. Perhaps it was too revolutionary for them!

Professor Hill left Westland to take up the Kennedy Chair of Engineering Science at the University of London and served in a liaison capacity for the Air Ministry during World War Two. In 1948 the professor retired to Northern Ireland, where he furthered a long-standing friendship with Donald Keith-Lucas, who the following year became Chief Designer for the Short and Harland Aircraft Company that had just completed its move from Rochester to Belfast.

Keith-Lucas's Ideas

The new chief designer was a very progressively minded man. His company's S.A.4 bomber design had been finalized and early construction was in hand on the shop floor. However, he was aware of that aircraft's limitations and believed that its operational envelope could be greatly improved if it had a highly swept wing. This could eliminate the drag of a conventional tail unit, as the original troubles associated with trailing-edge control-surface flutter on such an aircraft had by now become generally understood. Furthermore, Keith-Lucas considered that Geoffrey Hill's pivoting wing-tip concept, as used on his Pterodactyl IA design, could cure any new or unknown problems that might occur, although a vertical fin/rudder assembly would be necessary.

Although the idea was only at an embryonic stage, he submitted a design to meet Specification B.35/46, which had been put to almost the entire British aircraft industry, to produce a four turbojet-engined, high-altitude subsonic bomber. The company designation P.D.1 (Preliminary Design number 1) was given to the new submission, which was based on the established S.A.4 fuselage, with a redesigned rear end and having Geoffrey Hill's pivoting wing-tip concept incorporated in a highly swept wing, which had the four engines buried within its roots.

To illustrate the advanced thinking behind the design, when it was put before the Advanced Bomber Project Group, set up to consider the merits of the B.35/46 submissions (from which the Vulcan and Victor eventually emerged), the P.D.1 was thought to be far too radical.

Hill Joins Shorts

Professor Hill joined the Short and Harland design office, principally to look into a further problem that had become apparent when dealing with high-aspect-ratio, highly-swept wings, namely their tendency to twist under loads, which altered their aerodynamic shape. This jeopardized the lift properties when an aircraft made a rapid pull out of a dive or a tight turn at high speed. The lift at the tips lessened, thereby transferring extra loads to the rest of the wing, which resulted in an aeroelastic tendency to twist the structure so that the tips were pulled upwards towards one another.

As both Avro and Handley Page were building small-scale flying models of their respective B.35/46 submissions in order to investigate the designs' low-speed handling characteristics, both Keith-Lucas and Hill thought it would be prudent to do likewise. However, the MoS refused to provide funds for such a project, so the company's board of directors sanctioned private-venture finance in order to build a one-third-scale glider based on the P.D.1, and the whole project was undertaken in great secrecy, which was somewhat easier to achieve than could have been possible had the company been located on the British mainland.

The Aeroisoclinic Wing

Wind-tunnel models confirmed that Hill and Keith-Lucas were on the right track in placing the torsion box much further aft than usual. This enabled the wing's torsional and flexural axes to coincide, which meant that when the wing flexed, twisting was eliminated; when twisting was induced, the incidence remained unaffected. In order to enhance the process, the under-skin of the leading edge was separated from the lower edges of the box-spar, in order to avoid local buckling, and a small gap was left down the entire span, up to the tip-pivoting control section.

Professor Hill addressed the Royal Aeronautical Society's International Conference, held at Brighton in 1951, and described the principle of his design with the term 'aeroisoclinic wing', which set all the delegates talking.

The Short S.B.1

By the early summer of 1951, the one-third-scale glider was completed, under the Short designation S.B.1 and allotted the B-Condition registration G-14-5. It was built mainly of spruce, with light alloy to reinforce highly-stressed areas, together with the nose ribs and the pivoting tubes for the all-moving outer wing section.

This constituted more than a third of the total wing, which was made in one piece and was shoulder-mounted with a leading-edge sweep of 42.5 degrees. The trailing edge started from the root at zero degrees, then at a quarter span swept back at 30 degrees to the all-moving outer section, where the sweep decreased to 18 degrees. The wing outer section operated in unison as elevators and in opposition as ailerons. An anti-balance tab fixed to their trailing edge and pneumatically operated flaps were sited under the inboard wing section's unswept trailing edge.

The short-legged undercarriage consisted of main wheels attached to the fuselage at the centre of gravity, with a small nose bumper wheel and a similar unit under the rear fuselage. A pair of sprung skids was fitted just inboard of the wing's moveable outer sections, together with long ventral skids to protect the fuselage underside and there was a towline attachment point just ahead of the nose bumper wheel. The cockpit canopy was a simple sliding plastic unit sited ahead of the wing leading-edge root and the rear fuselage blended into a tall swept fin and rudder, with a short dorsal fairing. It was finished in an overall silver, with broad alternating black/yellow/black bands around the fuselage fore and aft, together with similar markings on the fin, while the wings had two alternating bands on each side. The reason for these highly-visible markings was to identify the S.B.1 as a glider. On 14 July 1951, Tom 'Brookie' Brooke-Smith piloted it for its first flight, launched by a winch at RAF Aldergrove. A similar flight was accomplished a few days later.

The S.B.4 at roll-out, before the B-Condition markings G-14-1 were applied. The single dorsal NACA intake for the two Turbomeca Palas axial-flow turbojets and their individual orifices, toed outwards at 10 degrees, are clearly visible, as are the covers for each wing's bearing, upon which the aeroisoclinic outer wing sections pivot. *Aeroplane*

As longitudinal stability was found to be satisfactory, preparations were put in hand for the first towed flight.

Towed to Disaster

Short had designed and built a large twin-engined carrier-borne reconnaissance bomber to Specification S.11/43, called the Sturgeon, but the Royal Navy's carrier policies were changed before it became operational, so the twenty-four Sturgeons built served as Sturgeon TT.2 target-tugs with Nos 703, 728 and 771 Squadrons. The prototype TT.2, VR363, was retained by the manufacturer and, on 30 July, 'Jock' Eassie was at the controls when it towed the S.B.1 into the air for the first time. Brooke-Smith was at the glider's controls when cast off at 10,000ft (3,000m) and he found its handling to be perfectly satisfactory.

However, the turbulence from the Sturgeon's two Rolls-Royce Merlin 140 engines,

each driving a six-bladed Rotol contra-rotating propeller, gave Brooke-Smith an uncomfortable ride before he cast off and he suggested the towline be lengthened before the next flight. For some unknown reason, this did not take place until 14 October.

From the moment that the Sturgeon started its take-off run, it became obvious that the longer towline had exacerbated, rather than reduced, the turbulence problem. Brooke-Smith attempted to get out of the violent wash and cast off before he had attained any real height or speed to generate lift. The glider came down, hitting the runway at over 80mph (130km/h) in a nose-down attitude. The injuries that 'Brookie' sustained included several crushed vertebrae and it was over six months before he was able to resume flying. He made it perfectly clear that he wanted nothing more to do with the combination of aeroisoclinic-winged gliders and tug-aircraft's turbulence.

The Short S.B.4

In spite of the severity of the S.B.1's crash, its fin/rudder assembly suffered remarkably little damage, so the company decided to build a new redesigned fuselage in which this tail unit could be included without too much difficulty. The problems with the glider, especially in getting it airborne, prompted the new fuselage to be designed around a power-source and a pair of Turbomeca Palas axial-flow turbojets, each producing 353lb (160kg) thrust, was selected, shortly before Blackburn Engines set up a production line to manufacture the engines under licence in the UK. In its powered form, the design was given the new Type number S.B.4.

The S.B.4 fuselage, which followed the lines of its predecessor to a certain extent, was built in three sections, with three different materials. The nose was fibreglass, the centre section was light alloy, and the rear section, including the fin/rudder

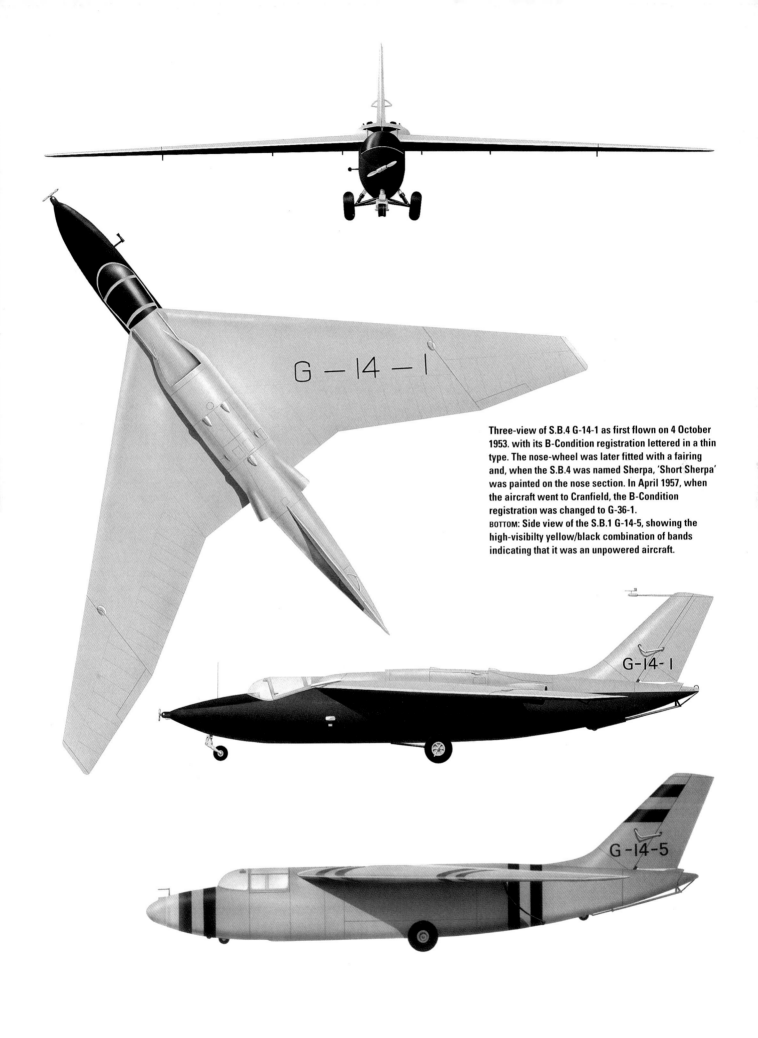

Three-view of S.B.4 G-14-1 as first flown on 4 October 1953. with its B-Condition registration lettered in a thin type. The nose-wheel was later fitted with a fairing and, when the S.B.4 was named Sherpa, 'Short Sherpa' was painted on the nose section. In April 1957, when the aircraft went to Cranfield, the B-Condition registration was changed to G-36-1.

BOTTOM: Side view of the S.B.1 G-14-5, showing the high-visibilty yellow/black combination of bands indicating that it was an unpowered aircraft.

G-14-1

G-14-1

G-14-5

assembly, was a spruce/plywood mix. The two Palas engines were installed on a false deck above the centre-section and each was toed out at 10 degrees to the fuselage centreline. An NACA-type intake, situated in a dorsal position behind the cockpit canopy and above the shoulder-wing, fed the two engines, while a 1gal (4.5ltr) fuel tank for ground starting, two recuperators for air starting and an oil tank were situated between the two engines.

The main fuel tanks, each holding 25gal (112.5ltr) were installed on the centre of gravity, below the engines, and these gave the S.B.4 a flying endurance of approximately fifty minutes. A V-G (velocity and gravitational force) recorder and automatic observer were fitted in the rear fuselage, with a nose-mounted windmill generator providing their power. Behind the generator, the nose section contained the pneumatic system's air bottles, a radio transmitter/receiver, battery and fuse boxes. The materials used in the aircraft's construction did not permit an ejector seat to be fitted, besides which there was not enough space in the cockpit for one. On the ground, the aircraft stood on a short, fixed undercarriage designed and manufactured by Palmer Tyre Ltd, who also handled the brake system and the flap-operating ram. The latter was quite ingenious, as on the approach the pilot selected 60 degrees flap and this automatically increased to 80 degrees just before levelling out.

Taken on 30 November 1953, four days before the maiden flight, this close-up of the port aeroisoclinic wing section shows it at the fully upward position. The ventral cable running to the fuselage rear end is for releasing the anti-spin parachute. *Aeroplane*

First Flights and a Name

Short had a liking for the combination of black and silver for, like the S.B.5 two years earlier, the S.B.4 wore this. Being a private venture, the aircraft received the B-Condition registration G-14-1, and in this styling it had its maiden flight in the hands of Tom Brooke-Smith from Aldergrove on 4 October 1953. Also like the S.B.5, the S.B.4 proved to be underpowered, but the structural limitations that imposed a maximum speed of 250mph at 5,000ft (400km/h at 1,500m) did not

Brooke-Smith pulls G-14-1 to a high angle of attack as he takes up station with the photographer's aircraft. Author's collection

Having by now received the name 'Sherpa', the aircraft's manoeuvrability is well demonstrated in these two shots taken during 1954. It is noticeable that the underwing G-14-1 registration had been thickened after the banking-to-port photograph was taken. Author's collection and *Aeroplane*

hamper the aircraft from being a very useful research vehicle in the evaluation of the probable low-speed handling of a full-size, high-speed aircraft employing the same flight control system.

In September 1954, just prior to G-14-1 making its one and only appearance at a Farnborough SBAC Display, it was christened the Sherpa. Various explanations have been given for the selection of this title. The fact that in the previous year, Mount Everest had been climbed by Edmund (later Sir Edmund) Hillary, together with a guide from the Sherpa people who inhabit the borders of Nepal and Tibet is often cited, as is the rather contrived acronym 'Short and Harland Experimental and Research Prototype Aircraft'. Whatever the reason, the name obviously had appeal with the company, for in the 1980s it was given to the eighteen C-23A USAF variants of the Short 330 utility transport.

At Farnborough, Brooke-Smith's demonstration generated considerable interest in the aeroisoclinic principle, but this interest seemed to stay at the event, for Short did not receive any further enquiries. Not to be daunted, Keith-Lucas drew up a private venture photo-reconnaissance design designated the P.D.8, together with the P.D.10, an aeroisoclinic-winged variant of the Supermarine Swift. A further application of the system was extended to Short's tender to meet Specification M.148T/NA39, in which

the design incorporated jet deflection for rapid take-off. This design was for a much lighter aircraft than the eventual winner of the contest, the Blackburn B.103 that led to the Buccaneer. In view of the latter's illustrious operational history with both the RN and RAF, it must be conceded that it was the correct choice.

University Challenge

Eventually, more conventional solutions were found to the difficulties initially encountered in high-subsonic flight, which negated the whole aeroisoclinic concept and, in April 1957, the S.B.4 Sherpa was handed to the College of Aeronautics at Cranfield, where its registration was changed to G-36-1 in order to fall in with the College's B-Condition serials.

At Cranfield, a former RAF flight lieutenant, A. J. 'Mac' MacDonald was the test pilot charged with flying turbojet aircraft and during one of his flights in 1958, several Palas turbine blades were ejected out of its jet-pipe. For Blackburn Engines, quantity production of the Palas had not quite met their expectations and it was another two years before the College received replacement engines, which were actually rebuilt units. With these installed, flying was resumed on a very occasional basis up to 1964, by which time the engines had reached their allotted hours and the aircraft was grounded. A year later, Professor

David Keith-Lucas joined the College as Professor of Aircraft Design, but too late to make any difference to the Sherpa's status.

The Concept's Demise

In view of Short's original high expectations for the aeroisoclinic-wing concept, its end was rather ignominious. From Cranfield, a large portion of the aircraft was transferred to the Bristol College of Advanced Technology as a test example for their laboratory work. The reasons why the whole aircraft did not get to Bristol are indeed bizarre.

The whole purpose for the S.B.4 was to test the wing concept but, because this unit was built as a one-piece item that was too long to fit in the vehicle used to transport it to Bristol, the wing was sawn in half! It is difficult to understand how such a foolish act could be undertaken on the premises of a well-respected college. In view of the standard of knowledge within Cranfield, surely someone would have realized how wrong this was.

The College of Advanced Technology used the fuselage and half a wing until May 1966, when the fuselage went to the Skyfame Aircraft Museum at Staverton, outside Cheltenham. The half-wing that Bristol had was destroyed in their wind tunnel, but Skyfame had already received the other half as a donation, so had aspirations of rebuilding a whole aircraft. These were

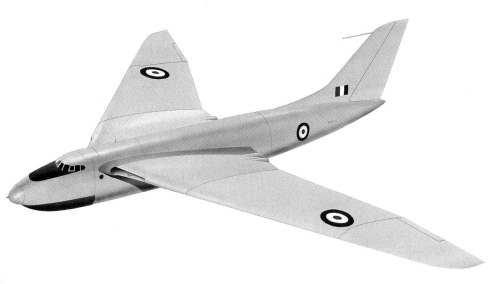

An impression of how Short's P.D.1 bomber design submitted to meet Specification B.35/46 could have looked. It was in effect the front and centre sections of a Sperrin married to an aeroisoclinic wing, therefore needing no tailplane to be incorporated. Author's artwork

Technical Data – Short S.B.1 and S.B.4 Sherpa	
Dimensions:	Span 38ft (11.5m); length (S.B.1) 30ft (9.14m), (S.B.4) 31ft 10in (9.72m); height 9ft 1in (2.76m)
Powerplants (S.B.4):	Two Blackburn-Turbomeca Palas turbojets, each producing 353lb (160kg) thrust
Weights (S.B.4):	Empty 3,000lb (1,360kg); loaded 3,125lb (1,417kg)
Performance (S.B.4):	Designed maximum speed 250mph (400km/h); operational ceiling 5,000ft (1,500m); maximum duration 50 minutes
Production:	One private-venture S.B.1 built, with registration G-14-5; one private-venture S.B.4 built, with registration G-14-1, later G-36-1

dashed when the museum had to close and the Sherpa's fuselage went to the Imperial War Museum at Duxford, where it lay in the corner of a hangar for many years. The remaining half-wing had previously been given to a farmer in Gloucestershire for storing, but who he was and the whereabouts of the farm remain something of a mystery.

In 1993, the derelict fuselage was given to the Medway Aircraft Preservation Society (MAPS), which on 5 June 1999 came under the auspices of the RAF Museum Cosford. At the time of writing, they have the fuselage stored at Rochester Aerodrome, without any plans for its future, which is understandable for, without even half a wing, it is akin to a frame without a Rembrandt.

CHAPTER SIXTEEN

Fairey FD.2 and BAC Type 221

Delta Metamorphosis

Just why the delta planform was accepted with so much enthusiasm in post-war Britain is hard to explain, but of all the research data brought back by the technical missions that examined German aeronautical research in 1945, this configuration was taken up with the most enthusiasm by several leading aircraft manufacturers.

When the MoS started to realize how far other countries were advancing compared with Britain, they at last turned their attention to providing the RAF with a supersonic fighter. English Electric and Fairey showed the greatest interest, which was enough for each company to eventually receive orders to produce two prototypes plus a static airframe each. English Electric's Teddy Petter opted for the highly-swept wing planform that materialized into the Lightning.

Triangular Preference

Fairey, on the other hand, had begun investigating the vertical-ramp-launched interceptor principle in 1946 and produced their delta-winged FD.1 to meet Specification E.10/47, as described in Chapter Eleven. Although this type of interceptor was discarded by the Air Ministry, the delta-wing data that the FD.1 provided greatly assisted its manufacturer when, in 1949, the Principal Director of Scientific Research (Air) intimated to Fairey that he considered the company should produce an aircraft for the sole purpose of investigating the unknown territory of genuine transonic flight, and Specification ER.103 was issued to them to cover the design and manufacture of such a vehicle. The requirement was for a single-seat aircraft to research all aspects of flying up to Mach 1.5 at altitudes between 35,000ft and 45,00ft (11,000m and 14,000m). The aircraft should be single-engined, preferably with reheat and it was stipulated that it had to be capable of exceeding Mach 1.3 in level flight at these high altitudes.

The FD.2

Basing their design on their delta-wing experience, Fairey submitted a design in the early summer of 1950. On 27 July they received Contract number 6/ACFT/5597/CB.7(a) to produce two flying prototypes, with serial numbers WG774 and WG777, plus a static-test airframe. An indication of the correctness of their design can be gauged from the fact that when the finished aircraft first appeared on the runway threshold, it was exactly as laid down in the original project office's submission. This appearance, though, was four years after the signing of the contract, for in the early 1950s the Korean war was raging and an official 'super-priority' status was placed on certain aircraft currently being built. Fairey had their GR.17/45 anti-submarine/strike aircraft in the early stages of production and this had to take preference, in order that it could enter Royal Navy service as soon as possible as the Gannet.

Therefore, it was the end of 1952 before the FD.2 started to be built at the company's Hayes factory in Middlesex. But it was worth waiting for. The aircraft that emerged at the end of September 1954 was one of the sleekest, best-proportioned aeroplanes that ever emerged from an aircraft factory anywhere in the world. At 4 per

On a wet hardstanding, the first prototype FD.2, WG774, awaits its maiden flight on 6 August 1954. Author's collection

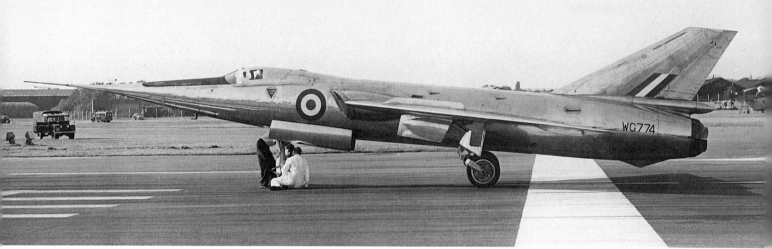

In September 1954, while attending its first SBAC Display, WG774 undergoes system checks before proceeding to the runway, as the nose-wheel receives some last minute attention. *Aeroplane*

cent, the wing's thickness/chord ratio was the lowest of any delta wing of that period and Fairey had to produce a lever-suspension undercarriage in high-tension steel mounting slim wheels with tyres of 225psi, in order that it could retract into the aerofoil section. Four integral fuel tanks were also located within the wings, which had a leading-edge sweep of 60 degrees out from the 52-degree swept engine intakes, set at quarter chord, while the trailing edge had zero sweep.

The designer's quest for minimal drag led to the fuselage diameter being just enough to house a Rolls-Royce RA.14R Avon turbojet, with a clearance of only 5in (13cm) between it and the outer skin,

while the cockpit's size was kept as small as was possible to accommodate a pilot seated in a Martin-Baker Mk 3 ejector seat, modified for a low-down installation within the cramped space. This position necessitated a hydraulically operated drooping front section which, complete with cockpit, lowered through 10 degrees to give a reasonable view on landing. Ahead of the windscreen, the nose was faired into a veritable lance of a pressure-head probe. A pair of airbrakes were ranged either side of the rear fuselage extremity that surrounded the engine jet-pipe. Above this, a broad fin/rudder assembly swept back sharply – a in-mounted tailplane like the FD.1's was considered at one stage, but was discarded.

Beauty in the Air and Dedication

WG774, in a polished natural metal overall finish with national roundels below the cockpit canopy and on the top surface of each wing, was transported to Boscombe Down where, following taxiing trials and system checks, Fairey's Chief Test Pilot, Peter Twiss, took it for a 25-minute maiden flight on 6 October 1954. Over the next four weeks, speed and altitude were cautiously increased.

On 17 November, Twiss earned the Queen's Commendation for Valuable Service in the Air. While flying at 30,000ft (9,000m), the Avon failed and the CTP

Rolling after landing, WG774 displays its trio of braking parachutes, after passing Westland Widgeon G-ALIK, Bristol's 173 XH379 and Sycamore XJ364, with Skeeter XK773 just visible above the parachute canopies. *Aeroplane*

had the choice of ejecting or attempting a 30-mile (50km) powerless flight in order to return to the A&AEE's airfield. With a test-pilot's instinctive dedication to preserving a valuable prototype, Twiss glided back to Boscombe Down, where he performed a forced landing with only enough hydraulic pressure to lower the nose-wheel and without airbrakes or the drooping front section lowered. The fact that the aircraft made a gliding flight of this length indicated just how right the FD.2 was aerodynamically.

The damage sustained on landing was comparatively slight so, after being taken back to Hayes, the wings from the static-test airframe were installed on WG774 and test flying was resumed in August 1955. During its enforced lay-up, the aircraft received several modifications, including a ram-air-driven hydraulic pump for emergencies such as had occurred, before its appearance at the 1955 SBAC Display, in a very polished condition.

Supersonic Flight and Record

On 28 October 1955, Mach 1 was exceeded without the use of reheat. It was calculated that, with the reheat in operation, the power available would almost double at 35,000ft; and the following month, Mach 1.5 (1,028mph, 1,654km/h) was achieved at that altitude. The FD.2 was indeed a fast aeroplane and consideration was given to it attempting to break the existing official absolute World Air Speed Record. This was held by the United States where, on 20 August 1955, a North American F-100C, piloted by Col H. A. Hayes, had established a speed of 822mph (1,322km/h).

In November 1955, it was decided that, as an exercise in high-speed precision flying, the FD.2 would attempt to raise the world record above the magic 1,000mph (1,609km/h) mark, with 38,000ft (11,600m) being agreed to be the most suitable altitude for the flight. As the weather had to be clear, in order that a good contrail could be made for recording the flight over the 9.7-mile (15.61km) course set between Chichester and the Royal Naval base at Ford on the Sussex

At Farnborough's 1956 SBAC Display, the first FD.2 taxis past the exhibition tent and hospitality suites, the lettering on the nose proclaiming that it holds the World Air Speed Record of 1,132mph (1,821.7km/h). *Aeroplane*

By 1957, WG774 displayed its record achievement with an overall magenta paint scheme, plus a white flash and lettering proclaiming its status. While landing, the rear fuselage air brakes were deployed and the front fuselage section drooped to improve visibility. Author's collection and *Aeroplane*

coast, everything was put on hold until the early spring of 1956.

Test runs over the course commenced early in March, when over 1,000mph (1,600km/h) was recorded during every flight and unanimous agreement was reached that a serious, officially monitored attempt should be made as soon as conditions were right. Saturday 10 March 1956 provided conditions good enough for the flight and at 11.30hr, two timed runs, each lasting thirty seconds, were made within half an hour of each other, to comply with new rules established by the Fédération Aéronautique Internationale (FAI) governing record attempts at high altitude. The average speed of 1,132mph

(1,822km/h) meant that the F-100C's record had been exceeded by 310mph (500km/h). This stood until 12 December 1957, when it was raised to 1,208mph (1,944km/h) by a McDonnell F-101 and the record went back across the Atlantic.

Second FD.2

A month before the record flight the second FD.2, WG777, had made its first flight, on 15 February. This was just as well, for when the Press descended on Boscombe Down a few days after the flight, WG774 was undergoing servicing in the A&AEE's hangar, so WG777's serial was hastily

changed to WG774 for the cameras, with no journalist being any the wiser! Following this service, both FD.2s were engaged in testing the many aspects of supersonic flight at all altitudes. These were temporarily halted for them to participate in the 1956 SBAC Display. Peter Twiss flew WG774, bedecked in an overall magenta colour scheme with 'Holder of the World Absolute Speed Record' proclaimed under a striking white flash, while his deputy, Jimmy Mathews, piloted WG777.

The desire to continue low-level supersonic test flying during the winter of 1956 brought about an arrangement to operate from Cazaux, near Bordeaux in south-west France. While the aircraft were at their temporary French base, supersonic speeds were flown as low as 3,500ft (1,100m). Design staff from Avions Marcel Dassault took an unusually keen interest, for their company had first flown the prototype of the MD.550 Mirage I on 25 June of the previous year. Their interest certainly paid off, for the Mirage I's development, the Mirage III fighter, was flying by the end of 1956! They were not alone in their thinking, for Fairey themselves had aspirations of a fighter developed from the research aircraft. In 1960, they submitted a fighter design to meet Specification F.155, based on the FD.2. This was to be powered by a de Havilland Gyron with reheat, plus a Spectre rocket motor on each side of the rear fuselage. The armament was to be a pair of wing-tip-mounted *Blue Jay* missiles, and speeds in the region of Mach 2.5 were calculated as being possible. However, this design, like so many others of that era, was rejected.

Alone

The FD.2s operated out of RAE Bedford with the Establishment's Aero Flight

When seen at Finningley's Battle of Britain Air Show on 14 September 1968, the second FD.2, WG777, was resplendent in an overall dark blue finish, with a white flash as first seen on WG774. It was parked alongside Vulcan B.2 XH559 and an unidentified Varsity. Dennis Robinson via *Aeroplane*

for another four years, before WG774 left to join the Concorde development programme. WG777 operated on its own until 1 July 1966, when a new official directive decreeing that all aircraft should be fitted with UHF radios ended its flying days. There just was not enough room in the sleek fuselage to take the required new equipment. WG777 had amassed only 198 hours 15 minutes' flying time, so it was decided to preserve the airframe, though system components and equipment were removed to put in store. It went to RAF Finningley as Instructional Airframe 7986M for a short while, before being transferred to the RAF Museum, Cosford, later in the year. It is still there today, but with its original serial number restored.

Concorde Assistance

WG774, on the other hand, began a new career. Two years of negotiations between Fairey and the RAE came to fruition on 5 September 1960, when the aircraft was flown to the former Bristol Aircraft Company, but now British Aircraft Corporation (BAC) plant, at Filton in Gloucestershire. Specification ER.193D had been raised and Contract number KD/2E/06/CB.7(c) covered Filton's work to convert the aircraft into a research vehicle to evaluate the ogee wing that had been designed for the Concorde. The original specification was later replaced by another, ER.221D, and from this, WG774 became redesignated as the BAC.221. The wings, which housed 505gal (227ltr) in four integral fuel tanks, had centre-sections with a 65-degree sweep, that developed from

Between 5 September 1960 and 7 July 1963, the metamorphosis of WG774 into the BAC.221 took place at Filton. It was first towed out with traces of its serial still visible and the Avon's reheat yet to be installed. Author's collection

Three-view of the first FD.2 WG774 before it broke the world's air-speed record.

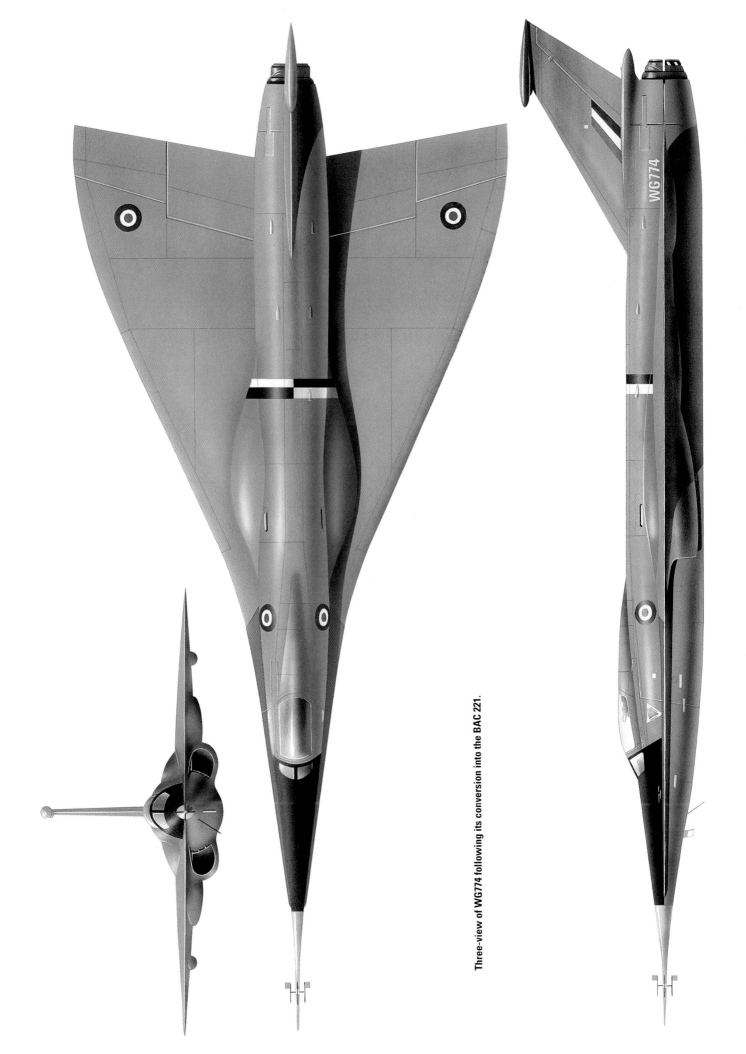

Three-view of WG774 following its conversion into the **BAC 221**.

When first flown on 1 May 1964, with BAC Filton Division's Chief Test Pilot Godfrey Auty at the controls, it was a strange mixture of some parts still in natural metal and others painted. It also showed that the complete nose-wheel door system still had to be fitted. Author's collection and Derek James

long nose-chines and carried on to smooth streamwise tips. The thickness/chord ratio of 4.5 per cent was slightly thicker than on the original FD.2 wings, but the leading edges were considerably sharper.

The conversions involved much more than just the new wings. The air intake geometry was altered to feed a new engine, the Rolls-Royce RA.28R Avon.

The fuselage was lengthened, though it retained the original airbrakes at the rear. New systems and telemetry, and a new cockpit canopy were fitted, but with the nose probe retained. Lastly, an entirely new long-stroke undercarriage was installed. This work took a lot longer than had originally been estimated (which was nothing new to the industry!) and was not

completed until 7 July 1963. However, nearly another year was to pass before the BAC.221 first flew. This was because of the initial decision to minimize cost: part of this economy resulted in there being no separate systems checking facilities. Consequently, all systems were made to flight specifications, which had to be checked on the aircraft during ground runs.

Another 'Maiden Flight'

On 1 May 1964, WG774 was at last ready to fly and it took off from Filton's long runway, which had been extended, it was said, in order to test fly the Bristol Brabazon airliner prototype of the 1940s. The fact that Bristol had hopes for their Type 182 expendable bomber, for which they got as far as partially constructing a retrievable prototype, may also have influenced the runway extension!

Trials of WG774 in its new configuration revealed that the longer nose created some lack of directional stability. This was corrected by extending the fin by 8in (20cm) which, in turn, required the bullet fairing on top of the fin, which contained a cine camera for recording wing air-flow pattern, to be extended as well. The new cockpit canopy improved visibility compared to the FD.2's, but the drooping front section was still necessary. As on the FD.2, an anti-spin parachute was housed in a bullet fairing at the base of the fin/rudder and there were new systems to investigate the characteristics of slender delta wings on take-off and landing. Although first flown in an unpainted state, by the time that Godfrey Auty demonstrated it at the 1964 SBAC Display, WG774 was resplendent in an overall dark blue finish, which it still retains.

Between this demonstration and the next, at the 1966 Display, the BAC.221 carried out a variety of trials at various speeds up to the planned Mach 1.6. After each, the results were compared to the theoretical data together with wind-tunnel readings. Trials were also made to perfect the devel-

By September 1964, the BAC.221 had been fully decorated in an overall dark blue and it stands on the threshold of Filton's 030 runway having engine ground runs prior to attending that year's SBAC Display. Author's collection

opment of an automatic throttle system that could maintain the aircraft's stability during the gradual reduction of speed and altitude on the landing approach. While these flights were useful in providing data about slender delta wings, the BAC.221's gestation time had been so long that it was really too late to supply test data that could

On rotation, the full extent of the aircraft's stalky undercarriage becomes apparent. Aeroplane

ABOVE: **WG774 makes a slow flyby with everything down, at the 1964 'Farnborough'.** *Aeroplane*

RIGHT: **Close-up of the BAC.221's starboard rear airbrakes, as displayed in the Concorde Hall at the Fleet Air Arm Museum, Yeovilton.** Author's collection

Technical Data

Fairey FD.2

Dimensions:	Span 26ft 10in (8.16m); length 51ft 7in (15.74m) including probe; height 11ft (3.35m)
Powerplant:	One Rolls-Royce RA.14R Avon turbojet, producing 9,500lb (4,300kg) thrust dry, 14,500lb (6,600kg) with reheat
Weights:	Empty 13,400lb (6,100kg); loaded 14,530lb (6,590kg)
Performance:	Maximum speed 1,147mph (1,846km/h) at 38,000ft (12,000m); maximum ceiling 45,000ft (13,700m)
Production:	Two aircraft built to Specification ER.103, with serial numbers WG774 and WG777

BAC Type 221

Dimensions:	Span 25ft (7.62m); length 57ft 7in (17.54m) including probe; height 13ft 9in (4.19m) with original fin, 14ft 5in (4.38m) with later fin
Powerplant:	One Rolls-Royce RA.28R Avon turbojet, producing 10,150lb (4,600kg) thrust dry, 14,000lb (6,350kg) with reheat
Weights:	Empty approximately 14,000lb (6,350kg); loaded approximately 15,000lb (6,800kg)
Performance:	Maximum speed approximately 1,200mph (1,930km/h)
Production:	One aircraft built to Specification ER.193D by conversion of FD.2 WG774

affect the Concorde, for that aeroplane's design had been frozen and construction of the two prototypes had already begun. Furthermore, the Concorde wings featured various twists, droops and cambers to assist the aircraft's cruise efficiency, that were not at all applicable to the BAC.221's test envelope.

Retirement

In June 1973, after nine years of very useful research flying as the BAC.221, much of this being conducted from RAE Bedford together with the H.P.115, and the previous six years as the FD.2, WG774's flying days came to an end. It went to the Museum of Flight at East Fortune airfield in East Lothian, where it was displayed for several years, before joining the H.P.115 once again, together with the first British Concorde, G-BSST/002, in the Concorde Hall at the Fleet Air Arm Museum at Yeovilton. The trio is still one of the Fleet Air Arm's prize exhibits today.

CHAPTER SEVENTEEN

Short S.C.1

Short's Early Riser

As with several initial researches into new aeronautical concepts, Short Brothers, with their wealth of experience accumulated since 1908, were in the forefront of pioneering when Short/Vertical Take-Off and Landing (S/VTOL) was first considered as a viable means of getting a turbojet-powered aircraft into the air from a small ground site as quickly as possible.

Uplift from Hucknall

By the early 1950s, the rapid development of the turbojet engine had reached the point where the difference between an aircraft's all-up-weight and its engine's thrust output was, in theory, closing to where there would be sufficient power to lift an airframe straight upwards from its parked position.

As the RAE was anxious to test this theory, collaboration with Rolls-Royce led to practical experiments that encouraged thought to be given to constructing a vehicle to take the concept one step further. This would be the proving of S/VTOL as a controllable operation. Rolls-Royce's chief installation designer, Stan Hart, headed a team charged with designing the vehicle and the result was an exercise in tubular construction that quickly earned the nickname 'Flying Bedstead'.

Officially designated the Rolls-Royce Thrust Measuring Rig (TMR), the work was covered by Contract number 6/ENG /5910/CB.13(c). The TMR was not considered to be an aircraft, hence the 'ENG' (engineering), rather than 'ACFT' (aircraft), prefix. Although no formal specification was issued, certain basic requirements were expected of the TMR. Its thrust-to-weight ratio when fully loaded was to be a minimum of 1.25:1, it was to be capable of lifting to a height of 50ft (15m) and moving in any direction within a 100sq ft (9.3sq m) area from its lifting point, and had to be capable of fifteen

minutes' sustained flying in order for meaningful research to be carried out.

The resulting structure had four corner legs, with oleos above small castoring wheels. The pilot was perched above the rig's two horizontally opposed Rolls-Royce Nene engines, which were installed to exhaust downwards at the structure's centre of gravity. Compressed air, using approximately 9 per cent of the Nene's compression-produced output, was tapped through a system of pipes, one projecting from each of the four sides, with a downwards-directed valve at each extremity, by which pitch, yaw and roll were controlled.

On 3 July 1953, the finished TMR left its Hucknall assembly shed to start a year of tentative trials, which commenced with its first tethered flight on 9 July. It was discovered that the rig fell short of the thrust-to-weight requirements, and its ratio of 1.19:1 when approximately 50 per cent of the fuel had been used had to be accepted. With such a radical experimental vehicle, complications were bound to be encountered and an early problem with the oleos not extending in unison, together with the scorching of the wheel's tyres, were overcome, the latter by the substitution of metal wheels.

Confidence in the TMR's capabilities increased so that, on 3 August 1954, Capt Ronald Shepherd successfully undertook the first free flight and, although the rig was not classified as an aeroplane, it was allocated serial number XJ314 two months before being transferred from Hucknall to RAE Farnborough on 13 January 1955. It stayed at Farnborough for eighteen months, before the research programme was taken over by RAE Bedford.

Almost a year before it went to Bedford, a second TMR had been completed, and from 19 August 1955 it carried out a year of tethered trials before making its first free flight on 12 November 1956, by which time it had acquired the serial XK426. The two rigs put in nearly a year's joint test flying before, on 16 September 1957, XJ314 crashed at Bedford, due to a failure of the

auto-stabilization system. It was rebuilt for exhibition purposes only and, after a period at Yeovilton, today it is to be seen at the Science Museum, Kensington.

Two months after XJ314's accident, the second TMR also crashed when, on 27 November it struck a gantry at Hucknall, resulting in a loss of control which the pilot, Wg Cdr H. G. 'Hank' Larson, could not rectify. He sustained a broken neck from which he died. This rig was not rebuilt, as the principle of S/VTOL had been proved, although the sale of its remains to a scrap metal merchant was an ignominious end to such a revolutionary vehicle.

Small Engines

Rolls-Royce started developing a short life/expendable turbojet engine in 1950, under the designation RB.82, to fulfill the power requirements of Vickers-Armstrongs' bomber, designed to meet Specification UB.109T, codenamed *Blue Rapier*. The engine was named the Soar and, although UB.109T was cancelled, the engine had superior thrust/weight and thrust/frontal-area ratios to any other turbojet of the era. It consisted of a single axial compressor and annular high-intensity combustion chamber, fitted within a length of 5ft (1.52m) and diameter of 1ft 3.8in (0.42m). With a dry weight of 275lb (125kg) and producing 1,810lb (820kg) static thrust, it was test flown as the Soar RSr.2 in a wing-tip installation on Meteor F.8 WA982 between 25 February 1954 and 22 March 1956; Rolls-Royce then ran down the Soar programme as it became aware that no production application was in view. WA982 was restored to standard at Hucknall and finished its career with Flight Refuelling Limited, in their programme of converting Meteor F.8s into U.16 radio-controlled drones that operated from Llanbedr in west Wales.

But the advantages of the Soar, with its high thrust/weight ratio, were not totally discarded for, within the MoS, thoughts were being crystallized on the advantages of a true S/VTOL aircraft and Rolls-Royce saw their small-engine programme as being more applicable to such a design than their original TMR deflection arrangement.

Consequently, under MoS sponsorship, they developed from the Soar the world's first direct-lift turbojet, designated the RB.108, with an 8:1 thrust/weight ratio and delivering 2,010lb (912kg) thrust in a true vertical installation. Because of Rolls-Royce's firm belief in the principle of multiple RB.108-type engines being employed for VTOL military aircraft, together with the company's chief scientist Dr. A. A. Griffith prophesying that civil aircraft could also benefit from such an installation, the MoS raised Specification ER.143.

Enter Short Brothers

Specification ER.143 covered the design and construction of a research aeroplane capable of making a vertical take-off on the power of the lift-engines alone, following which it should accelerate into a horizontal flight attitude, supported by its wings. It should have the ability to decelerate to a stationary hover, then execute a vertical descent landing under the control of the lift-engines. The Percival Aircraft Ltd at Luton tendered their P.94 design but, with their experience of tackling new avenues of aviation, Short Brothers

received Contract number 6/ACFT/11094/CB.7(a) on 10 July 1954 to produce two prototypes, allocated serial numbers XG900 and XG905. The RAE made demands that the aircraft must have the ability to make a rapid change-over from automatic to manual control and visa versa, which in itself occupied a considerable amount of time to perfect, in the general design of the aircraft.

The company had already made some preliminary design studies, so that their PD.11 submission was a small delta-winged aircraft, with a 54-degree sweep angle of the leading edge and 3 degrees on the trailing edge, employing a bank of four RB.108 engines in a vertical installation at the centre of gravity, plus a fifth in the rear fuselage for conventional flight. This was considered by the Ministry as worthy of taking to the hardware stage. As the primary concern of the design was to investigate vertical take-off, transition to conventional flight, then vertical landing from zero forward speed, the finer points of wing-borne flight, such as airspeed and range did not enter the equation to any great extent. Structural lightness, in order to produce the best thrust margin over all-up weight, was placed at the top of the requirements list, together with the minimal size of airframe necessary to carry the five engines, sufficient fuel for a worthwhile research flight endurance, plus a pilot to handle the whole package.

By 1954, flight on a vertical axis was the exclusive domain of the balloon and helicopter, so Short decided that the cockpit

layout of their research aircraft, which by then was designated the S.C.1 under the new SBAC nomenclature system, should follow existing helicopter controls wherever possible, thereby giving a sense of familiarity to the pilot. To meet the RAE's demands, a fail-safe design of servo-controls embodied three separate channels in parallel, so that any malfunction in any single channel could be contained by the remaining two until the pilot could take over. In the RAE's own words 'no single fault in the system should be catastrophic', which certainly contained no ambiguity whatsoever.

The S.C.1 Takes Shape

The finalized design materialized as a small and dumpy delta-winged, tailless aircraft that, at 25ft 6in (7.77m), had the shortest fuselage length of any turbojet aircraft since the Gloster E.28/39. Metal for XG900 was first cut in the spring of 1955 and construction progressed at a remarkably steady pace considering how unconventional the design was. A Folland lightweight ejection seat was installed in the cockpit, but this was later replaced by a Martin-Baker zero-zero seat. The pilot sat under a transparent canopy in the extreme nose section, which provided him with excellent all-round visibility except to the rear. A substantial boom projected over 5ft (1.5m) ahead, carrying the pitot head and the pitch and yaw vanes.

The first prototype S.C.1, XG900, started conventional flying at Boscombe Down on 2 April 1957. Only the horizontal-flight engine was fitted, with the yaw, pitch and roll nozzle housings blanked off. Author's collection

ABOVE: **When this photograph was taken, the four lift engines had been installed, with their nozzles protruding below the fuselage underside. At this stage only the manually controlled intake gills were operative and the lift engines' main intake via the dorsal mesh remained to be installed. The yaw, pitch and roll control systems are also not yet fitted.** Author's collection

RIGHT: **This schematic drawing illustrates the degree of plumbing required to make the S.C.1 a fully operating S/VTOL aeroplane.** *Aeroplane*

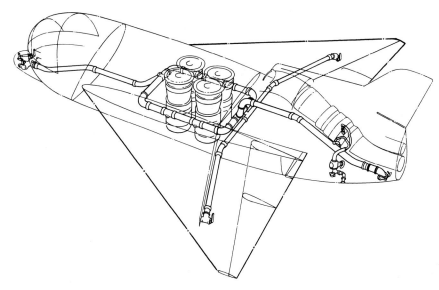

The entire fuselage centre-section was the bay for the four lift engines. The rear fuselage housed the conventional-flight engine which, because the RB.108 had been designed for working in a vertical position, had to be inclined at an angle of 30 degrees to the fuselage datum line, to obviate any modifications to its lubrication systems. Air for this engine was drawn via a dorsal intake, above which was sited a swept fin/rudder assembly. However, for its initial flight trials, XG900 was not going to have the lift-engines installed. It was considered necessary to prove it in a conventional flight mode before entering any vertical-axis programme – there was no point in getting airborne in a vertical trajectory and then being unable to fly anywhere else.

Carrying on their experience with the S.B.5, Short provided the S.C.1 with the ability to rake the main wheel legs of the fixed tricycle undercarriage into attitudes that were set and locked before the aircraft left the ground. For conventional take-offs and landings, the oleos were set in a forward-raked position, but it was considered that when making a vertical landing, there would be a risk of the aircraft tipping back onto its rear end, so for jet-lift trials, the legs were to be raked in slightly.

XG900 was taken from its Belfast assembly shop to the company's airfield at Sydenham at the end of November 1956, and on 7 December, RB.108 testing began. Progress was so good that Tom Brooke-Smith started taxiing trials ten days later; prior to this, the CTP had taken a concentrated course in helicopter handling, as well as experiencing control of the TMR at Hucknall. S.C.1 ground handling proceeded until February 1957, by which time everyone agreed that test flying could commence. However, Sydenham was considered inadequate for the maiden flight, so the long journey to Boscombe Down was started.

First Flights

On 6 March 1957, XG900 was lifted aboard the SS *Copeland* at Belfast Docks, to begin a squally two-day passage to Southampton, from where it was transported by road to the A&AEE's airfield. Further taxiing trials were conducted until, on 2 April, the first S.C.1 had its maiden conventional take-off and landing.

It could not be said that the aircraft was pleasant to fly, possibly because of its size and proportions, but this was not considered to be too adverse a situation, as its prime function was to evaluate the VTOL mode. There was also the possibility that when the lift-engines were installed its flying characteristics could change. The only serious aspect was a degree of directional instability, which was partially cured by the fitting of a substantial dorsal fin, running from the rear engine's air intake back to a position halfway up the fin leading edge.

The testing of XG900 as an aerodynamic airframe was successfully completed at Boscombe Down by the autumn of 1957 and it was expected that the aircraft would return to Belfast for the installation of its bank of lifting engines, but for economic reasons this was delayed until the following year. It could possibly have been because the second S.C.1, XG905, had been completed and this had its four R.B.108s *in situ*.

On 2 June 1959, XG900 moves away from the hovering control gantry and hovers to make its first vertical landing on the company's football pitch. Aeroplane

S.C.1 Number Two

The second prototype encompassed lessons learned on XG900 and had the dorsal fin installed while still being assembled. The four lift engines were linked together on transverse axles, in order to tilt in unison through a 35-degree arc rearwards to assist the transition to horizontal flight and forwards to provide deceleration in level flight, prior to a vertical descent to land. Both the top and bottom of the engine bay were open, with the top covered by a wire-mesh screen, to avoid the ingestion of foreign objects. Forward of this screen, manually-controlled, spring-loaded gills were opened to provide additional air to the engines during vertical take-offs and landings, but closed to reduce drag in conventional flight.

The four RB.108 lift-engines' jet-pipes slightly protruded below the fuselage underside and were fitted with shroud extensions around their leading edges, to assist directional flow. They were started by bleeding air from the propulsion engine and, although the basic airframe was small in overall size, a large part of the structural interior was taken up by an ingenious 'ringmain' trunking system that fed air bled from the engine compressors for pitch/yaw control, via four nozzles at the airframe's extremities. A nozzle in a bulged fairing under the lower nose section acted with a similar installation under the rear fuselage

to control pitch, while nozzles in bulged fairings under each wing surface, close to the tips, acted as roll controllers. All nozzles reverted to a partially closed position when the engines were closed down.

A lack of space within the fuselage dictated that fuel had to be carried in a sealed unit within each wing leading edge, which could be detached from the front spar by quick-release fasteners. These leading-edge fuel tanks were augmented by small additional bag tanks situated between the wing main spars.

First Vertical Flights

Confidence in the S.C.1's conventional flight mode was sufficient for the company to consider the Sydenham airfield as capable of handling the flight research programme, so XG905 was spared the stormy Irish Sea crossing. The lift-engines were run for the first time on 3 September 1957, and over the winter an overhead gantry, supported by substantial upright members, was constructed over a raised open-grid platform. This was considered necessary to channel away the lift engines' hot exhaust gases, as it was feared that if they recirculated to be redrawn into the intakes, there would be a drop in thrust; there was also the unknown factor of the effects of the lift-engines' jet efflux being directed straight onto Sydenham's tarmac.

Progress was cautiously made during the early spring of 1958 and on 23 May Brooke-Smith made the first hover flight, with XG905 tethered within the gantry. Experience enabled minor modifications to be made, as well as to introduce Jock Eassie, Brooke-Smith's deputy, and Sqn Ldr S. J. Hubbard from RAE Bedford into the programme. On 25 October 1958, the first free hover flight was made over the gridded platform, which was followed in November by the first landing away from the site (following a conventional take-off). This was executed on the company football pitch, which became quite a regular venue once the scorched grass had been accepted as a small price to pay for progress.

XG900 Back in Business

In the early winter of 1958, the first aircraft returned to Belfast from Boscombe Down to have its bank of lift-engines installed at last. Slight modifications were made, based on the experience with XG905, which involved some geometrical alterations to the intake gill's housing, as well as incorporating a bulged top to the cockpit canopy, which served as the entry hatch, replacing the original side door. The undercarriage oleos were fitted with fairings, but these do not appear to be permanent fixtures, as flights were sometimes made with them detached.

LEFT: A noisy demonstration as XG900, with the second prototype XG905, perform a duet at RAE Bedford, showing their differing yaw and pitch nozzle housings. *Aeroplane*

ABOVE: A fine air-to-air study of the first prototype flying with the dorsal manually controlled intake gills partly open and the lift engines pointing at the rearward extremity of their 35-degree arc of movement, thereby assisting horizontal flight. *Author's collection*

BELOW: Today, XG900 is displayed at the Science Museum, London, alongside a sectioned RB.108 and with a glazed screen around its yaw boom (to deter the younger generation from trying to swing from it!). *Aeroplane*

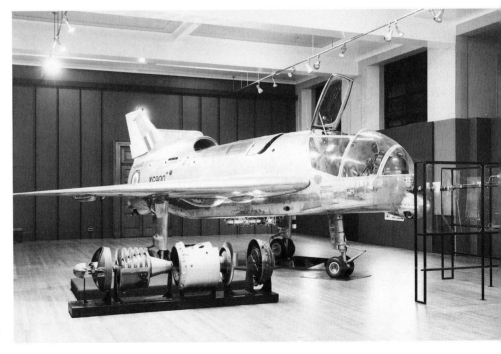

As the VTOL side of the S.C.1 had been satisfactorily proven by XG905, the first prototype did not need to go through the 'tethered-to-the-gantry' initiation, and both aircraft participated in developing the S/VTOL principle, employing separate lift and conventional flight power. These trials continued throughout 1959, but during the week of 7–14 September XG905 took time out to demonstrate how successful these trials had been. The first prototype had appeared at the previous year's SBAC Display as a static exhibit, but in 1959 the whole noisy, exciting process of vertical lift and landing was to be shown to the world's aeronautical fraternity. Unfortunately for Tom Brooke-Smith, on the first day no allowance had been made for the humble lawn mower.

XG905 was parked on a beautifully manicured stretch of grass in front of the viewing stands and the rear engine bled air to the four vertical engines. The aircraft gently rose, in formation with millions of grass cuttings that followed the airflow pattern to the intakes. The protective grill did its job by preventing the majority of the cuttings from getting into the engines, so a green carpet completely covered the grill, starving Rolls-Royce's excellent engines of air and XG905 made an ignominious return to Farnborough's airfield much sooner than scheduled.

XG900 Gets Posted

Complete transition was accomplished on 6 April 1960 at RAE Bedford, when lift-off was performed to a height of 100ft (30m),

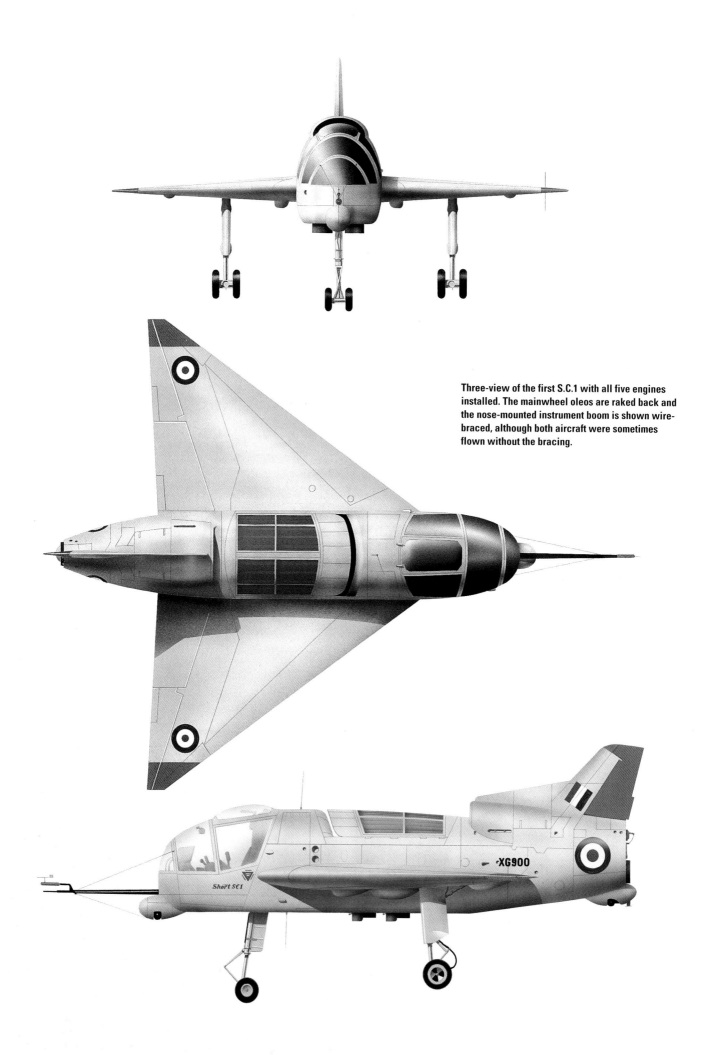

Three-view of the first S.C.1 with all five engines installed. The mainwheel oleos are raked back and the nose-mounted instrument boom is shown wire-braced, although both aircraft were sometimes flown without the bracing.

Short SC1

XG900

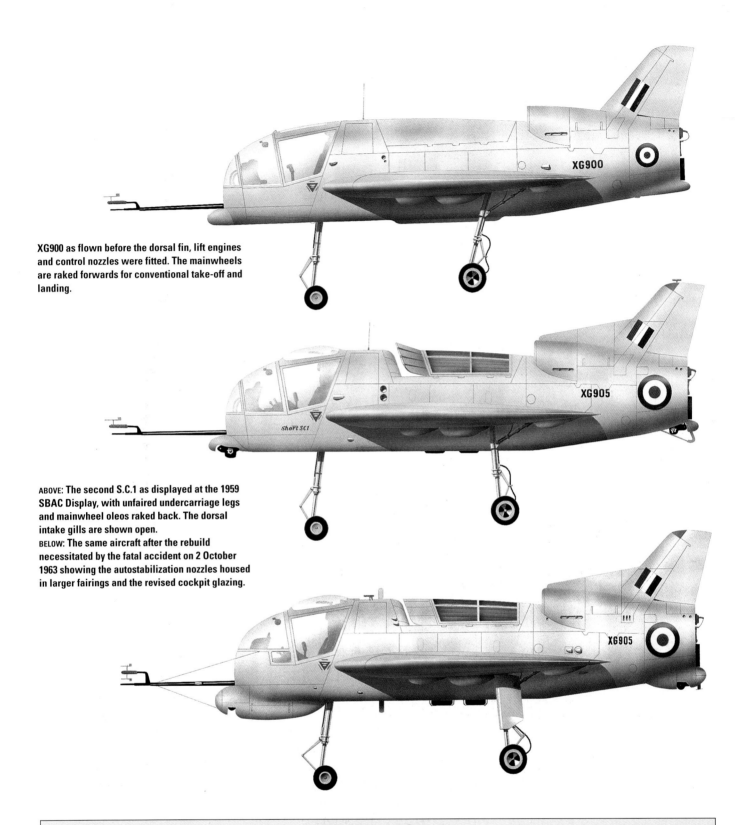

XG900 as flown before the dorsal fin, lift engines and control nozzles were fitted. The mainwheels are raked forwards for conventional take-off and landing.

ABOVE: The second S.C.1 as displayed at the 1959 SBAC Display, with unfaired undercarriage legs and mainwheel oleos raked back. The dorsal intake gills are shown open.
BELOW: The same aircraft after the rebuild necessitated by the fatal accident on 2 October 1963 showing the autostabilization nozzles housed in larger fairings and the revised cockpit glazing.

Technical Data – Short S.C.1	
Dimensions:	Span 23ft 6in (7.16m); length 25ft 6in (7.77m) excluding boom, 29ft 10in (9.10m) including boom; height 9ft 10in (3m) with main wheels raked forward, 10ft 8in (3.28m) with main wheels raked rearwards
Powerplants:	Five Rolls-Royce RB.108 turbojets, producing (vertical engines) 2,130lb (970kg) thrust each, (rear engine) 2,010lb (912kg) thrust
Weights:	Empty 6,000lb (2,700kg); maximum loaded (VTOL) 7,700lb (3,500kg); maximum loaded (S/VTOL) 8,050lb (3,650kg)
Performance:	Maximum speed 247mph (397km/h)
Production:	Two aircraft built to Specification ER.143, with serial numbers XG900 and XG905

ABOVE: This view of the unpainted XG905 clearly illustrates the four lift engines' installation and the shield placed in front of the fifth RB.108's intake when the lift engines were ground-run. *Aeroplane*

BELOW: Tom Brooke-Smith poses for the camera with XG905, which is fitted with individual shrouds around each lift engine orifice, to assist directional flow of their efflux. *Aeroplane*

inventory to join the RAE's Aero Flight at Bedford in April 1961. The aircraft was temporarily recalled in September 1961 to be demonstrated once more at the SBAC Display, but this time with Tayler at the helm, showing the constant level attitude possible during the transition cycle.

XG905 Takes a Life

While the first prototype was at Bedford, XG905 was returned to Belfast for the installation of an updated auto-stabilization system, in order to improve the aircraft's handling during moments of external fluctuations, such as sudden wind gusts, and the front nozzle housing was slightly extended to accommodate the new valve. By the summer of 1963, another RAE pilot, J. R. Green, had joined the programme at Sydenham on loan, to evaluate a new control device that had been fitted during the modification programme.

He performed nearly one hundred successful flights over a seven-month period until 2 October 1963 when, despite the triple safeguards incorporated in the S.C.1 before the first prototype was completed at the RAE's insistence, the gyros failed. XG905 was below 30ft (9m) at the time of failure and Green made a very quick attempt to revert to full manual control, but there was just not enough altitude for this to be successfully achieved and the aircraft flew into the ground, killing the pilot. The damaged aircraft was returned to the factory for repair and XG900 was grounded pending the findings of the accident board of enquiry.

Modifications to the systems were incorporated during the repairing of XG905 to ensure that such a sequence of events could not reoccur, and these were also applied to XG900. XG905 did not reappear for over two and a half years. In view of the modifications, it was considered prudent to fly the aircraft tethered within the gantry, which was the first time that it had used the safety construction. The flights commenced on 17 July 1966 and, following their satisfactory completion, the aircraft received a revised ground data link, together with a new Head-Up-Display (HUD). Almost a year after the commencement of the tethered flights, XG905 went to Boscombe Down during the first week of April 1967, and from the A&AEE it returned to RAE Bedford on 16 June to rejoin XG900, which by this time had resumed test flying.

with level flight being made across the airfield and back, before a vertical descent to 20ft (6m) was held, followed by a straight-up climb preceding level flight once more. A vertical landing completed the sequence and it was found that a wing-borne speed of 154mph (248km/h) was possible before the bank of lift-engines required relighting. Through improvements made to the air-bled valve nozzles, power output of the vertical RB.108s was gradually increased, to a point where each was delivering 2,130lb (970kg) thrust at sea level.

Tom Brooke-Smith retired from Short Brothers at the end of 1960 but not before, three months earlier, proving that the whole S.C.1 system worked in front of the visitors to that year's SBAC Display, thereby replacing the memory of the unfortunate episode at the previous Display; this was the first time that the full transition sequence had been demonstrated before the public. Denis Tayler left the RAE to become Short's new CTP and he mastered the final trials of XG900, before the aircraft was removed from the company's

RAE Trials Programmes

The Establishment flew both S.C.1s extensively for a variety of trials programmes, and the Blind Landing Experimental Unit (BLEU) at Bedford thoroughly investigated the techniques required for operating S/VTOL aircraft at night and in adverse weather conditions. These trials lasted over two years during which time XG900's airframe time was reached and it was restricted to ground running only. By 1971, the useful life of the S.C.1s as research aircraft had been completed and both left Bedford

RIGHT AND BELOW: The second prototype displays the modifications made to its control nozzle housings. It was photographed at RAE Bedford, alongside a Rolls-Royce 'Flying Bedstead', in April 1960.
Adrian Balch via *Aeroplane*

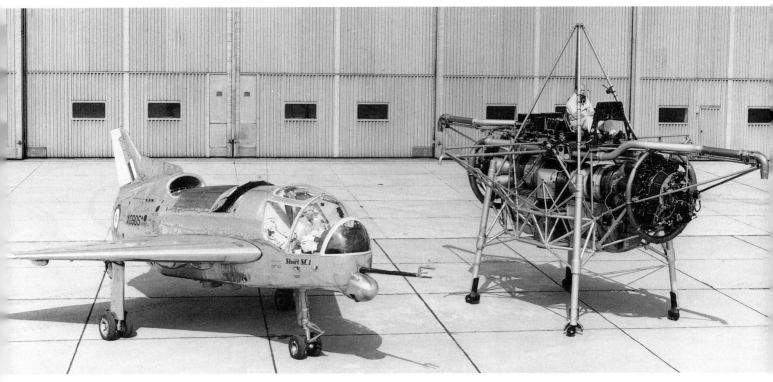

BELOW: In a conventional touchdown, XG905 deploys its braking parachute and shows that the main wheels are raked in the forward position. *Aeroplane*

ABOVE: **XG905 hovers above the special grid at Sydenham, with J. R. Green at the controls. The improved auto-stabilizer is housed in the modified housing under the nose and the rearward-raked main wheels are clear. This photograph was taken shortly before the aircraft's crash on 2 October 1963, in which Green lost his life.**
Adrian Balch via *Aeroplane*

BELOW: **After the crash, XG905 was repaired and various improvements were incorporated, including revisions to the cockpit glazing.** Author's collection

during the year. XG900 had a period at the Science Museum in London before going to the Fleet Air Arm Museum at Yeovilton, but at the time of writing it is back at the Science Museum.

XG905 was stored for a couple of years before appropriately returning to Northern Ireland, to become an exhibit at the Ulster Folk and Transport Museum at Holywood, County Down, about 7 miles from its place of birth eighteen years earlier. Both aircraft had been in a natural metal finish all their lives, although dayglo-red was added to their fins and wing tips and retained for many years.

The whole idea of hauling static engines around during conventional flight had been overtaken as early as 1957, when the development of the rotatable nozzles of the Bristol BE.53 established the lengthy pathway to the eventual Pegasus engine and the Harrier. But the S.C.1 concept was a valuable tool for the British aircraft experimental establishments and proved to be more practical than some projects undertaken in the United States and France, although it could never have been made into an operational service aircraft in the form in which it existed. Perhaps this is why it was more successful than the foreign projects, which were designed to run before they had learned to walk.

CHAPTER EIGHTEEN

Saunders-Roe SR.53

Saro's Mixed-power Flirtation

In the second half of the 1940s, the RAE engaged in a very comprehensive investigation of the projects that were in hand with Germany's Word War Two air ministry, the *Reichsluftfahrtministerium* (RLM), and recovered by the Allied technical teams at the end of the war. In particular, the rocket-propelled, small target-defence interceptors, such as the Messerschmitt Me 163 and Bachem Ba 349 Natter, led to Fairey's FD.1 programme, while research contracts for rocket motors were placed with Armstrong Siddeley Motors and the de Havilland Engine Company.

Rocket Motors

The two companies took different lines of approach. Armstrong Siddeley opted for a fuel mixture of liquid oxygen (lox), water and alcohol, and developed the Snarler, which gave 2,000lb (900kg) thrust and was flight-tested in the rear end of the Hawker P.1072 adaptation of VP401, the first prototype P.1040 (*see* Chapter Four). De Havilland concentrated on High Test Peroxide (HTP), which culminated in the 5,000lb (2,300kg) thrust Sprite motor, intended as a boost motor for their Comet airliner.

Both companies undertook exhaustive trials programmes with their respective motors, and each had drawbacks as well as advantages. The RAE favoured the lox system, principally on the grounds of it being much cheaper than HTP, but when their application into the design of an aircraft was considered, operational requirements ruled out the lox system.

Specification F.124T

Operational Requirement (OR) 301 was formulated in August 1951, generated by military intelligence's revelations of the USSR's progress in the fields of supersonic bombers and nuclear weapons. OR301

The first prototype, XD145, blasts into the air above Boscombe Down for its maiden flight on 16 May 1957. Just discernable in the background is the Meteor T.7 with Saro photographer Ben May aboard, vainly trying to get an air-to-air take-off shot. When he did eventually catch up and came alongside the SR.53, the burnt-out rocket motor was just producing a trail of steam. Saunders-Roe

A fine portrait of XD145 showing its very clean lines and the cut-out at the top of the rudder to allow for the movement of the all-flying tailplane. *Saunders-Roe*

called for the design of a small, uncomplicated, rocket-powered interceptor with an outstanding rate of climb. Basically, the Air Ministry was thinking about something along the same lines as the Bachem Natter of 1944, but with a much greater performance and a different retrieval process. The interceptor was required to make a glide descent, preferably back to base, or to land wherever possible on a built-in skid.

From OR301, Specification F.124T was raised in 1952, to which Avro entered their Type 720 design, Bristol its Type 178, Blackburn the B97/B99 projects and Short Brothers the PD.7. Of these, only Avro received an order, this being for two prototypes plus a structural test airframe, which answered a revised requirement embodied in Specification F.137D, but only the structural mock-up was partially completed.

At Saunders-Roe Limited, universally abbreviated to Saro, the Deputy Chief Designer, Maurice Brennan, had been asked by the Board to consider future paths of development that the company could take in order to produce an operational production aeroplane. Their rotary-wing progress was quite healthy, as the Cierva-designed W.14 had been taken over and was being supplied to three Services as the Skeeter. However, previous fixed-wing projects, the SR.A/1 and the SR.45 Princess, were impressive aircraft in their own fields,

but did not materialize into anything that could maintain a production line.

Brennan's thoughts crystallized into a small fighter that could use rocket-power to climb above an incoming supersonic bomber in order to make an interception – again, similarly to the Bachem Natter. Saro had a dynamic Chief Executive, Sir Arthur Gouge, and on learning of Brennan's idea, he sent an official written request to the Ministry of Supply for a copy of Specification F.124T to be forwarded to his company immediately. It is presumed that Saro's long-established

association with marine aircraft had placed them outside the MoS's initial consideration. The Ministry complied with Sir Arthur's request, but also stated that the company would not be paid for any design that it submitted!

Saro's Reply

When Maurice Brennan studied F.124T, its impracticalities became obvious and revealed the lack of official understanding of the operation of such an aircraft.

The full-span leading-edge slot can be seen as the aircraft flares out. *Aeroplane*

Although the ramp or very-short-run launching disposed with an undercarriage, it added greatly to the difficulties of landing. Obviously the Messerschmitt Me 163B concept had been studied by the MoS, but its operational altitude of 30,000 to 33,000ft (9,000 to 10,000m) did not take it too far from base, so gliding back was a feasible proposition. F.124T was placing an altitude of 100,000ft (30,000m) as the operational requirement, which could take an interceptor so far away from base as to make a gliding return out of the question.

The Ministry had foreseen such an occurrence and the specification's built-in requirement was for the design of a very large recovery vehicle to go and collect the grounded aircraft from wherever it had landed. This completely nullified the design concept of a simple, inexpensive supersonic interceptor, not to mention the ergonomics of such an exercise.

Saro submitted their answer to F.124T in every respect in April 1952, but also attached their own P.154 design, based on Brennan's own conception of what was required. This was a far less revolutionary aeroplane, and included aerodynamic features that had been approved by the RAE. It was a single-seat, mid-wing aircraft, employing a Saro-designed rocket motor running on HTP and kerosene and mounted in the rear fuselage. The aircraft also had a small turbojet engine, which answered a question already raised by several other company's designers when examining F.124T – 'How do you get a worthwhile amount of electrical power out of a rocket motor?' This turbojet would also enable the interceptor to return to base and, as a tribute to Maurice Brennan's logical thinking, the Air Ministry proposed that the other companies should also consider this factor.

Not only did Brennan propose the installation of a turbojet, but he advocated the fitting of an undercarriage so that on returning to base the aircraft could land, be refuelled and rearmed ready for the next sortie – in the same time that the original F.124T's recovery vehicle driver was mapping out how to get to the aircraft's location!

Official Acceptance

In just four weeks the MoS accepted Maurice Brennan's alternative design proposal and Saro received an Order to Proceed, followed on 8 May 1953 by Contract num-

This rear view shows the disposition of the two engine outlets, as well as the anti-spin parachute housing on top of the tailplane, partly obscured by an errant piece of rag. Author's collection

ber 6/ACFT/8703/CB.7(a) for three prototypes, allocated serial numbers XD145, XD151 and XD153. Specification F.138D was written around Saro's design, to which they gave the company type number SR.53. This was an out-of-sequence number that some have attributed to the year of their receiving the contract, but this has never been substantiated.

In October 1953, Maurice Brennan became Chief Designer on Henry Knowler's elevation to be the company's Technical Director. Now having overall charge of the SR.53 project, Brennan made it known that so far as he was concerned, lox was totally unsuitable for his design, no matter how the RAE and Armstrong-Siddeley emphasized the economic advantages. Brennan catalogued many grounds for the fuel not being appropriate for an operational aeroplane. It was far too volatile, thereby forming a risk to Service personnel. All the mechanical systems had to be maintained at a high temperature in order not to freeze up, and the aircraft could not remain on alert without the system being continually topped up which, again, was unacceptable in a front-line environment.

De Havilland Engines' research and testing proved that HTP was preferable. Despite its greater cost, Brennan stood his ground and it was finally agreed that Saro's rocket motor would be designed around HTP as its propellant.

Detailed Design

When it came to the turbojet engine, the MoS suggested that the Turbomeca Palas, giving 330lb (150kg) static thrust, would be suitable, but again, Saro did not agree. Such a power output would be totally inadequate for an operational interceptor and Brennan thought the Armstrong-Siddeley Viper a much more viable proposition. It produced 1,640lb (740kg) static thrust in its AS.V.8 form which, when supplementing the Saro rocket motor's designed thrust of 8,000lb (3,600kg), would make the SR.53 a genuine supersonic interceptor. However, while Saro's motor was still in the design stage it was learned that de Havilland Engines were obtaining a similar output from their Spectre motor and, as it was in an advanced state of development by then, it was decided by Saro to stop work on their indigenous motor design, in favour of the Spectre for their SR.53.

In the original design the Viper was positioned below the rocket motor, but when the drawing office got down to details, it was decided to transpose the installations. Another major change from Brennan's first thoughts lay in the pilot's emergency evacuation, which had originally been envisaged as the jettisoning of the whole cockpit assembly as one unit, to land by parachutes. However, detailed consideration of the mechanics and

Three-view of the second SR.53 as displayed
in the static park at the 1957 SBAC Display.

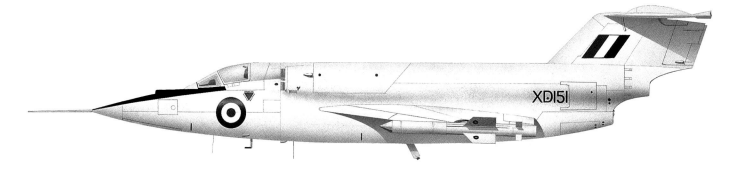

En route to the 1957 SBAC Display, XD145 still had bare wing tips, but by the time that the de Havilland Spectre projected it into the air to start its flying routine, dummy Firestreak air-to-air missiles had been fitted. *Aeroplane*

weight involved in such a procedure convinced the Chief Designer that a Martin-Baker Mk 3 ejector seat would be preferable. The offensive armament had been proposed as a battery of fifty rocket projectiles, but this too was superseded and a wing-tip launch rail was designed, to take a *Blue Jay* missile, as the Firestreak was originally known, on each side.

Competition and Rethinking

Saro was well aware that their SR.53 would probably be evaluated against the Avro Type 720, especially in the type of fuel used for the respective rocket motors, as Avro was using an Armstrong-Siddeley Screamer motor, running on lox. As the RAF was not really convinced that a rocket-powered

interceptor was required at all, Saro considered it was vital to get their aircraft flying as soon as possible. They determined that July 1954 was a realistic date, which gave them approximately thirteen months to produce one of the most advanced interceptors of the era, but almost before construction commenced, the whole idea of such an aeroplane was raising doubts in official heads.

The Central Fighter Establishment (CFE) laid down one important stipulation, namely that it was mandatory for any new fighter to be equipped with a satisfactory Airborne Interception (AI) radar. The idea of a Mach 2 interceptor's pilot having to make visual contact with his quarry at 100,000ft (30,000m) and rely on a ground control radar to position him for a successful missile launch was ludicrous.

Maurice Brennan sought the advice of the Royal Radar Establishment (RRE) over the matter and they informed him that the best system to meet his requirements was their AI-23, which was in production at Ferranti's plant in Scotland. The SR.53 was quite unable to have this large piece of equipment incorporated into its airframe and, furthermore, did not have the power to even get airborne with such a weight aboard. Therefore, as the design stood, it was a non-runner and a larger aircraft was called for, using the SR.53 as a test airframe to prove the concept of a high-speed, mixed-powerplant interceptor. Specification F.124T had required that there be 'provision for radar', which was understood at the time to refer to a gun-laying system even though it stipulated missile, not gun, offensive armament! It was obvious that no real thought had been given to this aspect and it appeared that officialdom was waiting to see what the designers came up with, in the hope that it would be acceptable. The one ray of sunshine so far as Brennan was concerned was the fact that Avro would have the same problem.

While the SR.53 had a turbojet to enable it to return to base, Brennan was of the opinion that such an engine should be capable of doing more. The Viper, while giving a return-to-base facility, was certainly not even capable of getting the aircraft off the ground and a larger engine, in combination with the rocket motor, would be a better proposition. Such an aircraft would also have a greater endurance, cruising on the power of its turbojet, with the rocket motor used solely for high-speed pursuit and interception. This idea evolved as the Saro SR.177, which is featured in the final chapter of this book.

Misplaced Optimism

The SR.53 was now purely a research vehicle for the mixed-power interceptor project. In view of this the third prototype, XD153, was cancelled in January 1954 on the grounds of economy, which also terminated all work on the Avro Type 720.

Saro's forecast made in early 1953, that the first aircraft would make its maiden flight in July 1954, was proving to be ultra-optimistic. In fact when that date arrived, the question of how to install all the required equipment into the small airframe was far from being resolved, while

de Havilland was having its own problems with the Spectre. A complete SR.53 rear fuselage was despatched to the engine manufacturer in the winter of 1954–55, but this suffered acoustic-generated damage that required both the rudder and elevator structure to be modified.

Eventually, all the respective problems were overcome so that, in June 1956, the elements of XD145 were transported to the A&AEE's airfield at Boscombe Down for final assembly. The finished aircraft had a slim fuselage with a pointed nose-cone, forward of which was a 7ft (2.13m) pitot boom. The pressurized cockpit was faired into the fuselage front section, with a small air intake on either side behind the canopy to feed the Viper 101. A large rectangular airbrake was faired into either side of the rear fuselage, ahead of the two orifices. A substantial fin, with a 41-degree leading-edge sweep, carried a round-tipped delta tailplane on its top and the wings, too, set at a 5-degree anhedral angle, were of delta shape, with the tips cropped.

With a 6 per cent thickness/chord ratio, each wing had an integral tank outboard of the undercarriage bearing member, carrying additional turbojet kerosene, but the primary HTP fuel was housed in five bag tanks that occupied the majority of the lower fuselage, under the Viper. A sixth tank in the same location carried turbojet fuel and the entire lower fuselage outer panels were removable for servicing the two engines. When XD145 was being ground-tested, trouble was experienced in keeping the fuel in the bag tanks, so the aircraft was first flown with only two tanks installed.

The tricycle undercarriage featured a 14ft (4.26m) wide track for the inward retracting main wheels, while the nose-wheel retracted forward into the underside of the nose section. Each wing tip had a launching rail for a de Havilland Firestreak missile, although not even dummies were fitted during early flight trials, and each wing had a full-span retractable drooping leading edge. The whole aircraft was painted gloss white, with a black anti-glare panel ahead of the windscreen.

First Flights

Hurn had been considered as the SR.53's operating base, the idea going so far as to have HTP storage facilities built, but as the mixed-power layout was a new venture, which had not been employed in Britain at that time, Boscombe Down, with its overall amenities and vast runway, was thought preferable. This became the aircraft's operating base throughout and Hurn was never used. By this time, Brennan's insistence on using HTP had been vindicated by the cost being considerably lower than in 1952.

For such a new generation of aeroplane, ground testing became, of necessity, a lengthy process. The Spectre was first fired in January 1957, with the Viper following suit three months later, by which time XD145 had been at Boscombe Down for ten months. Taxiing trials commenced at the beginning of May and on the 16th, almost three years later than originally scheduled, the aircraft had its maiden flight. Saro's Chief Test Pilot, Geoffrey Tyson, had retired in early 1956 and his deputy, Sqn

LEFT: **Today, the first SR.53 is housed among the experimental aircraft collection at the Royal Air Force Museum, Cosford, with the perforated airbrakes extended.** Author's collection

OPPOSITE PAGE:
The second prototype, XD151, attended the 1957 SBAC Display as a static exhibit, with dummy Firestreaks on its wing tips, plus a cine camera housing ahead of the windscreen. While at Farnborough, it attracted the attention of an RAF Service Policeman and a couple of onlookers. Alongside are Israeli Britannia 313 4X-AGB and an unidentified Hunter, the P.1 WG760, Heron G-AOGW and, in the far distance, Westland Widgeon G-AKTW with Herald G-AODF. *Aeroplane*

Ldr John Booth DFC, had taken over his mantle. The SR.53's maiden flight began the first programme for which he had full responsibility.

Considering the complexity of the design and its specification, early flight testing went very smoothly. The first air-to-air photographic session was held on the 27 May and the company's assistant chief photographer, Ben May, recalls the event thus:

> I was aloft in the only suitable chase-plane available, an early two-seat Meteor, doing tight turns for about fifteen minutes within Boscombe's boundary, waiting for the '53 to start its run along the vast runway. The neck-ache which I suffered for days afterwards was doubtless caused by the combined weight of a Rolliflex, a cine-camera and Weston meter being several times their real weight as a result of considerable 'g'.
>
> Eventually the '53 got the green light and my pilot, John Overbury, dived the old 'meatbox' towards it, arriving about a second after John Booth fired his rocket motor. My hoped-for cine shots of the little white plane sitting on that long orange flame, disappeared rapidly, as the '53 climbed to something like 30,000ft in a minute. We caught up with him at 25,000ft over Bristol, running cold on HTP only, trailing miles of steam! I managed to get a long cine shot and a few stills, before he shut down the Spectre. We then got really close and took what I believe are the only air-to-air shots of the aircraft.

Mach 1.3 was attained early in the flight-test programme and rate-of-climb figures, from brakes off to 50,000ft (15,000m) in two and a half minutes, exceeded the anticipated performance. Later in the programme, XD145 recorded Mach 2 at 40,000ft (12,000m) and a maximum altitude of 55,000ft (17,000m) was reached.

event. The second aircraft was very similar to its partner, except for a cine-camera housing ahead of the windscreen, and was finished in the same overall white gloss.

Much Testing and Tragedy

John Booth experienced rudder and tailplane buffeting when the airbrakes were deployed, but a comprehensive series of perforations in their surfaces cured the problem. During some flight tests, a pair of pods were attached to the wing-tip missile launch rails, each containing a cine camera and tape recorder.

The lack of thrust from the Viper became evident when more than 10 degrees of flap was extended as, with the wing leading edge flaps drooped, there was insufficient power to beat the drag and stalling was not an option with such a small turbojet. This again proved Maurice Brennan was right when he considered the Turbomeca Palas did not have enough power.

Booth started taxiing trials with XD151 during the early winter and on 8 December 1957 he took the aircraft up for its first flight. The aircraft had the full complement of HTP tanks and as it was now available to join the test programme, XD145 was taken into the hangar space that the A&AEE had allotted to Saro, to undergo minor repairs to damage sustained during a Spectre flashback; at the same time, it had all five HTP tanks installed. While this work was in hand, John Booth was kept busy flight-proving XD151. He made eleven flights in the second aircraft before tragedy struck on 5 June 1958.

For some reason which has never been fully established, Booth lifted the nose-wheel clear of the runway on take-off, but the rest of XD151 did not follow. The aircraft struck a concrete approach light pylon after over-running and exploded, killing its pilot. The AIB investigation established that the pilot had shut down the Spectre but had not opened the airbrakes or applied wheel brakes. The power of the Viper on its own was not sufficient to get the aircraft airborne and there were signs of the braking parachute being deployed, but without being able to have any effect on the situation. XD151 had been fully serviced prior to the event and the findings of the AID had to be that there would never be a conclusive reason for the disaster.

As John Booth was the designated pilot to the SR.53 programme, XD145 was grounded, although some reports suggest that it was flown once more and, as it joined the Rocket Propulsion Establishment at Westcott, Buckinghamshire in October 1959, this flight could possibly have been its delivery, or it could have been transported by road. After four years at Westcott, employed as the ground-running test-bed for various rocket motors, ownership of the aircraft went to the RAF Museum, but it was placed in store at Henlow, where it stayed for the next fifteen years.

In 1978, XD145 was delivered to the newly formed Brize Norton Aviation Society, where it was restored to static display standard over a three-year period. Then on 30 November 1981, it was handed over to the RAF Museum at Cosford. Today it is displayed among Cosford's collection of research aircraft, as all that remains of a protracted, but very promising, programme.

Two Aircraft and a Display

The second SR.53, XD151, was completed in August 1957, but was not ready for flying by the first week of September, when the annual SBAC Display was held at Farnborough. Therefore, it was transported by road and displayed in the static aircraft park, while John Booth took time out from the test-flight schedule to pilot XD145 in an exhilarating display of fast, noisy, low-level flying. It appeared early in the week with empty launch rails on its wing tips, but later had a pair of dummy Firestreak missiles installed, while the XD151 carried a dummy pair for the whole

Technical Data – Saunders-Roe SR.53	
Dimensions:	Span 25ft 1in (7.64m) without missiles, 28ft 1in (8.56m) with missiles; length 39ft 4in (11.97m) excluding pitot boom, 46ft 4in (14.11m) including pitot boom; height 10ft 10in (3.29m)
Powerplants:	One Armstrong-Siddeley AS.V.8 Viper 101 turbojet, producing 1,640lb (740kg) thrust and one de Havilland D.Spe.1A Spectre rocket motor, producing 7,000lb (3,200kg) thrust
Weights:	Empty 6,650lb (3,020kg); loaded 18,400lb (8,340kg) including 500lb (230kg) kerosene for Viper and 10,500lb (4,760kg) mixture of kerosene and HTP for Spectre
Performance:	Maximum speed Mach 2.1 at 60,000ft (18,000m); rate of climb at sea level 12,000ft/min (3,700m/min); rate of climb at 50,000ft (15,000m) 39,000ft/min (12,000m/min); normal service ceiling 60,000ft (18,000m); maximum endurance approximately 50 minutes
Production:	Two aircraft built to Specification ER.138D (later renamed F.138D), with serial numbers XD145 and XD151; a third aircraft (XD153) was cancelled before construction began

CHAPTER NINETEEN

Hawker P.1127

Towards the Kestrel

One of the darkest days ever for the British aircraft industry was Thursday 4 April 1957, when the Minister of Defence, Duncan Sandys, declared that all manned fighter aircraft development for the RAF was to be terminated forthwith. It was an action from which the industry never recovered and precipitated mergers and closures that continued over the following twenty years.

Almost in contradiction to the above is the fact that for the Hawker Aircraft Company the Defence White Paper was a blessing in disguise. Using its own money, earned from the sale and refurbishment of its Hunter fighter, the company had invested over a million pounds in designing its supersonic successor, the P.1121 which, despite being at the prototype-construction stage, was cast asunder at the time of the 1957 White Paper. Without the prospect of a customer, continuation was pointless and would be a further drain on the company's finances. Therefore, while the shop-floor was thriving the design office, which is the heart of any aircraft company, had time to spare when an unlikely project appeared via Bristol Aero Engines.

French Genesis

Short/Vertical Takeoff and Landing (S/VTOL) as a concept had been demonstrated in August 1954, when Rolls-Royce first lifted its Thrust Measuring Rig off Hucknall's tarmac and Short Brothers extended the principle into a more acceptable aeronautical shape in 1957, as related in Chapter Seventeen. However, the French aircraft designer, Michel Wibault, considered the carrying of idle engines during conventional flight to be an unnecessary weight penalty, and he drew up a system of rotatable nozzles for a single engine in his Gyroptere, based on the Bristol Orion engine, which was the most powerful turboprop engine at that time. Instead of driving a propeller, Wibault's design had the engine driving four separate centrifugal compressors via a shaft and multiple gearboxes. The Gyroptere was designed as a single-seat tactical strike aircraft, with a nuclear-weapon-carrying facility. The idea generated no interest whatsoever from the French authorities, so Wibault approached the Mutual Weapons Development Programme (MWDP), through which the USA was funding weapons development

for NATO. Through this his idea was forwarded to Bristol Engines' Technical Director, Stanley (later Sir Stanley) Hooker, via a mutual friend, Johnny Driscoll, for consideration.

Enter Bristol Engines

The merits of the idea instantly appealed to Hooker, but the mechanics of the system nearly produced a repeat of the French reaction, for the vast array of gears, shafts and compressors was daunting so far as a production engine was concerned. However, Sir Stanley had a team of young and enthusiastic designers, and they proposed discarding this engineering nightmare, replacing it with a 1.5:1 ratio reduction gear, driving two stages from the low-pressure compressor of their Olympus turbojet. The air drawn in through the Olympus's fan could be ducted through a

The first prototype is rolled out on 31 August 1960 for a photocall, devoid of markings, while the protective covering taped on the canopy and windscreen are still in place. Author's collection

simple swivelling nozzle on either side of the fuselage. The company designation BE.48 was allotted to the engine, but further thought led to a decision to use the Orpheus rather than the Orion, as this was a simpler and lighter unit. In this form, the engine was redesignated the BE.52.

Like all good design teams, Hooker's group did not sit back and consider the job done. They contemplated forming the front compressor into a constituent of the engine itself, using a common intake. The inner airflow was channelled to the core Orpheus, while the outer stream discharged through

For its first tentative hovering, XP831 was stripped of everything not specifically required, which included, externally, the nose probe, all undercarriage doors, the anti-spin parachute extended housing and the fairings for the outrigger wheels, in order to bring the weight below the engine's thrust output. The tethering lines are prominent, as are the metal intake lips that conform to the shape that the future inflatable ones would adopt when the aircraft manoeuvres in the vertical plane.
Derek James and *Aeroplane*

the swivelling nozzles and this brought about another type number, the BE.53. Wibault was in full agreement with Bristol's adaptation of his idea, to the extent of his joining Gordon Lewis, from Hooker's team, in applying for a patent for the first aeroplane powered by a BE.53-type engine.

US Air Force Col Johnny Driscoll's involvement in the project stemmed from his being a member of the Paris-based MWDP, after he had succeeded Col Willis 'Bill' Chapman to the post, and it was Col Chapman who Wibault had first approached with his Gyroptere, following the French rejection. The US-backed MWDP funded 75 per cent of the BE.53's development costs and the whole concept met the approval of Sir Reginald Verdon Smith, Chairman of the Bristol Aeroplane Company, of which Bristol Engines was a part. He sanctioned the 25 per cent funding short-fall and his action guaranteed the BE.53's future.

Enter Hawker Aircraft

The engine was now in a state of development where its marriage to an airframe was the next logical step. Bristol prepared a brochure on its BE.53 and submitted it to various aircraft designers, with the reaction being rather on a par with the French and Wibault. Sir Sydney Camm, Chief Designer of Hawker Aircraft, was singularly unimpressed, as the quoted thrust output of the engine was less than 9,000lb (4,000kg). Undeterred, Hooker made an official presentation of his BE.53 to Hawker Aircraft Limited and the Board passed the project to their design team, even though Camm thought the engine's quoted thrust was too low to be viable.

One of Hawker's younger engineers, Ralph Hooper, was finding it hard to face up to the cancellation of the P.1121, as he had made a considerable input to its design. He studied the BE.53 brochure and, together with colleague John Fozard, began sketching various airframes that could be designed around the engine, with the first firm proposal being a two-seat battle liaison aircraft, with a cold nozzle under the wing on each side of the fuselage and a single hot jet-pipe exhausting the Orpheus core engine from a ventral position under the rear fuselage section. But it was a 'tail dragger' and Hooper considered that all the engine's thrust should be used for vertical take-off and landing.

He recalled Camm's idea for the P.1040 back in 1946, where the Nene exhausted via a bifurcated jet with an outlet on either side of the fuselage and considered a similar configuration could be applied to the BE.53. The two cold nozzles of the battlefield liaison aircraft design were retained, but moved further forward, while the hot air exhausted through bifurcated nozzles situated under the wings. All four worked in unison to rotate through a 90-degree arc from a vertical to a horizontal rearward-facing position.

At first, Bristol thought the idea unworkable, but on further consideration came to realize the merits of such a layout. They amended the rather crude nozzles into cascades, which have been a big feature of the engine ever since. Development of the BE.53 was conducted at a rapid rate and in September 1959, a bare three years after the original drafting on the drawing board, a prototype engine was running on Bristol's test bench.

Shortly before Hawkers received the BE.53 brochure, Michel Wibault died and was denied seeing his Gyroptere idea evolve into a practical aeroplane. Although Camm initially dismissed the principle, he had enough faith in Ralph Hooper and

When the first prototype started hovering trials without the tethering lines the nose probe had been reinstated, but the undercarriage doors and outrigger fairings had still to be replaced. *Aeroplane*

John Fozard for them to continue developing their ideas and the company's number P.1127 was raised to their design, which was the only new project in the whole company. However, his faith in the young designers was sorely tested when they advocated a tandem undercarriage with wing-tip outrigger wheels. His design philosophy of wide-tracked, inwards-retracting undercarriages, applied ever since the Hurricane first appeared in 1935, was difficult to overcome. Despite Boeing having been successfully operating a tandem layout on their B-47 since 1946, as well as Dassault's Vautour since 1952, the concept was anathema to him and it took much persuasion on the part of Hooper before the configuration received the Chief Designer's approval.

Again like the French, official ministerial interest in the project was zero and certainly no funding was offered. The MWDP and Bristol financing was continued and instructions to proceed were issued in 1958 for the construction of six engines, to be produced to flight-clearance standard. Hawker Aircraft, for its part, had faith in their design to a point where they once again agreed to finance a project as a private venture and two prototype P.1127s were ordered, together with the cost of flight testing. It seems amazing today, that one of the most important developments in the operating of an aeroplane was brought about entirely without official understanding or assistance by the country of its origin. The Sandys' decree of 1957 could have been a contributory factor to this attitude and credit must be given to the fact that an official 'blind eye' was taken, because the

Posing in front of XP831 are the two pilots principally involved in making the P.1127 a success. Bill Bedford (on the left), sporting a bow tie and suede shoes with his flying suit, stands beside the more conservatively attired Hugh Merewether. *Aeroplane*

When first built, the prototype had inboard cut-outs on its flaps in order to clear the jet efflux, but they were found to be unnecessary and were later removed. XP831 now has its out-rigger fairings fitted, together with revised metal intake lips conforming to the shape required for level flight. *Aeroplane*

BELOW: The aircraft was fitted with inflatable intake lips, together with an identity statement on its nose, when Bill Bedford flew it to make its first landing aboard HMS *Ark Royal* in February 1963. Derek James

P.1127 was billed as a ground-attack aircraft rather than as a fighter.

Wind-tunnel models were tested to determine the flow patterns from the four nozzles during their transition from the vertical to rearward-facing attitude. In this respect, one ministerial concession was made and these tests were conducted in their wind tunnels. Also, in the United States, NASA took a great interest in the project and offered all their research facilities to Hawker Aircraft.

NATO Aspirations

One reason for the United States' interest lay in the fact that NATO was looking for a new aircraft, and this alone encouraged the Air Staff to consider the P.1127 principle as a future replacement for the Hunter. They went so far as to raise Operational Requirement 345, but were of the opinion that it was not an operational aircraft in its present form. NATO had raised their Basic Requirement 3 and issued NBMR-3 to aircraft manufacturers all over Europe. Hawker tendered a stretched P.1127, titled P.1150, which incorporated plenum-chamber burning in an uprated BE.53, which by this time had received the name Pegasus.

There followed a protracted saga, created by increasing demands of NBMR-3, and Hawker answered them with an improved P.1150, the P.1154, in which an entirely new engine was proposed, this being the BS.100, which was at the advanced design stage in the newly-formed Bristol Siddeley Company. A thrust in the region of 33,000lb (15,000kg) was forecast for the BS.100 and Hawker's design employing the new engine was adjudged the winner of NBMR-3. However, the ever-nationalistic French thought their Dassault Mirage III-V Balzac equally commendable and gave NATO notice of their intention to continue with this aircraft's development, which resulted in NBMR-3's demise. The fact that the Balzac did not progress beyond the prototype stage was really only incidental, for France had achieved its object of not seeing a British aircraft win the NATO contest!

Service Interest, At Last

By 1963, both the Royal Air Force and the Royal Navy had woken up to the potential of Hawker's P.1154. Two Operational Requirements were written around the project, one being a single-seat Mach 2 S/VTOL strike aircraft for the RAF, while the RN requirement was for a two-seat S/VTOL carrier-borne interceptor, which they stipulated should have a Mach 2.5 capability.

Besides the P.1154, Admiralty House had an interest in the McDonnell Phantom II, and maybe it was to convert this interest into hard fact that they made continual demands to Hawker for alterations to their aircraft. Whatever the true reason, the Senior Service pulled out of the P.1154

ABOVE: Here XP831 is joined by the second P.1127 prototype, XP836, which has fairings around its outriggers and the metal high-speed intake lips, while the first prototype still carried the metal lips conforming to the fully inflated profile. Derek James

BELOW: The retractable dorsal ram-air turbine for the hydraulics is in the deployed position on the static XP831, now sporting outrigger fairings. It has rubber inflatable lips installed for the hovering shot. Derek James

programme in 1964. The RAF's ambition to have it as an operational strike aircraft was not deterred by the Admiralty's withdrawal, although research and development costs had started to rise at an alarming rate. In the middle of 1964, a General Election saw Harold Wilson lead a Socialist government into power and one of the pledges in their election manifesto was to reduce defence spending. Consequently, almost before they had warmed the seats on the Government side of the House, the axe was dropped on the BAC TSR.2 strike aircraft, the Armstrong Whitworth AW.681 STOL transport aircraft and the P.1154.

Progress

While the P.1154 saga was unfolding, work on the subsonic P.1127 had been steadily continuing and Bristol had delivered the first flight-cleared Pegasus 2 during the summer of 1960. Official backing had at last been declared, with Specification ER.204D being written around the two prototypes, which were given the serials XP831 and XP836. The specification was issued to Hawker Aircraft on the last day of February 1960 and four months later, on 27 June, the company received Contract number KD/2Q/02/CB.9(c) from the Ministry of Aviation (MoA), which included a third airframe for static test purposes, although it is believed that the funding of the two prototypes was still borne by Hawker Aircraft.

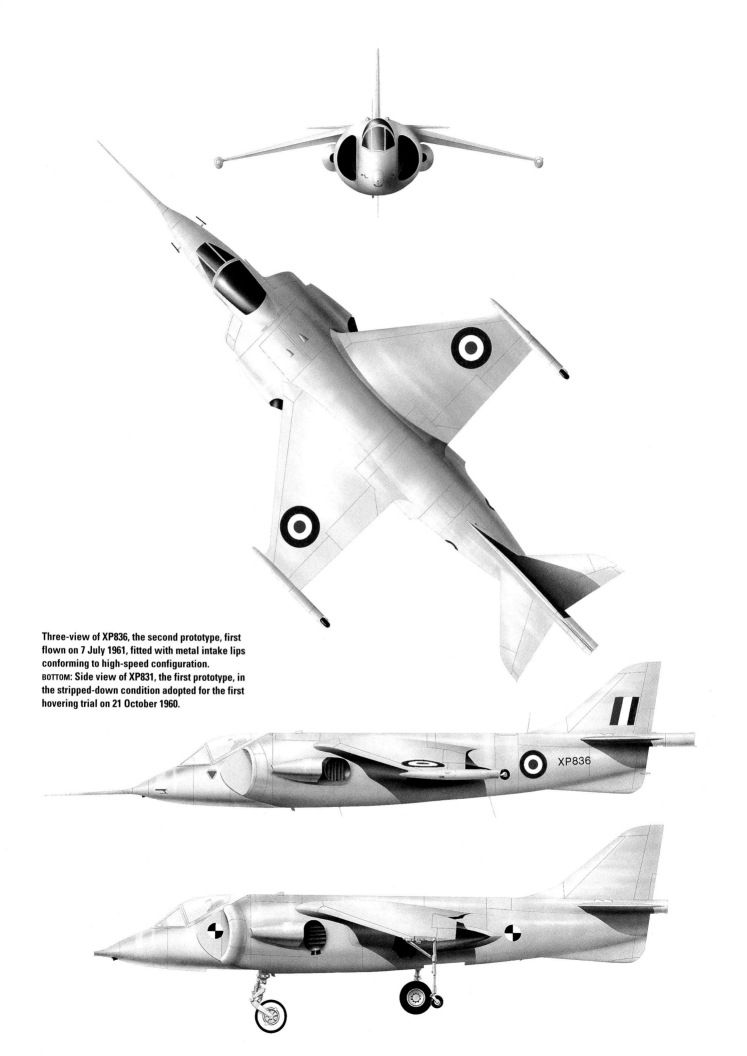

Three-view of XP836, the second prototype, first flown on 7 July 1961, fitted with metal intake lips conforming to high-speed configuration.
BOTTOM: Side view of XP831, the first prototype, in the stripped-down condition adopted for the first hovering trial on 21 October 1960.

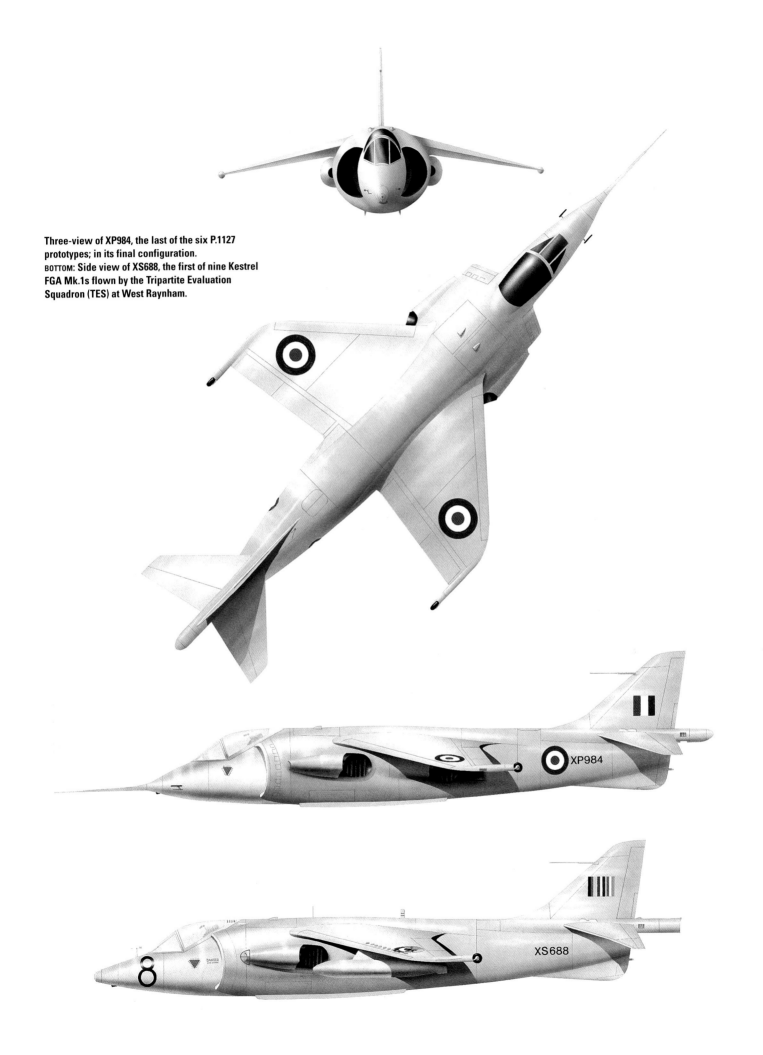

Three-view of XP984, the last of the six P.1127 prototypes; in its final configuration.
BOTTOM: Side view of XS688, the first of nine Kestrel FGA Mk.1s flown by the Tripartite Evaluation Squadron (TES) at West Raynham.

XP984

XS688

The tare weight of XP831 reached parity with the Pegasus's thrust output, but by August 1960, when the aircraft was rolled out at Dunsfold, by dint of subtle modifications an additional 1,000lb (450kg) had been squeezed out of the engine which, although it did not reach the 1.5:1 ratio of Hooker's original goal, was a step in the right direction. Ground running of the Pegasus 2 commenced on 31 August.

In appearance, the first P.1127 looked a far more operational aircraft than the Short S.C.1 which, to be fair, was purely a research vehicle. It sat in a nose-high attitude, with the shoulder-wings, which had a sharp angle of sweep on their leading edge, set at a marked angle of anhedral. The tandem undercarriage on the fuselage centreline had a single 10.25in (26cm) diameter nose-wheel which retracted forwards, and a side-by-side pair of 11.4in (28.7cm) main wheels that retracted rearwards. At either wing tip, a thin outrigger leg supported a wheel of 4.5in (11.4cm) diameter, which retracted rearwards into slim, bullet-shaped housings, with the wheels uncovered.

The tail assembly featured a swept fin and rudder with a single-piece tailplane.

An extension of the rudder trailing edge led to a ventral fin, with a built-in tail bumper. A considerable amount of research had centred round the pair of large air intakes positioned either side of the cockpit section, for it was considered that the airflow into the Pegasus would vary between vertical and horizontal flight, although this had yet to be confirmed in a wind tunnel. The intakes were to have inflatable rubber lips, but on roll-out XP831 had metal lips conforming to the shape that the inflatable units would adopt during vertical flight, which was to be the aircraft's first test programme.

Pitch and yaw control was to be via valves at either wing tip, together with one in an extended parachute housing running rearwards from the tailplane and another at the underside tip of the nose section. Two 90-degree rotatable nozzles on either side of the fuselage centre section were the aircraft's driving forces, with the front pair drawing cold air from the engine's low-pressure fan, while the rear pair exhausted from the high-pressure compressor, directed outwards by the bifurcated jet-pipe at the engine's rear.

Tentative Hovers

A grid-covered pit had been built at Dunsfold, in order to dissipate the hot jet efflux so that it was not re-ingested into the Pegasus, and XP831 was first positioned over the grid on 21 October 1960.

Hawker's Chief Test Pilot, Neville Duke, had retired in 1956 as a result of spinal injuries received when crash-landing a Hunter at Thorney Island the previous year. His deputy, Flt Lt 'Bill' Bedford, stepped into the CTP post in October 1956 and it was he who was to become the leader of the P.1127's team of test pilots. On 21 October, following a series of taxiing runs to evaluate the steerable nose-wheel and the braking system (which was only installed on the pair of wheels), Bedford began a series of hovering trials, with the aircraft tethered to three weights positioned below the platform's grid.

The first hovering was a series of precarious operations, for the pilot found it difficult to maintain position and keep the aircraft away from the tethering lines. In view of the small margin of thrust available over the aircraft's weight, everything that was considered unnecessary was removed from the airframe. These included all the undercarriage fairings, doors and jacks, the nose-mounted instrument boom, all radio sets, the dorsal ram-air turbine, the airbrake, the rear parachute installation and all the cockpit conditioning systems. A Perspex windscreen replaced the heavier glass one and

The second prototype, XP836 had a short career for, having first flown on 7 July 1961, it crashed on 14 December of the same year. It is seen here fitted with metal intake lips to the level-flight profile and deploying its ribbon braking parachute on landing at Dunsfold. *Aeroplane*

meticulous calculations showed that, with a gross weight of 9,243lb (4,192kg) including the pilot, sufficient fuel for just three minutes' hovering could be carried.

Bedford had tested the temporary telephone line to the ground crew prior to lift-off and the testing of the control surfaces together with the auto-stabilizing system had used half the available fuel, so that the P.1127's 'first flight' lasted exactly 1¾ minutes. XP831's second hovering flight was made on 24 October, with Hugh Merewether, Bedford's deputy, at the controls. During the flight the tethers broke, so an early amendment to the system was a doubling of its strength. It was also found that the rigid outriggers caused a problem, so they were modified to incorporate temporary sprung extensions before Bedford made the third flight, on 3 November.

Further tethered test hovers were carried out until 19 November, when two untethered lift-offs were carried out from the grid platform. Three days later, the first vertical take-off from tarmac was accomplished. By this time, both pilots had become experienced enough for at least 75 per cent of the fuel to be burnt in actual hovering.

More Progress and More Aircraft

After all the years of apathy, it was encouraging to Hawker Aircraft when, before the end of 1960, their MoA contract was extended to include an additional four aircraft, allocated serial numbers XP972, XP976, XP980 and XP984. Furthermore, they would all be covered by defence expenditure! Early in 1961, taxiing showed a juddering problem with the brakes on the main wheels, which were a pair of standard Sea Hawk wheels fitted either side of a new oleo leg, and the malfunction continued until there was an undercarriage collapse on 4 February. A repositioning of the brake-pad units around the discs cured the juddering, and at the same time the outriggers were locked to prevent any more of the shimmy tendencies that had been encountered. However, the shimmy problem returned after the aircraft had been to RAE Bedford for extensive taxiing trials, and this time shear pins were fitted to alleviate the unpleasant defect.

On 13 March 1961, the next milestone was passed, when XP831 made its first conventional flight from a normal take-off, which was another step into the unknown. Although vertical take-off, hovering and vertical landing had been mastered within the limited time allowed by the restricted fuel load, how the P.1127 would handle as a conventional aeroplane had yet to be established. This shows how unorthodox the whole P.1127 conception was, for this was five months after it had first become airborne (or thrust-borne). Bill Bedford made the first conventional flight, with a Hunter used as the chase 'plane. The undercarriage was retracted at 500ft (150m) and, with a full fuel load carried for the first time, XP831 climbed to 25,000ft (7,600m) where speed was gradually increased to Mach 0.8. The aircraft handled beautifully and the ailerons provided a very quick rate of roll – in fact, it was a typical Hawker aircraft. The pilot found that a nose-down pitching took place when the flaps were lowered, so when

In this view of the third prototype, fitted with metal intake lips, the revised wing with streamlining at the tips and the filled-in formed cut-outs in the flaps are clearly seen. The ventral strakes have yet to be fitted.
Derek James

XP972 has a horizontal tailplane, inflatable intake lips and rectangular rear-nozzle heat shields. The latter were interchangeable with the pen-nib variant on the majority of P.1127s. *Aeroplane*

he brought the prototype in for a conventional landing, he adopted a long, flat, flapless approach.

Despite the encouraging first conventional flight, many problems still existed, with the centre-of-gravity being particularly fickle. Quite a juggling act was required as, with an increase in power the CG moved forward to stabilize conventional flight, but it became too far from the thrust line when the nozzles were rotated for vertical manoeuvring. Too much air was drawn off for the pitch and yaw trimming to handle with the nozzles in a vertical attitude, so that the thrust was barely sufficient to remain airborne. But between them, Bedford and Merewether evolved a handling sequence that alleviated these tendencies. Serviceability of the aircraft was good by any standards and, for such an unorthodox aeroplane with all its complexities, this was bordering on the remarkable.

The whole P.1127 programme benefited greatly when Bill Bedford gave XP836, the second prototype, its maiden flight on 7 July 1961. Although XP831 had made further conventional flights since 13 March, a new schedule was drawn up so that XP836 undertook the majority of normal flight testing and XP831 concentrated on hovering trials, with the two pilots sharing the workload. With the installation of a new variable-bleed reaction-control system on both aircraft, power control became much easier to manage and flypasts at 50ft (15m) along Dunsfold's runways enabled vertical landings to be accomplished from this height,

onto a pre-selected landing site. At last, the P.1127's two realms of unconventional and conventional flight were uniting into a successful aeroplane.

On the morning of 12 September 1961, those associated with the programme since its genesis, including Ralph Hooper and John Fozard, travelled down to Dunsfold to witness both pilots performed full routines from vertical take-off, transition to conventional flight, deceleration to the hover, finishing with a vertical-thrust-maintained landing. Representatives of the Ministries had also been invited, but they were late and the demonstration began before their arrival. They were none too pleased about this, but a company explanation, made with tongue-in-cheek, that the transition was accidental due to an unexpected rapid acceleration down the runway, appears to have placated the situation and things were settled over the mandatory luncheon!

New Realms and First Loss

Investigations began into short take-offs and it was soon apparent that operating in this way enabled greatly increased payloads to be carried, compared with straight vertical rising. During December 1961, Mach 1 was marginally exceeded in dives and XP831 reached Mach 1.2 in one dive from 40,000ft (12,000m). But on 14 December, exuberance was moderated when Bill Bedford had a front nozzle detach itself from XP836. An emergency landing at RNAS

Yeovilton was attempted but, although the undercarriage was down, the aircraft was flying at about 200mph (320km/h), which was too high for a full deployment of the flaps. The aircraft went into a slow roll that could not be corrected and the CTP had to eject through the canopy. A few days later, the offending nozzle was retrieved by a farmer going through his orchard and a fault in the nozzle's plastic was found to have been responsible. From that day on, cold (i.e. front) nozzles matched their hot (rear) counterparts and were manufactured in steel.

XP831 underwent changes to its intake lips during the course of its testing. Inflatable rubber lips were fitted, activated to full-blown configuration on take-off, then sucked down to a sharper leading edge during conventional flight. However, continuance of the operation produced ripples in the rubber, inducing them to tear at higher speeds and, although considerable development work was carried out to stiffen the rubber structure, together with improving the venturi sucking pump, the situation could not be completely resolved. Therefore it was literally back to the drawing board for a compromise fixed metal lip to be designed; the inflatable rubber lips were cast into the box of 'good ideas at the time'.

New Engines and Aircraft

During 1962, XP831 had its Pegasus 2 replaced by a Pegasus 3, developing 13,500lb (6,100kg) thrust, which was 1,500lb (700kg) more than its predecessor. The Pegasus 2 had been in the aircraft for well over a year, although not the same actual engine, for attrition was rather high and the return of engines to Bristol became a regular occurrence, which was not really surprising considering how unconventional the unit was.

Then, in February 1963, the aircraft was demonstrated by Bedford and Merewether to the Royal Navy at Portland, which was followed by the CTP making the first landing on a carrier deck. HMS *Ark Royal* was the historic recipient and routines were flown from the carrier during the day. However, it was another sixteen years before this became a normal operational procedure!

An addition to the programme had been made on 5 April 1962 when Hugh Merewether made his first maiden flight,

At the 1962 SBAC Display, the air show fraternity saw the first of the P.1127 routines that have extended to the present day with the Harrier. The first prototype, hovering to face the crowd line, was joined by the third prototype XP972, which was the first to have an anhedral tailplane. Both aircraft were fitted with inflatable intake lips and carried the combined markings of the RAF, USAF and West German Luftwaffe, which would be applied to the Kestrel derivative of the P.1127, when they joined the Tripartite Evaluation Squadron (TES) formed in August 1965. *Aeroplane*

in the third prototype, XP972. This had a modified wing and, when demonstrated at the 1962 SBAC Display, together with XP831, it was seen to be the first P.1127 to be fitted with an anhedral tailplane. However, XP972 was destined not to have a great input to the test programme, for on 30 October it suffered an engine failure and Hugh Merewether was forced to make a wheels-up landing at the nearest airfield, which was No. 22 Squadron's base at Tangmere, from where they operated with Whirlwind HAR 10s. The damage sustained in the landing was sufficient for XP972 to be returned to Kingston for repair, but this was deemed uneconomic and on 15 September 1964 the aircraft was struck off charge.

Three months before XP972's forced landing, on 12 July 'Bill' Bedford took the fourth prototype, XP976, into the air for the first time. Further changes had been incorporated into this aircraft, with the wing-tip leading edges having further sweep to improve transonic flight characteristics. It initially flew with a Pegasus 2, but from the fourteenth flight onwards, it was powered by a Pegasus 3. This was later replaced by a Pegasus 5, developing 15,500lb (7,000kg) thrust. With the increase in the number of aircraft, two new pilots were introduced to the programme during XP976's evaluation. They were David Lockspeiser and Duncan Simpson, who were to feature strongly in the type's development over the years, during which time they were joined by former RAE Bedford test pilot Flt Lt John Farley. The fourth prototype was used in

trials of short and vertical take-offs from grass, by A&AEE pilots, as well as head-up-display (HUD) evaluations by the RAE, before being retired in 1965.

The Final Pair

'Bill' Bedford piloted both XP980 and XP984, the fifth and sixth prototypes, for their maiden flights. XP980's was on 24 February 1963 and almost one year later, on 13 February 1964, XP984 took to the air. The gap between their first flights occurred because the Pegasus 5, fitted in XP984 for ground-running purposes only, received damage to its fan blades and had

to be returned to Bristol for repair. On returning to the airframe, a bearing malfunction was suffered when the ground running was resumed and the waiting for the replacement bearing occupied a longer time than anyone had foreseen, or wished.

The fifth prototype, powered by a Pegasus 3, incorporated a new hydro-mechanical nose-wheel steering system. It was delivered to the A&AEE at Boscombe Down for evaluation as a service aircraft, during which time it was flown with and without 100gal (450ltr) external drop tanks. Various Establishment and foreign pilots flew the aircraft as, on 16 January 1963, a Tripartite Agreement had been signed between the UK, USA and the

The TES upper-wing roundel is shown to advantage in this nice air-to-air shot. *Aeroplane*

XP984 was the sixth P.1127 prototype and the first to be built to the Kestrel profile, with the outrigger wheels moved further inboard to accommodate the revised wing-tip shape and a new tailplane featuring two angles of sweep on the leading edge.
Author's collection

Federal German Republic, to operate a Tripartite Evaluation Squadron (TES). Eighteen aircraft, given the name Kestrel, were ordered for the unit, but this was amended to nine before construction had begun. After its return to Dunsfold from the A&AEE, various trials were conducted with XP980 until it returned to Boscombe Down in January 1966 for semi-permanent use. During forced-landing practice the aircraft was damaged, and it was relegated to undercarriage load trials in rough ground in 1971.

XP984 was built more to Kestrel standard than the previous five prototypes, incorporating a true swept wing on both leading and trailing edges, with the tips conforming to the final evaluated shape. Metal intake lips, revised to be efficient at all speeds and attitudes, were fitted, while its Pegasus 5 underwent a stringent programme of strain gauging. On 19 March 1965, Merewether was flying XP984 when it had a complete engine failure while performing a supersonic dive. Through brilliant flying, he was able to make a dead-stick landing at Thorney Island, where Transport Command's No. 242 OCU operated with their Argosy C.1s.

XP984 was repaired and early in 1966 it had a further wing change, this one conforming to the shape for the proposed squadron-service aircraft that was to become world famous as the Harrier. It undertook a new series of carrier trials on HMS *Bulwark*, after which it began a new series of operating trials that were relevant to the Harrier and, as such, beyond the scope of the P.1127 programme.

Epilogue

For such a revolutionary and new aeroplane, the fact that the time from the start of its hovering tests on 21 October 1960 to the delivery of the first Kestrel FGA.1 to the TES at West Raynham on 8 February 1965 was a little over four years was a remarkable achievement. Much more had to be done before it was cleared for service as the Harrier GR.1, but the whole principle of an operational aeroplane embodying true S/VTOL ability had been proved.

This had not been accomplished without setbacks, with both XP836 and XP972 being lost, but at no cost to their pilots. A very large number of modifications were made in the course of the evaluations. The fin and tailplane area was increased, although the angle of anhedral was actually decreased. The rear nozzle heat shields were changed in shape for a while and ventral fuselage strakes were fitted at an early stage, to increase pressure beneath the aircraft during low-hovering. Vortex generators were attached to the wing upper surface and when originally flown, XP831's flaps had large cut-out sections, but these were filled in early in its test programme, never to reappear, while the air intake geometry in particular received many subtle changes.

Besides the two aircraft lost, there were several mishaps, one of the more embarrassing being the crash-landing of XP831 while Bedford was demonstrating at the Paris Air Show on 16 June 1963. The cause was a foreign object entering the nozzle actuating system, which made them rotate while the pilot was in hovering mode. A heavy but acceptable landing could have been achieved, had not a substantial concrete structure been in the way.

Of the P.1127 prototypes, XP831 is today displayed at the Science Museum, XP980 is a part of the impressive number of aircraft to be seen at the Fleet Air Arm Museum, Yeovilton, and XP984 resides at the Brooklands Museum outside Weybridge. Only XP976 was actually scrapped following its retirement, which shows that by the mid-1960s, the preservation of aircraft had at last been recognized as a meritorious activity.

Technical Data – Hawker P.1127	
Dimensions:	Span 24ft 4in (7.40m) (XP984: 22ft 10in/6.96m); length 41ft 2in (12.56m) (XP984: 42ft/12.08m); height 10ft 3in (3.12m) (XP984: 10ft 9m/3.27m)
Powerplant:	XP831, XP836 and XP872: one Pegasus 2 turbofan, producing 10,600lb (4,800kg) thrust XP831, XP976 and XP980: one Pegasus 3 turbofan, producing 13,500lb (6,100kg) thrust XP980 (ground running) and XP984: one Pegasus 5 turbofan, producing 15,500lb (7,000kg) thrust
Weights:	Empty, maximum 10,200lb (4,630kg) (XP984: 11,000lb/5,000kg); loaded, maximum 15,500lb (7,030kg) (XP984: 19,000lb/8,600kg)
Performance:	Maximum speed 715mph (1,150km/h) (XP984: 750mph/1,210km/h); normal service ceiling 49,800ft (15,200m) (XP984 55,000ft/16,800m)
Production:	Six aircraft built to Specification ER.204D, with serial numbers XP831, XP836, XP972, XP976, XP980 and XP984

PART THREE

1961 to 1964

CHAPTER TWENTY

Handley Page H.P.115

Slender and Slow

While the advantages of supersonic flight were considered to be mainly in the sphere of military aviation, both the National Physical Laboratory (NPL) and the RAE had accumulated a large amount of high-speed data that, in 1956, generated thoughts of supersonic flying being possible for civil airliners. The Ministry of Aviation (MoA) set up the Supersonic Transport Aircraft Committee (STAC) to integrate the recommendations of the individual government establishments with those of the aircraft industry. The Committee's first meeting was held at Farnborough on 5 November 1956, under the chairmanship of Morien (later Sir Morien) Morgan. As head of the Aerodynamic Flight Section at the RAE, he had formed the Advanced Bomber Project Group (ABPG) in the summer of 1947, to evaluate the designs submitted in response to Specification B.35/46, which gave birth to the V-Bomber force.

A Trio of Designs

Duncan Sandys' White Paper in April 1957 had focused the aircraft industry's design teams in the supersonic airliner market, with Avro, Bristol and Handley Page all taking up the challenge in submitting project designs. A. V. Roe had already considered a supersonic development of their Vulcan as the Type 735, powered by eight turbojets; in answer to the STAC proposals, they put forward a further development of the 735, with the company designation Type 760. Bristol's proposal was in fact a number of different projects, varying in size and configuration,

all grouped under the title Type 198. One early design featured an M-shaped wing planform for a Mach 1.3 aircraft powered by six Olympus 591 turbojets. When the STAC set the operational requirement at Mach 1.8, the M-wing was replaced by a slender delta with the six engines installed on the wing's upper surface.

By 1959, the STAC had raised its sights to an airliner capable of Mach 2.2, which was the limit of the acceptable effects of

An impression of one of the Handley Page designs to meet the original Specification X.197T, taking the wooden glider to the stage of having an engine. The position of the pitot boom indicated why the pilot requested its repositioning. Author's artwork

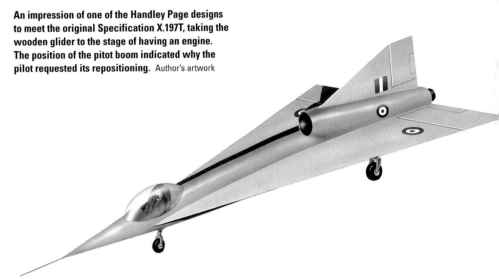

kinetic heat temperatures on the aluminium alloys of the day. Bristol repositioned the engines to the underside of their delta wing design, which was aimed at carrying 122 passengers in executive comfort over a range of 3,600 miles (5,800km) at 60,000ft (18,000m), with an all-up-weight of 385,000lb (175,000kg).

Handley Page submitted two proposals, the long-range Mach 1.8 H.P.109 and the medium-range Mach 1.3 H.P.110. However, by the beginning of the 1960s they, together with A. V. Roe, had withdrawn from the project, leaving just the Bristol Aeroplane Company. With the trans-Atlantic route as the goal, plus the realization that the size of aircraft being envisaged would produce a sonic boom of unacceptable severity, the company abandoned its

Type 198. A new design with the designation Type 223 was prepared, with a smaller fuselage carrying 100 passengers and powered by four higher-rated Olympus engines. The London to New York route was the target and it was calculated that the Type 223 would be able to operate at the Mach 2.2 limit set.

Anglo-French Agreement

No one can pretend that the British and French aircraft industries made natural bedfellows. However, Sud-Aviation had been developing a design under the title of the Super-Caravelle and, as its design parameters were similar to those being worked on by the British, the designs that emerged on either side of the English Channel bore a resemblance to each other. The Bristol 223 design was virtually finalized when, in the autumn of 1962, the almost unimaginable happened and the two countries' governments agreed to work together on a supersonic airliner. The Joint British-French project was signed on 29 November 1962 and Con-

corde was born – with the French having the final word by having the name finishing with an 'e'!

Ideas for Wing Testing

To embark on the production of an airliner with the performance stipulated meant that completely unknown territory had to be traversed before a myriad of questions could be satisfactorily answered. Research was needed to determine the flying and handling characteristics of such an aeroplane. With the wing established as an ogival planform, Bristol converted the first Fairey FD.2, WG774, into the BAC Type 221, to investigate the wing's behaviour at

the high-speed end of the flight envelope (see Chapter Sixteen).

However, in the United States, thoughts had also turned to civil supersonic flying and wind-tunnel tests on slender delta-wing planforms had concluded that handling at low speed would present problems that made the whole concept unacceptable. The RAE refuted the American conclusions, and W. E. Gray from the Establishment's team at Farnborough carved, by hand, model gliders that were flown off the 72ft (22m) high roof of the old 1907 Balloon Factory's hangar. From that height, the models' flight-path and flying time were long enough to provide accurate data. Obviously this could only be limited, but it was sufficient to warrant

ABOVE: Photographed before its maiden flight, the H.P.115 carries service markings and serial number but no ejector-seat warning triangle, as the Martin-Baker Mk 4 lightweight seat has yet to be installed (though the guide rails are in position). Derek James

BELOW: The fabric-covered wooden leading edge is discernable by the lack of reflections cast on the rest of the starboard wing. Author's collection

the Establishment proposing that an uncomplicated piloted slender-wing glider would provide even more data, as well as supplying information on the slow-speed properties of the ogival wing.

In order to complement the BAC 221's high-speed researches, Specification X.197T was raised in March 1959, to cover the design and construction of a slender delta-wing glider, to be built by Slingsby Sailplanes in conjunction with the RAE. Slingsby drew up a basic design for the glider at their Kirbymoorside works, but when Handley Page's deputy chief designer, Godfrey Lee, attended a meeting at the RAE, he thought Slingsby's proposal totally unacceptable and returned to his project office

The slimness of the whole design can be seen to advantage in these early air-to-air shots.
Handley Page Association

to draw up the type of glider that he thought was required. Although Bristol submitted its Type 215 glider, as well as designs from Fairey and Miles Aircraft being offered to meet the specification, Lee's design was accepted as being superior and the company allocated their Type number 115 to the project.

The Handley Page H.P.115 was designed as a glider but with a development potential that would allow the fitting of a small turbojet engine if necessary, in order to broaden the trial's parameters. The aircraft was a slender delta wing with a leading edge sweep of 74.7 degrees, to which was attached a basic fuselage to carry a pilot and instrumentation, a fin/rudder assembly and a fixed undercarriage. Provision was made for the wing leading edge to be detachable from the front spar, in order that alternative configurations, including a cambered and

an ogival leading edge, could be fitted. Various aircraft were considered as possible tugs for the glider, including the Canberra and the Gannet, but when the company submitted its brochure to the MoA, the glider was illustrated being towed by a Handley Page Hastings, naturally!

The 115 Receives Power

Although the idea of a glider seemed feasible to start with, its limitations were soon apparent. Take-off and landing could not be fully investigated, nor could its handling during a 'Dutch roll'. Consideration was given to fitting a small rocket motor, until the impracticalities of carrying rocket fuel within a wooden structure were recognized and the rocket idea was quickly discarded. Power was now to be

supplied by a small turbojet, and although redesigning would mean completing the aircraft later than originally scheduled, it was considered that it would prove to be a more useful research vehicle. In response to the changes, on 21 December 1959 the new Specification ER.197D was raised and Handley Page received Contract number KD/2N/02 for cover the construction of a powered H.P.115, for which serial number XP841 was reserved.

The chosen engine was the Bristol Siddeley Viper 9, producing 1,900lb (860kg) static thrust. The Viper had originally been an Armstrong Siddeley engine, designed to power target drones, before that company merged with Bristol Aero Engines to form Bristol Siddeley. It was in production as a family of small turbojets to be used in a variety of different aircraft, which was to include the Jet Provost and the GAF

Jindivik. It had been originally hoped to have the 2,460lb (1,120kg) thrust Viper 11 for the H.P.115, but this was not available at the time. Hunting's Jet Provost T.3 was in production, powered by a Viper 8 producing 1,750lb (790kg) thrust, and the Viper 9 was a limited production, up-rated version of this engine.

The Viper was positioned in a nacelle situated at the rear of the H.P.115, above the wing surface, with a bullet fairing inside the circular intake. A substantial cropped-delta-shaped fin/rudder assembly was mounted above the nacelle, while the pilot sat in a cockpit very close to the nose, under a bubble-shaped one piece canopy. Ahead of him, a long pitot boom projected from the pointed nose tip.

Change of Design and Material

Godfrey Lee's design was submitted to the MoA and their first reaction was that the whole nose section, complete with the bulbous canopy, would seriously interfere with the generation of the wing vortex. Furthermore, the RAE's designated pilot, Sqn Ldr Jack Henderson, when viewing the proposed shape, strongly objected to the pitot boom being immediately in line with his body: he thought that in the case of a taxiing mishap, if the boom hit an obstruction or another aeroplane there was a distinct possibility of his being impaled. To overcome these criticisms a

RAE Bedford's ownership of XP841 is well established and one of the numerous smoke/dye dispensing units that were fitted is shown in position, as is the substantial strutting required to hold the pitot boom in place. Author's collection and Handley Page Association

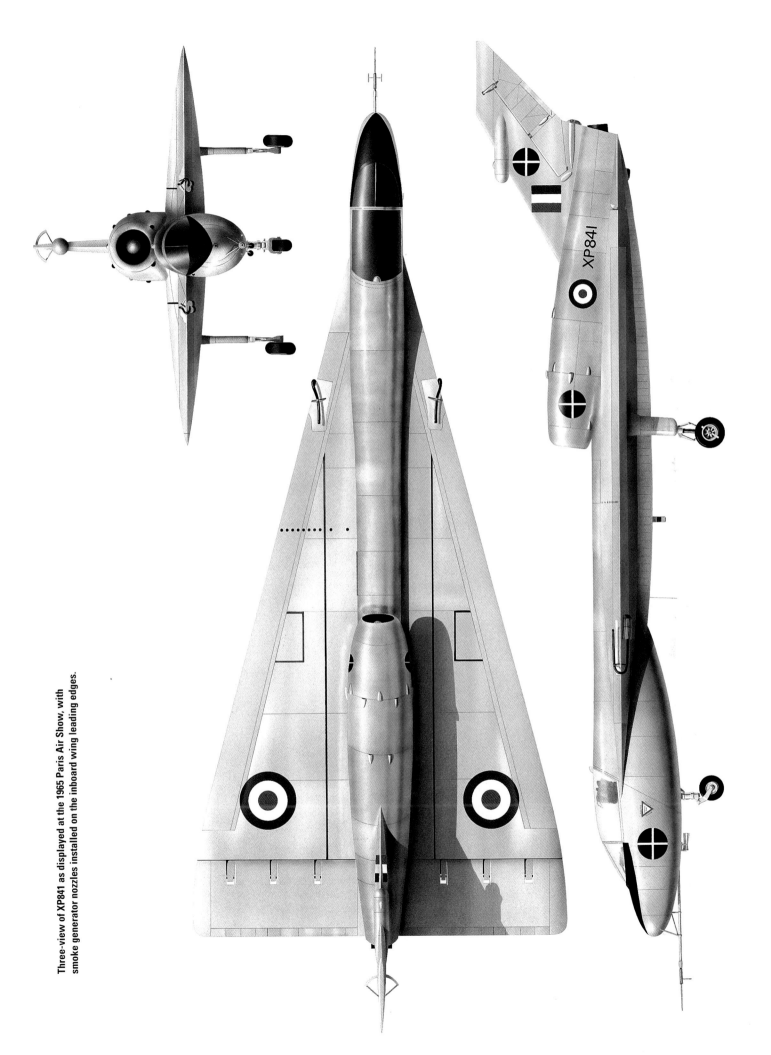

Three-view of XP841 as displayed at the 1965 Paris Air Show, with smoke generator nozzles installed on the inboard wing leading edges.

completely new front section for the pilot, sited lower on the aircraft's datum line, was designed as a slab-sided nacelle with a rounded nose, under which the pitot boom was supported by auxiliary structures.

The new configuration received official approval, but the fact that the construction was to be of wood raised some doubts, for expertise in this material was a fast disappearing art. There was also the fact that Lee had been informed of a 2,500lb (1,130kg) weight limit imposed by the MoA and the penalty for exceeding this figure was the loss of the contract.

Therefore, much to everyone's undisguised relief, it was decided that the H.P.115 would be made of metal. This was a material that everyone understood, and construction commenced at the company's Park Street works in the north London suburb of Cricklewood. RAE Bedford's Aero Flight Department liaised throughout the work and Sqn Ldr Henderson became involved as completion was approached. He spent much time in a simulator, programmed with wind-tunnel data, plus results from the free-fall model tests made from the hangar roof at Farnborough. A similar approach had been made when Short's S.B.5 was under construction, although the simulator supplied pessimistic readings compared to those obtained when flying the actual aircraft, and the Establishment hoped that this would also prove true when the H.P.115 took to the air.

In order to save time and money, it was proposed that an existing undercarriage should be used if possible. Investigations showed that the main wheels of the piston-engined Percival Provost could be used and this was confirmed by the unit's manufacturer, Palmer, although they recommended slight alterations. They also suggested that their nose-wheel unit designed for the Jet Provost would suit the Handley Page aeroplane, after being modified to make it a fixed installation. Agreement was reached with Palmer and the undercarriage units were delivered to Park Street.

Early in 1961, the completed airframe was transported by road to RAE Bedford, where the Viper 9 was installed. During construction it was decided to retain wood for the wing's leading edges, and they were manufactured in fabric-covered timber to a design where they could be easily removed when alternative leading-edge shapes were tested. Both the elevons and the top section of the rudder were also

fabric-covered. The cockpit was fitted with a Martin-Baker Mk 4 ejector seat, compatible with escape at ground level and low airspeeds. A total fuel capacity of 140gal (630ltr), carried in two wing tanks and one in the fuselage, meant that flight testing would have to be limited to a maximum of forty-five minutes per sortie.

Work-Up and Flight

The aircraft's arrival at Bedford heralded many months of intensive taxiing, with the speeds gradually being increased as confidence in its behaviour grew. Various positions of the centre of gravity, readings of tyre and brake temperatures, and deployment of the braking parachute, housed under the rudder's trailing edge, all had to be explored. Jack Henderson wanted to gain as much 'feel' and data as possible on what the Establishment regarded as a radical new aeronautical shape. Flight recorders were installed, in order to provide traces of every attitude, speed and height variable that it was thought the aircraft could possibly attain.

By the middle of August 1961, it was felt that all the ground-testing possible had been made, and Sqn Ldr Henderson considered that he knew the aircraft's characteristics enough to make a maiden flight. Calm weather conditions were required for the maiden flight as, although heavier than the previously-stipulated 2,500lb, it was still a light aeroplane. On 17 August, conditions were ideal and in the afternoon, XP841 became airborne for the first time. The flight lasted thirty minutes, which was long enough for Henderson to discover that all the prophesies of poor handling characteristics from the United States were completely groundless. He, the RAE and Handley Page were delighted with the maiden flight's results.

Display and New Ownership

The rest of August was taken up with further flight testing until 3 September, when the aircraft was flown to Farnborough to participate in the year's SBAC Display for a week – the flying characteristics of the slender delta wing at low speeds were appreciated by the technical experts assembled there from around the world. Then it was back to flight-testing to complete the manufacturer's trials programme.

With these completed, XP841 was transferred to the MoA's Air Fleet (of which the Aero Flight was a part) on 23 October 1961, to start the duties that were its whole *raison d'être*. Camera-reference markings, in the form of solid black circles containing white crosses, were applied to the fin, engine and cockpit nacelles. A true flight programme envelope was drawn up, and in all respects the H.P.115 was a far more pleasant aeroplane to fly than had been expected.

Although the Viper 9 was an uprated version of the Viper 8, it only produced 150lb (70kg) more thrust, so at 1,900lb (860kg) the power limited the maximum speed to just over 200mph (320km/h). A minimum touchdown speed of 103mph (166km/h) was possible while holding an acceptable angle of incidence, but in day-to-day operations the landing speed was slightly higher, at around 115mph (185km/h). At a flight-incidence angle of approximately 30 degrees, flying speeds as low as 70mph (110km/h) were regularly achieved without any loss of control, while almost instantaneous recovery could be made from any tendency to 'Dutch roll'.

Long and Busy Life

Over a four-year period from its delivery to the Aero Flight, XP841 produced a great wealth of low-speed handling data, relative not only to the Concorde programme, but to delta-wing research in general. Besides Jack Henderson, RAE pilots Angus McVitie and Ron Ledwidge took part in the various trials programmes, while American astronaut Neil Armstrong came over to Bedford from NASA to experience the aircraft's abilities.

Roland Beamont went to the RAE's airfield on 19 August 1963, where he received a very extensive briefing from Henderson before making two flights in the aircraft. He summarized the flights by declaring that the H.P.115 was 'a pleasantly responsive aircraft with adequate longitudinal and directional characteristics in the range of flight conditions checked'. He found 'adverse yaw was no more obtrusive than on the [English Electric] P.1'. Beamont told this author that he found it most enjoyable to fly and was surprised how little there was to do once you had got into the cockpit. With his vast number of hours at the controls of Canberras and the P.1, this is understandable.

Although XP841 had attended the previous year's show, at the 1964 SBAC Display it demonstrated the airflow over the upper wing surface by having its smoke dispensers in action. The undercarriage's wide main-wheel track is seen to advantage. Author's collection

More Demonstrations and an Injury

XP841 had its full share of attendances at the SBAC Displays, with the original one in 1961 being followed by a repeat in 1962 and a final presentation in 1964, which was the first of the biennial Displays. At the latter, the aircraft was fitted with smoke generators that ejected over both inboard upper wing surfaces, used in airflow-visualization trials as a replacement for the earlier wool tufts.

Two months after the 1964 Display, XP841 suffered its only major accident: on 20 November, it hit a runway obstruction while taking off from Bedford, which resulted in the port undercarriage unit being spread outwards at an angle of 60 degrees. Both the tower's duty controller and the pilot of a chase aircraft who witnessed the accident thought that Jack Henderson should eject, but he had enough confidence in the aircraft's handling to opt for a landing once fuel had been burned off. On touching down, the pilot held the port wing high for as long as possible, to limit the damage. As a result, a speedy repair was made without too much delay to the trials programme.

The biennial 'Farnboroughs' alternated with the Paris Air Show, and so that it did not miss out on a public demonstration, XP841 participated in the French capital's 1965 show, where it was observed to have had changes in the contours of the smoke generator nozzles. In fact, during its test-flying life, three different nozzles were fitted, with at least one of them ejecting red ink and kaolin dye instead of smoke.

A different set of trials was started in 1966, when the H.P.115 was fitted with Hartmann noise generators plus microphones, to investigate sideline and overhead vortex decibels associated with slender delta wings. This particular series of tests was a part of the Concorde development programme and several different positions were used for the unit's installation. Some time during its life, XP841 had the underwing perforated airbrakes removed, as the very low speeds at which it was capable of flying made them superfluous.

Engine Wear Brings Exodus

The only real problem encountered with the H.P.115 during the whole of its test-flying career was engine wear. Due to its low thrust, the Viper 9 had to be nearly always operated close to, or at, full power for every sortie, which produced a much higher level of wear than had been anticipated. In addition, there was considerable compressor deterioration, brought about by the ingestion of smoke generated during the visual vortex tests. After each smoke-trial, the whole engine had to undergo a washing procedure and,

inevitably, compressor performance gradually deteriorated. By the second half of 1965, a new Viper 9 had to be installed.

Naturally the new engine was subjected to the same effects, but it did last until 1973. By this time, the aircraft had come to a point where its input into slender delta-wing handling evaluations did not justify the installing of a third engine, so it was placed in storage at RAE Bedford.

On 31 January 1974, XP841 flew for the last time. This was a delivery flight to RAF Colerne, where several historic aircraft were stored at that time, prior to being allocated to specific museums. For the H.P.115, this was an eighteen-month sojourn before being transported by road in June 1975 to the Aerospace Museum, as Cosford was called in those days. It remained among Cosford's research aircraft collection for several years, but when the Fleet Air Arm opened its dedicated Concorde display, XP841 was transferred to Yeovilton and today stands alongside Concorde 002 G-BSST and BAC.221, thereby displaying the research work that was undertaken at both ends of the flight programme when the supersonic airliner was being developed.

Technical Data – Handley Page H.P.115	
Dimensions:	Span 20ft (6.09m); length 46ft 6in (14.17m) excluding nose boom, 50ft 4in (15.36m) including nose boom; height 12ft 9in (3.88m)
Powerplant:	One Bristol Siddeley, Armstrong Siddeley designed, ASV.9 Viper, producing 1,900lb (860kg) thrust
Weights:	Empty 3,880lb (1,760kg); loaded 5,050lb (2,290kg)
Performance:	Maximum speed 201mph (322km/h); minimum speed 70mph (113km/h); maximum endurance 45 minutes
Production:	One aircraft built to Specification ER.197D, with serial number XP841

CHAPTER TWENTY-ONE

Bristol Type 188

High-Temperature Hopeful

Although the Bristol Aeroplane Company Ltd was a late-comer in the pure-turbojet field, it produced an aeroplane that was beautiful but brutal-looking, with high research ambitions that were not realized, although it was through no fault on the part of its manufacturer. Furthermore, it was the last aircraft that was constructed under the 'Bristol' banner.

True Pedigree

On 19 February 1910, wealthy Bristolian Sir George White formed a company for his single-minded purpose of manufacturing and flying aeroplanes. He acquired the former depot of the company that had evolved from the electric tramways that he had pioneered, the Bristol Tramways Company. Situated at Filton, on the outskirts of Bristol, the spacious buildings were ideal to satisfy the manufacturing side of his ambitions and he established a flying school at Brooklands, with a secondary base for tuition at Larkhill. From the year of its foundation, the company designed and produced aeroplanes that are at the very core of British aeronautical history. The 'Boxkite', F.2A/F.2B, Bulldog, Blenheim and Beaufighter all put the Bristol name in the forefront of aviation development and the ill-fated, underpowered Brabazon is still the largest landplane ever built in Britain. The company's Bristol Aero Engine offshoot has been even more prominent, supplying power units for aircraft worldwide.

With this pedigree, it appears surprising that the company did not turn to the turbojet until twelve years after 'Gerry' Sayer had made his historic flight in the Gloster E.28/39. It can be argued that the company was preoccupied with the Type 175 Britannia, born of Brabazon Committee recommendations, as well as entering the helicopter field, although the Project Office first put forward unsuccessful proposals for a long-range, high-speed bomber in 1946.

Further Ambitions

In 1951, Specification UB.109 was issued and Bristol put forward their Type 182. The specification, code-named *Blue Rapier*, was for a radio-guided, steam-catapult-launched, expendable bomber, capable of cruising at 600mph (970km/h) over a 400-mile (640km) range, with a 5,000lb (2,300kg) warhead. Designed together with the engine company, it was to be powered by the new BE.22 disposable engine giving 3,500lb (1,600kg) thrust. A new material, Durestos, had been developed for aircraft construction, which was much lighter and cheaper than the alternative, welded steel. Bristol's estimate was £600 per airframe as the structural cost, and the MoS began thinking in terms of a production total of 20,000 aircraft!

In order to start flight testing as early as possible and bearing in mind the time required to develop moulding techniques to form the Durestos sections, two metal, non-expendable prototypes were put in hand, powered by the Armstrong Siddeley Viper. However, in 1953, the whole UB.109 concept was consigned to the well-stocked drawer marked 'good ideas at the time'.

The one positive thing to come out of the project was the further development of the BE.22 as a non-expendable engine, which eventually became the very successful Orpheus.

Type 188's Origins

With the abandoning of UB.109, the Air Staff concentrated their thoughts on the matter of ultra-long-range supersonic reconnaissance aircraft, equipped with very advanced electronics, to operate in conjunction with the high-altitude V-bomber force that was being established. It was to be capable of operating at altitudes that would make it invulnerable to existing and future interceptors or anti-aircraft missiles. Operational Requirement 330 was taken up by four companies and Avro emerged victorious with their Type 730. This was a canard design, with a stainless-steel, brazed-honeycomb construction, powered by eight Armstrong Siddeley P.176 engines. Specification RB.156D was raised to cover the design and many changes took place over the next two years, from which emerged the fact that new materials were being proposed, not the least

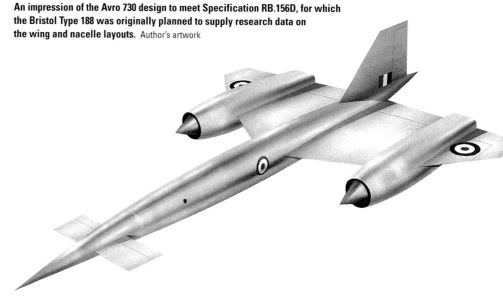

An impression of the Avro 730 design to meet Specification RB.156D, for which the Bristol Type 188 was originally planned to supply research data on the wing and nacelle layouts. Author's artwork

The first Type 188, XF923, stands with external fire extinguishers installed in large bulged fairings on the starboard side of each nacelle. Although there was provision for having the braking parachute in the tip of the rear fuselage, on XF923 it was carried in an external housing on the port side of the rear fuselage; it is receiving attention in this shot.
Author's collection and *Aeroplane*

of these being stainless steel, which needed to be tested.

New Frontiers

In 1953, Britain's experience of flying sustained Mach 2.5 missions was non-existent. Specification ER.134 was raised to cover the design and manufacture of a research aeroplane, to investigate the effects of long periods of high-frictional temperatures on an airframe. Several companies showed an interest, but it was Bristol Aircraft that came up with a viable project in their Type 188 proposal, for which the company received an Order to Proceed. In January 1954 they received Contract number KC/2M/04/CB.42(b) for three airframes, two with serial numbers XF923 and XF926 being the flying prototypes, the third to be a static-test airframe. The aircraft's principal task was to prove the Avro 730's construction material, together with flight testing the wing planform and nacelle shape.

Design work and static material testing at Bristol occupied the next three years, with a complementary amount of airframe work being expended by Avro, until April 1957, when the infamous Sandys' White Paper landed on the aircraft industry.

OR330, Specification RB.156D and the Avro 730 were discarded, and the portions of airframe that had been completed were cut up for use around the works as dump-bins for metal scraps.

A Change of Role and Headaches

The proposed shape of the Type 188, incorporating Avro 730 elements, was abandoned and the design amended to the shape required for a pure research aircraft, to be used to evaluate the effects of kinetic heating for prolonged periods of supersonic flight. A further stipulation injected into the requirements was that, as it was to be a research aircraft, it should have the capacity to accept different engines without structural changes.

From the beginning, the use of stainless steel presented enormous difficulties. It took a considerable amount of investigation by Bristol into the steel industry before the grade of metal, with the necessary uniformity and strength, was eventually guaranteed through a collaboration with Firth Vickers. But that was only one part of the saga. Having established the right grade of steel, getting it in large enough sheets with the required thickness and flatness tolerances created further problems. Then, as if these were not enough, the coupling of sections required that all screws, bolts and rivets had to be formed from materials that were compatible with the high temperatures that were anticipated in fulfilling the specification, although these temperatures had yet to be accurately confirmed.

To meet the great number of complications, Bristol eventually developed a technique of argon arc-welding, that became known as 'puddle-welding', which was the regulated fusion of the steel, employing an arc with its electrodes surrounded by the inert gas argon. Research in this field had also been made by Armstrong Whitworth Aircraft at Coventry, which resulted in them giving generous assistance to Filton, which was repaid by Bristol subcontracting the manufacture of the tail assembly, cockpit canopy and outer wing sections to the Coventry-based company.

An Act of Faith

When the Avro 730 was a live project, it was scheduled to be powered by the new Rolls-Royce RA.24R engine, producing 14,430lb (6,540kg) thrust with reheat. Therefore, when the Type 188 was conceived, being a part of the Avro 730's research programme, it was to feature a scaled-down wing/nacelle assembly for the RA.24R. With the killing of the reconnaissance aircraft, the Rolls-Royce engine went with it. Another victim of the government's action was the Saunders-Roe SR.177 interceptor, which was designed around an even newer engine, the de Havilland DGJ.10R Gyron Junior, from

The degree of work carried out on the structural test airframe could not be more graphically demonstrated than it is here. Author's collection

BELOW: Almost a year was spent on Gyron Junior ground-running trials, during which time this photograph was taken. Blanking strips were positioned over the suction-relief doors at the front of the nacelles, while the external fire extinguishers had yet to be installed. Author's collection

which a thrust of 14,000lb (6,350kg) was promised, with reheat. About a dozen of these engines were in various stages of construction and, as they were now going spare, without any future application in sight, the MoS decreed that the Type 188 was to be powered by the de Havilland engine.

Therefore, the situation was that a new airframe, powered by an engine chosen because it was surplus to immediate requirements, was going to undertake research into a totally unknown sphere of flight. This must have been one of the greatest acts of faith upon which British aviation ever embarked. Based on design calculations, it was anticipated that the Bristol 188 would be the world's fastest conventionally operated aircraft, bearing in mind that the North American X-15 was designed to be air-launched – although Kelly Johnson in the Lockheed 'Skunk Works', was possibly unconvinced. He had the SR-71 on the drawing board.

Testing Times

A series of wind-tunnel tests was conducted while the three airframes were being constructed. These were augmented by the launching of rocket-propelled free-flight models by the RAE at their Aberporth facility, in what was then known as Cardiganshire. As a result of these trials, various changes in the aircraft's configuration were implemented. The wing centre section was redesigned to a more rectangular planform, having swept fillets at both the fuselage and nacelle joining points. Large horn-balanced ailerons were sited outboard of the nacelles, which in effect provided moving wing-tip control surfaces. The fin chord was greatly increased and the all-moving tailplane was repositioned on the fin's top. The author saw the first aircraft in an advanced state of construction at Filton and was surprised how the sharp wing leading edges were covered by custom-built gloves. With the wing having a 4 per cent thickness/chord ratio, it is possible that the gloves were as much to provide protection for the workforce, as to prevent inadvertent damage to the wing. The finish was just about as smooth as it can get and was a lot smoother than any other aircraft that the author had previously seen: no fillers used to smooth panel joints, or copious coats of paint rubbed down to a smooth finish. Just well-constructed, virgin metal and a credit to its makers.

Roll-out and Frustration

When XF923 first saw the light of day, on 26 April 1961, it looked impressive from every angle. The long, narrow fuselage had a cross-section that was determined by the smallest elliptical area that could accommodate a Martin-Baker Mk 4 ejector seat. The tricycle undercarriage, situated well behind the cockpit section, had a nose-wheel featuring twin side-by-side wheels, with the whole unit retracting forwards into the lower nose section, while thin, single main wheels retracted into the wing centre-section which, because of its low thickness/chord ratio, required slight bulges in the lower skin surface. To the front, a sharply tapering nose-cone was extended by an instrument boom projecting nearly 7ft (2m) ahead of it. At the rear end of the fuselage, an enormous fin/rudder assembly, with a 65-degree swept leading edge and a cropped delta appearance, carried a tailplane with a generous area. The fuselage tapered at the end to a sharp tail-cone, housing the braking/anti-spin parachute, although for some reason the first prototype carried its parachute in an additional external housing in the port side. The main airbrakes were unusual in that they were in tandem, on either side of the rear fuselage; when activated, the front pair hinged outwards from their tops, while the rear pair were hinged at their bases. When deployed, they presented substantial perforated faces to the airflow; they were designed in this manner because of the rapid actuation required when the aircraft was flying at high Mach numbers.

Either side of the fuselage was a massive engine nacelle, which was nearly half the length of the fuselage itself and almost the same diameter. Pointed variable-positioning centre-bodies projected from the circular intakes. The diameter of the jet outlets at the rear was greater than that of the intakes.

The length of the fuselage and nacelles was visually accentuated by the short wingspan and the narrow thickness/chord ratio. With the wings being so thin, it was impossible to fit fuel tanks in them, so the total capacity of 1,000gal (4,500ltr) was carried in two fuselage tanks positioned fore and aft of a centrally sited equipment bay. A second equipment bay was located between the forward tank and the cockpit, while a third was sited in the nose. These bays contained telemetering and electronic recording apparatus, and one of them housed the

cockpit refrigeration system. The state-of-the-art electronics were for transmitting data to a ground control room, manned by an engineer and a pilot, thereby reducing the workload of the airborne pilot. While such equipment is commonplace today and even extends to Formula 1 racing cars, for 1961 it was very ahead of its time.

From the day of roll-out at Filton, almost a year of frustration was to occur, mostly centring on the Gyron Junior engines. During ground runs, the engines produced many surging problems and a considerable amount of time was spent experimenting with the intakes, together with the variable centre-bodies, but with only partial success. At the other end of the nacelles, the reheat units produced problems of their own, but to a large extent these were solved.

Flying at Last

Due to the engine problems, it was February 1962 before Bristol's Chief Test Pilot, Godfrey Auty, started taxiing trials. He had taken over when Bill Pegg retired in 1960, after twelve years of test-flying that had included nearly all the Brabazon trials. After XF923's initial taxiing, there followed several weeks of adverse weather, with high winds being the major cause of holding back on the maiden flight. They abated by 14 April and Auty lifted the aircraft off Filton's runway for the first time. The flight, which was in essence a delivery flight of the aircraft to Boscombe Down, was not without its moments of drama, as the radio suffered intermittent malfunctions and a hydraulic pipe sprang a leak. In fact, in retrospect it can be seen that the Type 188 was giving notice that it was going to be far from a trouble-free aeroplane. Twenty-five minutes after take-off Godfrey Auty landed at Boscombe Down, from where the aircraft was going to operate during early test flying.

The next six months were spent in evaluating the Type 188's low-speed handling characteristics, followed by a gradual increase in speed, until Mach 1 was exceeded. However, problems of engine surge escalated at supersonic speeds, and during its time at the A&AEE only nineteen sorties were flown. Then, in the first week of September, XF923 had a flying slot in the SBAC Display programme. It certainly gave a favourable impression at low level with its fast, silent approach, followed by a cacophonous departure, but this belied the true picture.

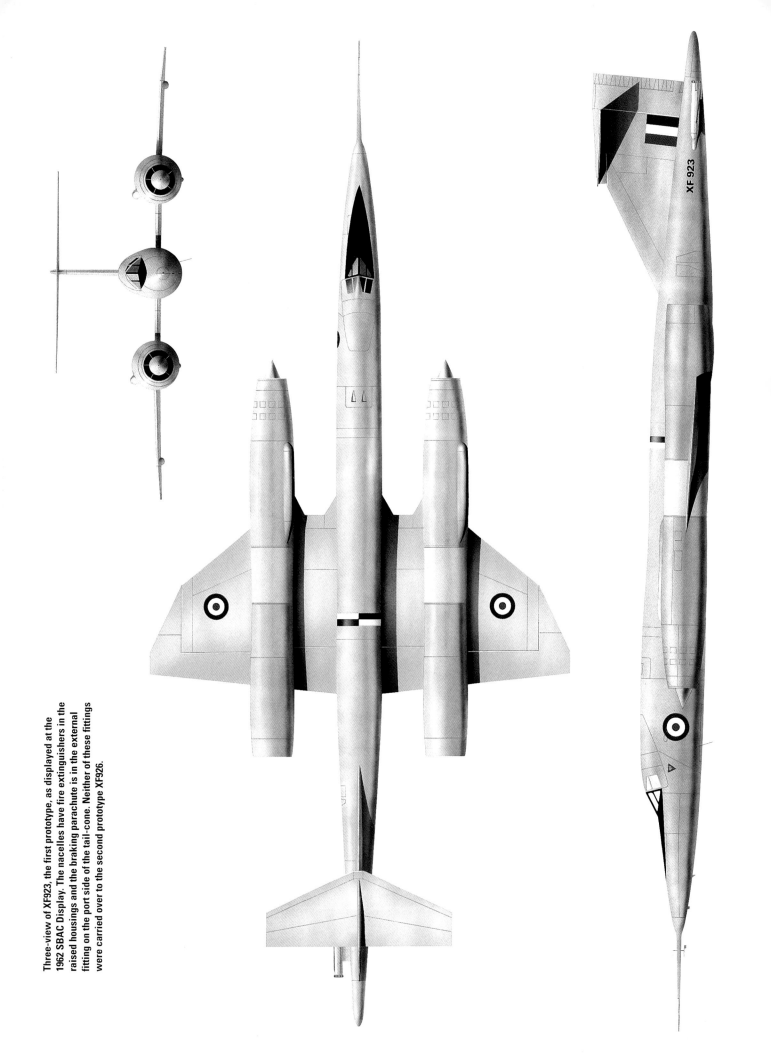

Three-view of XF923, the first prototype, as displayed at the 1962 SBAC Display. The nacelles have fire extinguishers in the raised housings and the braking parachute is in the external fitting on the port side of the tail-cone. Neither of these fittings were carried over to the second prototype XF926.

XF 923

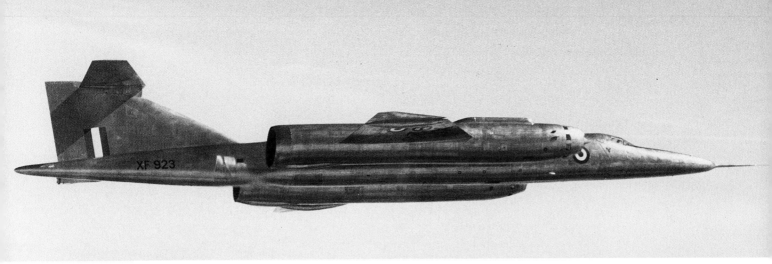

TOP: **On 14 April 1962, the first Type 188 had its maiden flight, shown here with the airbrakes on the rear fuselage slightly deployed.**
Aeroplane

ABOVE: **The braking parachute is activated from its external housing on touchdown. It can be observed that the line is quite short, with the canopy consisting of multiple ribbons.**
Author's collection

Two's Company

XF923 flew back to Filton on 15 November, but was only flown a few times during the winter. In the early spring of 1963, the second prototype, XF926, emerged from the assembly hall and had its first flight on 29 April. The aircraft was very similar in appearance to its predecessor, except that the external braking parachute housing, and the fire extinguishers carried in bulges on the first prototype's engine nacelles, had been deleted.

Two aircraft meant twice the trouble in relation to the engine surging problem, and by this time it had become patently obvious that the Type 188 was not going to fulfil the requirements of Specification ER.134, which called for an aircraft capable of maintaining Mach 2 long enough to obtain worthwhile data. The fact that this was not going to be possible was underlined by the Gyron Junior's excessive fuel consumption, which was very different from the figures anticipated by de Havilland

Engines. The highest speed attained was Mach 1.9 and this could not be held for more than two minutes, before the fuel limitations required the aircraft to decelerate and return to base. Possibly this was just as well, for the surge phenomenon made the aircraft very difficult to control at the higher speeds.

Enforced Retirement

The obvious answer to the whole dilemma was a change of engine, with its associated redesign of the intakes. Although the ability to do this had been stipulated in the specification, in reality it presented financial implications that had not been considered back in 1953.

In addition to these constraints, the Air Staff had changed their priorities and the days of the high-altitude, high-speed bomber had gone. February 1964 saw the official declaration that the V-bombers were to operate at low level, and a few

months later the whole Type 188 programme was ended, with less than fifty hours' flying being made by the two aircraft in a total of seventy-eight sorties. The poor performance of the Type 188 was to a large extent outside the manufacturer's control and, in retrospect, far from providing data on kinetic heating, the aircraft's main contribution was proving the feasibility in the UK of real-time telemetry whereby test data can be evaluated as it occurs. The total expenditure of £20 million was a lot of money in the mid-1960s and, while by today's standards it was 'small beer', it did exceed the combined Brabazon and Princess programmes by nearly £5 million.

Both prototypes were consigned to the Proof and Experimental Establishment at Shoeburyness, but fortunately someone with authority stepped in and XF926 was reprieved. The airframe was refurbished and eventually presented to Cosford, where today it is displayed among their research aircraft collection – but the engines are not included!

TOP: **Another shot taken during XF923's prolonged engine ground-running trials, with the suction-relief doors open and everyone well equipped with ear-muff sound diffusers.** Author's collection

ABOVE: **The second Type 188, XF926, touches down at Filton after its maiden flight on 29 April 1963, shepherded home by Hunter F.6 XF509. The braking parachute was housed in its proper location at the end of the rear fuselage and the nacelles show that their suction-relief doors are closed, as well as them not having external fire extinguishers.** *Aeroplane*

Technical Data – Bristol Type 188	
Dimensions:	Span 35ft 1in (10.69m); length 71ft (21.64m) excluding nose boom, 77ft 8in (23.68m) including nose boom; height 13ft 11in (4.23m)
Powerplants:	Two de Havilland DGJ.10R Gyron Junior turbojets, each producing 10,000lb (4,500kg) thrust dry and 14,000lb (6,350kg) thrust with reheat
Performance:	Maximum speed achieved Mach 1.9
Production:	Two aircraft built to Specification ER.134, with serial numbers XF923 and XF926

CHAPTER TWENTY-TWO

Hunting H.126

High-Lifter from Luton

The airport at Luton had comprehensive aviation connections long before the Greeks came bearing cheap-flight seats. In 1936, Capt Edgar Percival relocated his aeroplane design and manufacturing company to Luton from Gravesend, where it had been founded four years previously.

From their pre-war success with the Gull series evolved the Proctor, one of the RAF's principal communications aircraft. This was followed by production of 1,356 Airspeed Oxfords and 245 de Havilland Mosquitoes, which kept the company well occupied throughout World War Two. Luton's aviation activities increased in 1940 when Napier's Experimental Engine Installation Unit had to leave Northolt, on Fighter Command's orders, and set up alongside Percival's works. During the war, one of the activities that kept the Unit busy was the modification work necessary to keep several Folland 43/37 engine test bed airframes supplied with engines to test.

After the war, the two companies' work became intertwined through research work that had started at the National Gas Turbine Establishment (NGTE), situated at Pyestock, on the northern side of the RAE's Farnborough airfield.

The Percival/Napier Association

Towards the end of 1950, Napier started design work to produce a system of rotor-tip power for use by helicopters. Next door, Percival Aircraft had established a Helicopter Division, whose research centred on a system whereby a gas-turbine's gases could be ducted through the rotor blades, to exhaust at the tips. One year later, appreciating that they were thinking along similar lines, the two companies combined their efforts to fulfil Specification EH.125D, which had been written to cover the design and building of a helicopter using the rotor-tip exhausting concept.

Percival received Contract number 6/ACFT/7054/CB.8(a) on 8 May 1952 to produce the ten-seater Percival P.74, powered by a pair of Napier Oryx engines. This was a small single-shaft turbo-gas-generator with a twelve-stage compressor that, in its first Nor.1 variant, produced 750 gas horsepower for a fuel consumption of 0.68lb/hr/ghp.

Company politics came into play in 1954. Percival Aircraft had been a member of the Hunting Group since 1944 and the company was now renamed Percival Hunting; from now on, the P.74 project was completed under the new company banner. When it emerged, the helicopter had a dumpy body, coming to a point at the rear, where a small tail rotor was fitted. Above the fuselage, a large three-bladed rotor with hollow blades carried exhaust gas outlets at each tip. Because of their non-existent experience in helicopter flying, Percival Hunting borrowed Fairey Aviation's chief helicopter pilot, Ron Gellatly, together with his co-pilot, John Morton, in 1957, to undertake the test-flying programme of the P.74, which carried the military serial XK889. However, the P.74 proved totally incapable of leaving the ground, so the two Fairey pilots went home and the whole concept was abandoned after just three hours' ground running.

Uplifting Thoughts

In the early 1950s, the NGTE started researching the different applications to which the power of the turbojet engine could be applied. By 1952, some of these thoughts had crystallized into researching the deflection of engine exhaust through thin slots at a wing's trailing edge, to increase the limiting lift coefficient to more than twelve, in order to improve landing and take-off performance. The original concept of channelling all the efflux as a high-velocity 'jet-flap' was replaced, after further research, by the idea of directing a smaller percentage of the flow through a

number of nozzles around a radiused trailing edge. The rest of the exhaust would be directed through a conventional jet-pipe. There followed two years of experimentation with models, by the end of which it was appreciated that the system could not be taken further without installing it in an aeroplane for flight-testing.

The most cost-effective way to achieve this was by modifying an existing aircraft, and the de Havilland Canada DHC.3 Otter appeared best suited to meet the requirements. The Pratt & Whitney Twin Wasp radial piston engine would be retained to provide conventional flight power, while a pair of Rolls-Royce RB.108s would be installed inside the fuselage to power the jet flaps. However, by 1957, it was considered by the Establishment, in liaison with the RAE, that a modified Otter would not be the most efficient way of furthering the principle, and it was accepted that the proper course would be to have a purpose-built aeroplane designed. Another two years were taken up with calculations and costing until, in May 1959, Specification ER.189 was raised in order that things could proceed.

New Name and an Order

Not only was the P.74 scrapped in 1957, but the name Hunting Percival followed suit, with the company becoming Hunting Aircraft; Edgar Percival went his own way, to found the Edgar Percival Aircraft Company. Hunting became involved with the NGTE in its jet-flap research, and drew up several different designs that it thought would provide the aircraft that the Establishment required. Because of the experience gained in jet-flow ducting with the P.74, and despite the failure of that particular project, Hunting was considered to be well placed to build an aeroplane to Specification ER.189D. Consequently, on 16 June 1959, the company received Contract number KD/23/01/CB.10(c), without the specification being

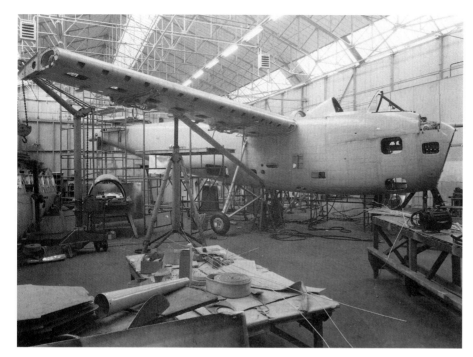

The H.126 during construction between 1959 and 1962, with the large hole showing at the end of the wing being where the ducting will emerge to be fitted with a roll-control valve. *Aeroplane*

put out to tender with other manufacturers. The contract covered all design work, together with the building of two prototypes, given serial numbers XN714 and XN719. Hunting's designation H.126 was applied to the project and it was considered expedient for the company to maintain close co-operation with RAE Bedford throughout the programme. As things turned out, the H.126 was the one and only indigenous design to be manufactured and flown by the company on its own – at least until it was handed over to the RAE's Aero Flight.

Construction Commences

With Hunting putting forward numerous configurations, considerable deliberation took place between them, the RAE and the NGTE. The design considered best was an aircraft with a well-strutted shoulder wing of high aspect ratio and a fixed tricycle undercarriage. Although the design was accepted, the question of which engine would best suit the operating requirements, while fitting into a rather limited space, took nearly two years to solve. The Bristol Siddeley Orpheus 805, rated at 4,850lb

(2,200kg) static thrust was eventually selected, although it was considered advisable to derate the engine for the H.126's purposes. Approximately 20 per cent of the turbojet's output would be lost in the labyrinth of ducting that was going to run from the engine to twenty-two outlets in the airframe.

Metal was first cut in the autumn of 1959, but this only heralded three years of construction that was required to produce the aircraft. While this seems an inordinately long time, the second airframe was also started in this time. It was the conveyance of hot exhaust through the wings and fuselage structure that presented a whole new raft of engineering challenges. Various materials were tried, including steel, but standard light-alloy stressed skin was eventually used through the whole construction. This required that very good ducting insulation was maintained within the wings, while an efficient system of heat-reflective shielding had to be incorporated within the fuselage.

The H.126 is rolled-out from the Hunting assembly shop in August 1962, with all the cockpit glazing, and the nose intake, masked prior to the aircraft receiving its vivid yellow colour scheme. *Aeroplane*

The three ducts within each wing were individually lagged before being covered with a steel reflective shield, after which they were insulated in a tunnel within the wings, that itself was internally lined with yet another steel reflective shield. Cool air, drawn in via slots under both wings' leading edges, circulated within the tunnel, which reduced the installation's radiant temperature from the 600°C of the jet gas, to a 170°C reading taken outside the tunnel. This would be further reduced once the aircraft was airborne, as the airflow would reduce the temperature of the wing structure to approximately 60°C.

Many months were spent on flap and aileron experimenting. With 600°C exhaust gases being ejected across the top surfaces and the lower skin being only about 60°C, the great problem of differential expansion had to be overcome in order to maintain the aerodynamic profile. This aspect alone epitomizes Hunting's abilities, for they ran a specimen section on test for over 100 hours to obtain the right result.

The Orpheus was situated unusually far forward under the cockpit floor, so that the exhaust gases would be able to be deflected into the wings without too many changes of direction. This was achieved by the jet efflux flowing via a 90-degree deflector, into a distributor that was colloquially referred to as the 'dustbin'. From this, 60 per cent of the gases flowed down the three ducts in each wing to discharge through fishtail outlets, with a small amount being ducted to a roll nozzle at each wing tip. On each wing, the whole of the trailing edge, apart from the tip, was occupied by a narrow-chord flap and aileron, with the latter effectively being an extension of the flap. They could be lowered in unison, although each had their own operating jacks inside prominent fairings. The exhaust gases flowed in a thin sheet over the flying surfaces, no matter what their attitude.

Forty per cent of the engine's exhaust bypassed the 'dustbin'. Thirty per cent provided direct thrust through a rectangular-sectioned orifice on each side of the lower fuselage centre-section. The final 10 per cent was channelled down a pipe to a pair of yaw nozzles positioned one on each side of the fuselage, and a pair of pitch-control nozzles installed in an extension of the rear fuselage. They operated so that as power was increased, the natural pitch-down effect was balanced by an upwards pitch from the low thrust-line, which resulted in trim changes being minimal.

XN714 with Hunting's Chief Test Pilot, 'Olly' Oliver, at the controls. No one could say that XN714 was a pretty aeroplane, but it was very functional in the research programme for which it was designed; it existed virtually unmodified during its whole life. Author's collection

High-Ratio Cauldron

The large amount of high-temperature gas being directed around the inside of the H.126's airframe dictated that a comprehensive fire-warning set-up should be installed. This requirement was met by the American Fenwall system, which was triggered to be activated at 405°C, which was marginally above the duct-lagging temperature. In order to give a comprehensive warning system, 130 thermo-couples were positioned within the airframe, which provided exact overall monitoring coverage virtually anywhere in the airframe.

Earlier in the 1950s, the French Hurel-Dubois H.D.34 had employed a high-aspect-ratio wing and in 1956–57, Miles Aircraft had converted Aerovan G-AHDM, in conjunction with Avions Hurel-Dubois, to have a similar wing, renaming the aircraft the Miles H.D.M.105. The H.126's wingspan was not as great as the H.D.34's, but it did have an aspect ratio of 9:1 and was set at a 4-degree angle of dihedral. Initially, it was designed to have 8 degrees of dihedral, but during construction the lower angle was considered more acceptable, so that when XN714 was first rolled out from Hunting's assembly shop at Luton in 1962 in an unpainted condition, it certainly was a large but strange-looking aeroplane, and this was not really enhanced when it was later painted an overall vivid yellow, apart from the flying control surfaces, which remained natural metal. Its uniqueness was guaranteed for,

during the time of construction, the second aircraft was cancelled and the work that had already taken place was scrapped. The multiple main-wheel struts, together with a substantial strut running from the lower fuselage to each wing, plus a strut supporting the nose-wheel, gave it an appearance of antiquity that was enhanced by a pitot boom projecting from the upper nose section, reminiscent of a unicorn.

But it Flies

XN714's taxiing began at Luton, with Hunting's Chief Test Pilot, Stanley 'Olly' Oliver, at the controls, seated on a Martin-Baker Mk 4 ejector seat under a large bulging canopy. Oliver had served with the RAF and the Fleet Air Arm before taking an Instructor's Course at the Central Flying School, Little Rissington. He graduated from the Empire Test Pilot's School's No. 9 course before joining Hunting.

RAE Bedford built a simulator to demonstrate flight characteristics in the 55–140mph (90–225km/h) speed range and Oliver considered that, as the simulator was a fairly basic structure, if he could master it then the actual aircraft should not be too difficult. One thing it did prove was that the simulator's reaction to an engine failure confirmed the Hunting design team's original calculations.

Luton was ruled out as the base from which the H.126 could make its maiden flight or even undertake the flight trials

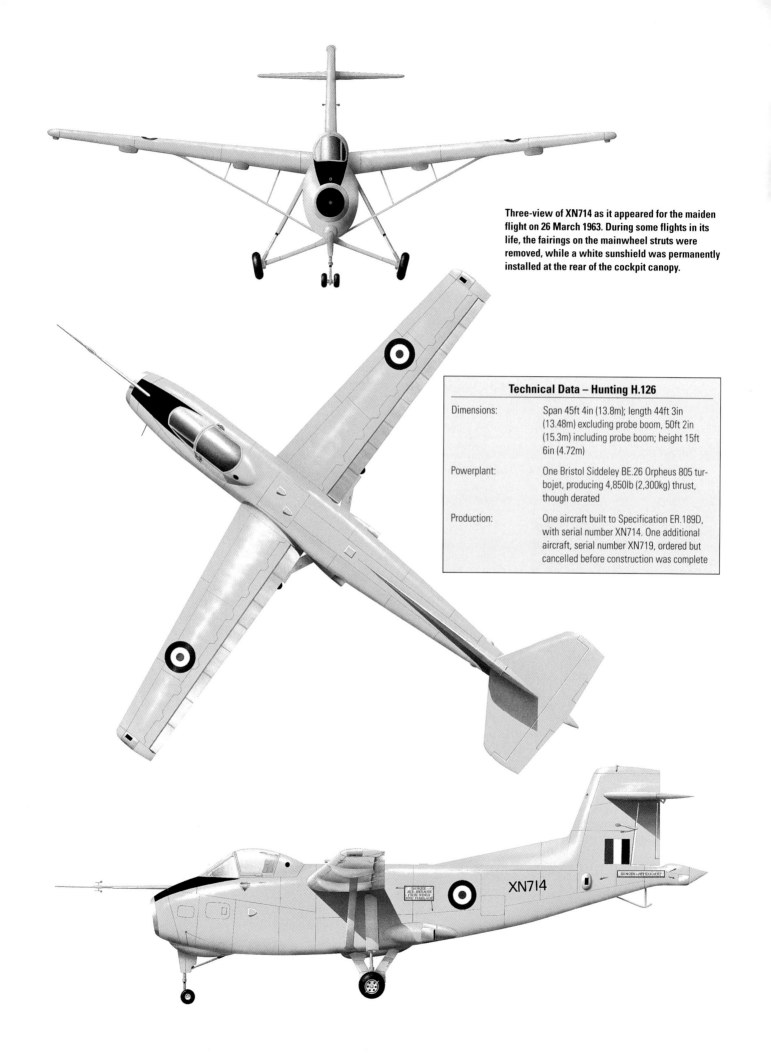

Three-view of XN714 as it appeared for the maiden flight on 26 March 1963. During some flights in its life, the fairings on the mainwheel struts were removed, while a white sunshield was permanently installed at the rear of the cockpit canopy.

Technical Data – Hunting H.126

Dimensions:	Span 45ft 4in (13.8m); length 44ft 3in (13.48m) excluding probe boom, 50ft 2in (15.3m) including probe boom; height 15ft 6in (4.72m)
Powerplant:	One Bristol Siddeley BE.26 Orpheus 805 turbojet, producing 4,850lb (2,300kg) thrust, though derated
Production:	One aircraft built to Specification ER.189D, with serial number XN714. One additional aircraft, serial number XN719, ordered but cancelled before construction was complete

XN714

XN714 has substantial areas of wool tufting during this particular flight from RAE Bedford. It can be seen that the pilot has been afforded some protection from the sun's glare, in order to make instrument-reading easier. Author's collection

failed, which brought about several more days of delay while the fault was rectified.

On Tuesday 26 March, with the weather conditions much more favourable, Oliver made a twenty-minute maiden flight following a take-off run of about 600yd (550m). During the flight, two Meteors of the RAE Aero Flight flew as chase aircraft and their pilots observed, as did spectators on the ground, that the H.126 took people's minds back to the Armstrong Whitworth Whitley, by flying in a distinct nose-down attitude. This came about following the aircraft lifting off at just over 90mph (145km/h) and flying close to the ground until a climb-away speed of 140mph (225km/h) had been reached.

Flight-test Programme

XN714's flight test programme proceeded over the succeeding eighteen months without any major malfunctions, the jet-lift system in particular proving to be very reliable. The general flying characteristics were good, although there was a self-induced directional lateral wander tendency, which was accompanied by a gentle lateral rocking in sympathy with the wandering. This was accepted as a nuisance rather than a problem, and the pilot came to accept it because it was basically manageable. However, the stall was not so friendly, as Olly Oliver recalled in conversation with the author:

programme. Principal among the reasons for its exclusion was the fact that it lay within Heathrow's flight path, coupled with the airfield being very active with both commercial and flying club training aircraft, many of the latter not being fully equipped with radio facilities. Therefore, once the taxiing had been completed, with speeds up to about 12mph (20km/h) below the 'unstick' speed, XN714 was dismantled in the early winter of 1962 and transported to RAE Bedford where, after being reassembled, it sat out the rest of the 1962–63 winter, during which there were particularly heavy snowfalls. By early March, conditions had improved enough for taxiing to be resumed and a few short hops were made, during one of which the anti-spin parachute was deployed from its rear-end housing. Unfortunately its jettison mechanism

> One thing that stands out in my mind is that, power off, the 126 was a gentle staller, regardless of the flap angle. Put on the power, however, and it became a very changed aircraft and perhaps the only one I have flown where you could say that there was NO stall warning. One second you were flying; the next you would be upside-down – and the rate of roll in this manoeuvre was quite sprightly!

On 13 October 1964, XN714 went to Boscombe Down for a series of tests in the Establishment's wind tunnel, where the path of an aircraft's canopy was monitored after being jettisoned. In view of this being a particularly important aspect for aircraft with tall fins and high-set tailplanes like the H.126, it seems surprising that the aircraft had been flying for over eighteen months before these tests were conducted. Following Boscombe Down, the aircraft returned to Bedford and also made several sorties from Luton, now that its flying characteristics were known factors.

The unpainted orifice of the Orpheus engine is seen to effect, as are the danger-warnings placed adjacent to areas where hot exhaust will be encountered. *Aeroplane*

Seven months later, in June 1965, XN714 was demonstrated at the Paris Salon, held at Le Bourget. For the event, it was piloted by 'Dizzy' Addicott, as Oliver had been transferred to Wisley in support of the BAC One-Eleven development at the end of 1963, following the fatal crash of the first prototype on 22 October. This is not as strange as it appears, for in 1960 Hunting Aircraft had been absorbed into the British Aircraft Corporation (BAC) conglomerate; the One-Eleven had started life, in 1956, as Hunting project H.107. Several other RAE test pilots became involved with the H.126 flight testing, including John Farley and Ian Keppie, who later became the RAE's designated pilot for the aircraft.

Visiting Uncle Sam

In mid-1967, plans were prepared for XN714 to go to the National Aeronautics and Space Administration (NASA) for a series of full-scale wind-tunnel tests. These plans took another year to materialize, and in the summer of 1968 the aircraft flew up to the Hawker Siddeley Group's factory at Holme upon Spalding-Moor, in Yorkshire, in readiness for crossing the Atlantic. Again, things moved very slowly and it was 3 April 1969 before the aircraft was dismantled to fit into the hold of Short Belfast

XR366, which transported the jet-flap tester to the Ames Flight Research Center at Moffet Naval Air Station in California.

The aircraft was at Ames for twelve months, but just what it did there has not been well documented. Whether it was flown at all is doubtful, for no pilots connected with the aircraft in the UK went to Moffet, nor were they asked to brief any American pilots. However, it returned to Holme upon Spalding Moor in crates, and after six months in storage, still in its crates, it was transferred to RAE Bedford.

Retirement and Retrospect

At Bedford, the dismantled aircraft stayed in its crates for a further eighteen months before it was struck off charge in June 1972, as the whole jet-flap concept had been abandoned and, judging by the way that the H.126 had been allowed to languish for the previous two years, one feels that this had been conceived a lot earlier. Two years later, the still-crated XN714 was taken up by Cosford's museum and, after over four years of being encased in timber, it was not in too good a condition, which resulted in Cosford having to reassemble the aircraft for static display only – but it did receive a new coat of yellow paint.

Asked if he thought the H.126 had fulfilled its purpose, Olly Oliver's reply was

an unequivocal 'Yes. It demonstrated flight at unprecedented lift coefficients.' Standard wings at that time produced lift coefficients in the order of 1.5, while XN714 produced a figure of around 7, which was unique for wingborne flight in that era. When asked why the principle had not been extended, Oliver replied 'It may have been in great measure because of the difficulty of providing the pilot with some warning of the onset of flow breakaway [stall warning] because the penalty for overstepping the mark in that direction was, or could be, catastrophic.'

In retrospect, besides Oliver's comments, the thick wing section was a non-starter for either commercial or military aviation, and the idea of filling a wing structure with red-hot ducting, heat shields, expansion joints, and so on, might have provided a warning that, no matter what the system's attributes were, they would prove to be an engineering nightmare.

Today, XN714 is still at Cosford, resplendent in its yellow coat of paint, representing yet another project that 'seemed a good idea at the time'.

On 3 April 1969, the disassembled H.126 was manoeuvred into the hold of Short Belfast C.1 XR366, for delivery to NASA's Ames Flight Research Center at Moffet Naval Air Station, California. *Aeroplane*

PART FOUR

CHAPTER TWENTY-THREE

Cancelled Projects

In the time-span covered by this book, literally thousands of designs emerged from the fertile minds in the project offices of the British aircraft industry, and a large proportion of them progressed no further than the drawing board. While obviously this broad figure includes designer's ideas that changed in the course of perfecting a particular project, official vacillation was responsible for so many wasted months and years, not to mention vast sums of taxpayer's money. Operational Requirements and Specifications were issued, to which the industry responded with continuing enthusiasm, only to be frustrated by ever-changing requirements that were so often, in the end, terminated by cancellation. Also it must be admitted that some proposals put up by the designers were non-starters – but everyone is entitled to their bad day!

A bench-mark has been set, whereby only projects that progressed at least to the mock-up stage have been presented in this chapter, which includes three designs that got no further than the mock-up, two more that advanced to the construction stage and one that flew for seven months. The Technical Data information given has, to a large part, been based on manufacturer's estimated design figures.

Miles M.52
Scheduled First Flight 1947

It was a very bold move on the part of the Ministry of Aircraft Production (MAP) when, in the autumn of 1943, they drew up Specification E.24/43 for a high-speed research aircraft and this high speed was thought of as being in the order of 1,000mph (1,600km/h) at above 35,000ft

One of the many models produced during M.52 development was this stainless steel one, which shows the general configuration in which the finished aircraft would have appeared. The rear orifice is as the prototype was to be finished, but it is believed that a longer rear fuselage aft of the tail assembly was envisaged.
Author's collection

(11,000m). Possibly because all the major British aircraft manufacturers were working flat out to supply the Services with contemporary aircraft, Miles Aircraft at Woodley, with no experience in the field of high speed, were chosen to convert the Specification into hardware.

There is no doubt that the company had a talented and imaginative design team under the directorship of the Miles brothers, and they accepted Contract number SB/27157/C.23(c) on 13 December 1943 with great enthusiasm. Two prototypes were called for: one for static testing and one to be produced for flight evaluation, and the company designation

M.52 was bestowed upon the project. Unusually, both airframes received serial numbers, with RT133 being for the flight airframe and RT136 for the static test vehicle. A small design team was set up in great secrecy within the company and a close liaison with RAE Farnborough was to be maintained throughout.

By early 1944, the company had prepared a preliminary design, which showed a cylindrical bullet-shaped fuselage, tapering at both ends. The air intake for the proposed W.2/700 engine, a variant of the Power Jets-developed turbojet, specifically modified for the M.52, was to be annular-shaped, immediately behind a pressurized cockpit set in a capsule that featured a sharply-pointed nose-cone. This capsule would be detached from the airframe by explosive charges in the case of an emergency, and slowed down by parachute until the velocity had reduced sufficiently to allow the pilot to bale out in a conventional manner. The unswept, bi-convex wings were to be very thin and semi-elliptical with cut-off tips, while the tail assembly consisted of a similar-shaped fin, but a straight-edged, slightly swept tailplane. A tricycle undercarriage would have all its units retracting into the fuselage and the engine was sited immediately behind the cockpit. Because of the thin wings, all fuel was to be carried in tanks positioned around the engine, which would have a long jet-pipe taking the exhaust to an orifice well aft of the tail assembly. This would be shortened at a later date when the proposed reheat had been installed.

Performance calculations were a delicate balancing act between the gross weight and the thrust output from the W.2/700. The output was estimated as 2,375lb (1,077kg) thrust at 40,000ft (12,000m), which would enable a speed of 700mph (1,100km/h) to be achieved at that altitude, for a gross weight of 6,500lb (3,000kg) including fuel, and it was calculated that this speed could be raised to 1,000mph at 60,000ft (18,000m) on the power available.

The full-size **M.52** mock-up, showing the circular aperture in which the port wing main spar would be inserted, and the positioning of the W2/700 engine. Author's collection

Inevitably, the preliminary all-up-weight increased as the design was developed, so that by the middle of 1944, it was 7,500lb (3,400kg) and still rising. This was partly due to the engine installation having to be revised and the fact that an extra 70gal (315ltr) of fuel had to be accommodated. There was also the complication that further studies of the wing design showed that the planform, as initially drawn up, would not be as efficient as a straight-edged wing, which would produce better lift coefficients at high altitude. A set of test wings was constructed, to be test-flown on

Miles M.3B Falcon L9705 and, due to their ultra-thin section, the aircraft was dubbed the Gillette Falcon. Flight-testing commenced at Woodley on 11 July 1944, with Hugh Kennedy at the controls, but a large part of the trials programme was conducted at RAE Farnborough, where it was considered that the wing shape was acceptable at the more critical low-speed end of the flight envelope, although it was pointed out that landing, without flaps, on the narrow-tracked undercarriage proposed, could present problems. The high-speed end had to be dependent on slide-rule calculations, made in association with results achieved with models tested in the company's own specially built wind tunnel.

The fitting of an all-flying tailplane was advocated fairly early in the design stage and it was proposed such a unit should be test-flown on a modified Spitfire. This did not materialize, however, partly because by the end of 1944 it was becoming evident that E.24/43 was not going to be met by the design proposed at that time. The drag at 600mph (1,000km/h), flying at an altitude of 36,000ft (11,000m), would be greater than the available thrust, although calculations showed that at higher altitudes thrust would be adequate. It was the getting to the higher altitude, and therefore speed, that presented the problem. A dive from 60,000ft (18,000m) might enable such a speed to be reached, but it would be at the expense of nearly all the available fuel and, while a rocket-booster was considered, its fuel consumption on the climb would be too high. Air-launching from such an aircraft as the Lancaster was given momentary consideration, but was rapidly decided to be impractical. All-in-all, the problems seemed insoluble.

Several small-scale aerodynamic models of the **M.52** were air-launched from a Mosquito. Here a model is seen attached in a ventral position on the aircraft, together with RAE pilot Sqn Ldr D. A. C. Hunt on the left and 'boffin' Mr C. B. Loche Bayne.
Philip Jarrett

Nevertheless, a mock-up of the fuselage had been constructed by early 1945 and this gave evidence of another problem. The pilot's capsule was designed with a diameter of only 4ft (1.2m), which ruled out a tall pilot. Furthermore, once the pilot had got inside, his seating angle would place his feet and shoulders on the same level, with the retracted nose-wheel housing jutting up between his legs, while visibility through the sharply slanted windscreen was decidedly limited, to a point where on the approach it was virtually nil.

When the various Allied technical missions trawled through German aviation research data in 1945, the extensive use of swept-wing designs for high speeds cast doubts on the M.52's configuration in the minds of the official aerodynamicists, although Miles was not informed of this changing opinion. They beavered away at developing what they had designed and this produced another problem: cost. So far the M.52 had cost nearly £75,000 and it was thought that at least another £250,000 would be necessary in order to get the project to a flight-testing stage. The Director General of Technical Development, Sir Ben Lockspeiser, voiced his opinion that progress had not been as rapid as originally envisaged when E.24/43 was issued and Miles were given the contract. To enable further funding to be expended, he would have to get Treasury approval and they blanched at the very thought.

Consideration was given to continuing with the project as an engine development test bed but, as the W.2/700 was specifically developed for the Miles design, the idea was dropped. Therefore, on 25 February 1946, Sir Ben gave notice to the company that the project was to cease forthwith, citing financial constraints as the principal reason, but adding his own view that he did not consider the M.52 would be able to produce supersonic research data in the foreseeable future.

In retrospect, it is clear that Britain lost its momentum in the field of supersonic flight at that time and it is obvious that Whitehall had no appreciation of what such pioneering work would cost. The American aircraft industry was not blinkered by such an outlook, and made great use of the data extracted from Germany. They were further aided by the benevolence of the Ministry of Supply, who donated all the data and results that Miles had achieved, in an act of blind generosity.

Technical Data – Miles M.52	
Dimensions:	Span 26ft 10in (8.19m); length 39ft (11.8m) in first configuration, 36ft 4in (11.09m) in revised configuration; height 11ft 7in (3.53m)
Powerplant:	One Power Jets-developed W.2/700 turbojet, producing 2,375lb (1,077kg) thrust at 40,000ft (12,000m) (estimated figures)
Weights (estimated):	Empty 5,955lb (2,700kg); loaded 8,655lb (3,925kg)
Performance (estimated):	Mach 0.9 in level flight at sea level, with Mach 1 exceeded in dives from various altitudes
Production:	One mock-up partially completed and some construction on one airframe being built to Specification E.24/43, with serial number RT133

Supermarine Type 545
Scheduled First Flight 1954

When Hawker Aircraft proposed a supersonic variant of the Hunter, with greater sweep and powered by either a reheated Sapphire or Avon to meet Specification E.105D.2, it was given the company designation P.1083. They received Instructions to Proceed (ITP) on 26 February 1952, with hopes of having the first prototype in the air by July 1953.

Before the shortcomings of the Swift had become apparent, Supermarine was heavily involved in meeting the same specification, based on a supersonic version of the Swift, although it was in essence an entirely new design. The Supermarine aircraft's calculated performance was superior to the P.1083 and, as Hunter production orders would keep Hawker occupied for several years to come, Supermarine received the go-ahead to produce their Type 545, at the expense of the Hawker design.

The aircraft had a compound sweep planform, with the inner section being swept at 50 degrees, the mid-section at 40 degrees and the outer section at 30 degrees. The thickness/chord ratio varied from 8 per cent at the root, to 5½ per cent at the tips, with fillets at the fuselage junction. The lower part of the fuselage centre section at the wing junction was flattened, in order to improve airflow and cure the losses of airflow over the wings that were experienced with the Swift in certain attitudes at low speed. Drawings indicate that a four-gun armament (presumably 30mm Aden cannon) was to be installed in the lower front section, but no provision for this was made on the first prototype.

The fuselage was area-ruled alongside the wing, and the nose intake featured an oval centre-body that produced two separate intake lips. The cockpit was situated well forward of the wings, with a large one-piece canopy cover, and the swept fin-rudder assembly had a dorsal fairing running up to the fin leading edge, with a rear-fuselage cooling intake at its beginning.

Power was scheduled to be provided by a Rolls-Royce RA.14R Avon axial-flow turbojet for the first aircraft, which was to be the first of two prototypes carrying serial numbers XA181 and XA186 respectively. The first prototype was offered as a Mach 1.3 aircraft, while a Mach 1.6 variant was put forward for the second Type 545 at the design stage. This was to be powered by a Rolls-Royce RA.24R Avon, with a proposed follow-up variant having a Rolls-Royce RB.106. For these more powerful engines a new fuselage was designed, with a large chin air intake replacing the smaller split intake on XA181 (rather reminiscent of the North American F-86D), and the tail-cone was enlarged to accept the reheat that either engine would employ.

Construction of XA181 began during 1952, but progress was marred by a succession of delays. Furthermore, revised calculations of the available thrust versus drag were showing that the aircraft would only achieve its design speed of Mach 1.3 in a dive, which was far from the Specification's requirements. The maiden flight had been scheduled for the spring of 1954, but the delays put this back. This was unfortunate for the company as by the end of that year, the Swift's problems were appearing thick and fast. This prompted the gradual cancellation of that aircraft mark by mark, although the Swift FR.5 continued in service with Nos 2 and 79 Squadrons until they disbanded in 1960.

The Swift's shortcomings had an effect on the Type 545, even though it was an entirely different aircraft. On 9 November 1954 the second prototype, XA186, was

ABOVE: **The almost completed Supermarine Type 545 prototype, for which serial number XA181 had been allocated, went to the College of Aeronautics in 1955 and is seen in their hangar in company with a Canadair-built Sabre, Tempest II LA607, Saro SR.A/1 G-12-1 and one of the six Wyvern TF.1s built.** Cranfield University Press

In this view at Cranfield, the future XA181 can be seen to have had the rear fuselage section detached and numerous maintenance panels removed. Cranfield University Press

cancelled while still in an early stage of construction. XA181 was far more advanced and was allowed to continue, with the new Specification E.7/54 being written around it as a research aircraft for the RAE. However, this requirement was dropped, and in the late winter of 1955 the whole Type 545 project was killed off. The first prototype airframe, in a virtually completed state, was transferred to the College of Aeronautics at Cranfield for instructional purposes. It remained there for nearly five years until, in 1960, it was scrapped, although a cockpit canopy is believed to be held by the Midland Aircraft Museum at Baginton.

Technical Data – Supermarine Type 545	
Dimensions:	Span 39ft (11.88m); length (XA181) 47ft (14.32m), (XA186) 48ft 6in (14.78m); height 14ft 4in (4.35m)
Powerplant:	(XA181) One Rolls-Royce RA.14R Avon turbojet, producing 9,500lb (4,300kg) thrust dry, 14,500lb (6,600kg) thrust with reheat (XA186) One Rolls-Royce RA.24R Avon turbojet, producing 11,250lb (5,100kg) thrust dry, 14,350lb (6,500kg) thrust with reheat
Weights:	Empty 13,860lb (6,290kg); loaded 17,260lb (7,830kg)
Performance:	Maximum speed (XA181) 723mph (1,163km/h), (XA186) 760mph (1,223km/h); operational ceiling 54,000ft (16,500m)
Production:	One aircraft almost completed to original Specification F.105D.2, later amended to E.7/54, with serial number XA181; one aircraft partly built to Specification E.105D.2, with serial number XA186

Avro 720
Scheduled First Flight 1956

Intercepting the high-altitude bomber became one of the Air Staff's priority considerations around the end of the 1940s and, with the Messerschmitt Me 163B being rather fresh in their minds, together with the Bachem Ba 349 Natter, the rocket motor was considered to be the best power-source whereby this could be attained. Operational Requirement 301 was raised on 21 January 1953 with the aspiration of designing an interceptor capable of attaining 60,000ft (11,000m) in 2½ minutes and able to glide back to base, again as the Me 163B. The later calculations of Saro's Maurice Brennan would prove the impracticality of such a consideration (*see* Chapter Eighteen), but in the early 1950s, the rocket-powered interceptor was the 'flavour of the month' and Specification F.124T was issued to A. V. Roe, Blackburn, de Havilland and Fairey Aviation. Saro's involvement came about through the personal request of the company's vice-chairman, Sir Arthur Gouge.

Avro's opinion right from the start was that in view of the performance of the modern bomber, the specification should be addressed by a supersonic aircraft. Their preliminary calculations pointed to a performance in the order of Mach 1.3 as being the target at which their design should be aimed. To this design the company bestowed the designation Type 720. The only two rocket motors that could provide such a performance were Armstrong Siddeley's Screamer and the Spectre being developed by de Havilland Engines. They were designed around different fuel systems, with Armstrong Siddeley opting for lox (liquid oxygen) plus kerosene, and de Havilland going down the road of High Test Peroxide (HTP), also mixed with kerosene. Both motors were delivering 8,000lb (3,600kg) thrust on test, which would enable Avro's Type 720 to be supersonic at any altitude above 40,000ft (12,000m) and would provide an interception endurance of approximately five minutes. Avro and Armstrong Siddeley having been founder members of the Hawker Siddeley Group since 1936, it is not surprising that the company selected the Screamer.

The company had Type 698 Vulcan airborne on 30 August 1952 and their aeronautical thoughts at that time were mainly in a triangular mode, so it was understandable that they should think the tailless delta

The full-size Avro Type 720 mock-up stands on its trestles, with a weapons pylon in position under its only wing. Harry Holmes

When the degree of finish that was applied to the mock-up is seen, it is understandable why this has sometimes been misidentified as the nearly completed first prototype. Harry Holmes

configuration right for the interceptor project – which was true. The data obtained through the Type 707 trials (*see* Chapter Eight) was readily available, especially regarding the all-important low-speed handling characteristics. The interceptor design featured a tapered delta planform with a thin section and a 60-degree angle of sweep on the leading edge. The fin/rudder assembly followed suit and the circular-sectioned fuselage tapered from a thin pointed nose to a rear end that surrounded the rocket-motor orifice. A small, raised cockpit with multiple framing was

faired into a dorsal spine that ran to the fin leading edge; the latter housed the tail and rocket-motor controls. The armament would consist of sixty-four 2in (5cm) unguided rockets, set within a centre-section ventral bulge containing four sixteen-rocket packs which, when empty, could be unplugged and replaced by new, loaded packs during re-arming.

For some time the Hawker Siddeley Group had been conducting trials of honeycomb sandwich construction, in which two thin sheets of metal were bonded to either side of a light metal section that was built in multiple small sections with their edges at right angles to the outer sheets. The result was a light structure with the stiffness that enabled it to be used as an aircraft's cladding, and Avro considered the material ideal for the operating conditions expected of the Type 720.

In order to get a prototype flying, and knowing that the rocket-motor development still needed time, Avro suggested using a Rolls-Royce Derwent turbojet which, although not being able to provide anything approaching the Screamer's performance, would get the aircraft airborne for the exploration of the gliding characteristics to be made. This proposal was discarded when the type's operational conception was altered by the introduction of an auxiliary turbojet, largely resulting from Maurice Brennan's researches at Saro.

The most suitable turbojet was the axial-flow Armstrong-Siddeley Viper which, in its ASV.8 form as the Viper 101, produced 1,640lb (740kg) thrust at sea level. Avro received the new Specification F.137D, together with a contract to cover the redesign work, the building of two flying prototypes given serials XD696 and XD701 and a structural test airframe.

The basic design of the Type 720 was followed and, by a clever adaptation of the lower fuselage, the Viper was housed in a ventral duct running from an intake positioned below the cockpit, to an exhaust outlet below the wing trailing edge. The rocket armament was replaced by two infra-red homing Firestreak missiles carried on external pylons, one beneath each wing. A tricycle undercarriage had the nose-wheel retracting rearwards into a bay set aft of the intake within the ventral ducting. The main wheels retracted forwards, with the oleos turning through 90 degrees to allow the wheels to lie flat within the thin-sectioned wing.

Avro built a mock-up of the newly-configured Type 720, which has caused a number of conflicting views to be expressed over the years. The mock-up was placed in the company's experimental shop, with the starboard side of the fuselage close to a wall, which meant that only the port wing was constructed. The mock-up was photographed with the undercarriage apparently retracted and also with the nose-wheel, together with the port main wheel, in the down position. Whether they were actuated by hand or just attached in a lowered position for the photographs, is

uncertain. The cause of the differing opinions lies in the fact that the mock-up was metal-clad, most likely to gain forming experience with the honeycomb outer skinning. Also, Avro went to the lengths of painting service markings, the first prototype's serial (XD696) and even an ejector seat warning triangle adjacent to the cockpit canopy, which made it appear very realistic. The elevons were hinged and the result was convincing enough for the mock-up to be captioned as the 'almost completed' first prototype on several occasions, although careful study of the photographs show that it was always mounted on stands, while one three-quarter front shot reveals the absence of the starboard main-plane. The finishing touch was most likely the dummy nose probe.

De Havilland now started development of the Gyron Junior, which prompted the use of this turbojet being considered for a slightly redesigned Type 720 to meet OR.337 and Specification F.177, which had been raised. This work was put in hand in the Project Office, who produced drawings of a larger aircraft, with a Vee-windscreen and a longer, area-ruled fuselage, that could accommodate an Airborne Interception (AI) radar in its nose section. In order to get this project moving, it was proposed that the available Bristol Siddeley Orpheus turbojet be fitted in the prototype, while the new de Havilland engine was being developed up to operational standard. The Firestreak missile armament would be retained and a naval variant, the Type 728, was also put forward. Saro was declared winner of OR.337 with their SR.177 (*see* later in this chapter), and Air Staff enthusiasm for mixed-power interceptors was on the wane: on 21 April 1955, they recommended the cancellation of the whole Avro Type 720/728 programme. Although

of no real consolation to A. V. Roe, Sandys' Defence White Paper two years later put the brakes on the Saro project and on Christmas Eve 1957 (no sentiment in business!) the Ministry of Supply officially cancelled the entire programme.

Inevitably finance came into the equation, which had a large bearing on the Air Staff's attitude. There was also the uncertainty and impracticality of operating aircraft in squadron service, employing a lox/kerosene fuel combination, with all its volatility. Although it is believed that the static test airframe was completed, very few assemblies of XD696 were made so that, with the cancellation, everything, including the test airframe, was scrapped.

Hawker P.1121
Scheduled First Flight 1958

When Hawker Aircraft's Project Office became short of work, following the Hunter being transferred to the Drawing Office, the company's Chief Designer, Sir Sydney Camm, sanctioned work on the design of a large supersonic fighter, on a private-venture basis. Given the project number P.1103, the aircraft was to be powered by a reheat-equipped de Havilland Gyron, which was the first true supersonic turbojet to be developed in Britain. The Air Ministry had issued Operational Requirement 323 in March 1954 and Hawker submitted their P.1103 design in response to the Requirement.

In 1956, as has so often happened in the history of the British aircraft industry's dealings with the official bodies, Hawker found that the goalposts had been moved: the Air Ministry now wanted a dual-purpose aircraft, able to take on strike operations as well as interception. In view of this, OR.323 was scrapped, but the Deputy

Technical Data – Avro Type 720	
Dimensions:	Span 27ft 3in (8.3m); length 43ft 3in (13.18m) excluding nose probe, 48ft (14.63m) including nose probe; height 12ft 7in (3.84m)
Powerplants:	One Armstrong Siddeley Screamer rocket motor, producing 8,000lb (3,600kg) thrust, and one Armstrong Siddeley ASV.8 Viper 101 turbojet producing 1,640lb (740kg) thrust
Weights:	Empty 7,812lb (822kg); loaded 17,575lb (7,970kg)
Armament:	Two de Havilland Firestreak missiles
Performance:	Maximum speed Mach 2; operational ceiling 60,000ft (18,000m)
Production:	One aircraft partially built to Specification F.137D, with serial number XD696. Building of second aircraft, XD701, not started.

Chief of Air Staff Air Marshal Thomas (later Sir Thomas) Pike thought the P.1103 was worth amending to the new role, and as it was Hawker Aircraft who was footing the bill, they encouraged the company to consider a modified P.1103 to meet a new requirement, OR.329.

Camm considered that the redesigned P.1103 would be a two-seater aircraft, equipped with a large 40in (100cm) radar antenna and powered by a de Havilland Gyron fed by a ventral intake with an internal bullet fairing. Two wing-mounted rocket motors would provide good acceleration on take-off and in the climb. The armament was to be a pair of *Red Deans*, an enormous air-to-air missile with an 8ft (2.4m) wingspan, developed by the Guided Missile Division of Vickers Armstrong. In April 1956, Hawker Aircraft was informed that Fairey Aviation's 'Delta III' had been the successful submission to OR.329, which had been updated to Specification F.155T. However, on 11 March 1957, the Delta III joined the ever-growing pile of cancelled projects.

Hawker's Project Office worked on the Air Ministry's recommendation and almost redesigned the P.1103, with the result being given the new designation P.1121. By May 1956 the design had become a single-seat strike aircraft, which was still on a private-venture basis, but the company's Board took the brave step of agreeing to a prototype being constructed in Kingston's experimental shop. This commenced on 24 January 1957, alongside a full-size mock-up, which showed the P.1121 was going to be a big aeroplane. In fact, it would have been the longest single-seat fighter in the history of the RAF, had it gone into operational service.

A large, deep, split ventral air intake, with a long nose section protruding above it, would aspirate the Gyron. The nose was to house an AI.23 radar unit or cameras, dependent on the mission being flown. Mid-set wings featured a 40-degree sweep on the leading edge, which was emulated by the low-set, all-moving tailplane. A large fin/rudder assembly had a 63-degree sweep

on its leading edge; this sat on a long dorsal spine-housing running from the cockpit, in which the tail flying control runs were installed, as was a rear-fuselage cooling duct, leading from a small intake on either side of the spine. Although no undercarriage was featured on the mock-up, it is known that the nose-wheel retracted rearwards into a bay in the intake's underside, with the main wheels retracting rearwards into the lower fuselage. This layout gave the P.1121 a narrow main-wheel track, which

was entirely contrary to previous Camm fighter designs. A large retractable airbrake was fitted on either side of the upper rear fuselage, with a third carried on the underside centreline, behind the nose-wheel bay. A braking parachute housing extended aft above the large jet-pipe outlet, in which a reheat installation would have been fitted.

The mock-up also carried a long instrument boom extending forward from the pointed nose-cone and the wings were clean, devoid of the proposed multi-purpose

From this view of the full-size mock-up, the size of the P.1121 can be appreciated, as can the enormous ventral air intake that was intended to feed the finished aircraft's Gyron turbojet. Michael Stroud

Taken shortly before the P.1121's cancellation, Hawker's experimental section has the mock-up in the background and the systems mock-up on the right, while in the centre foreground are the nose and centre section elements of the first prototype that had been built thus far, behind two Hunter sections. Michael Stroud

pylon that was to be fitted, one on each side. These would carry a mixture of Firestreak air-to-air missiles, external fuel tanks or tactical weapon pods, again depending on type of mission was to be flown. On the production aircraft, it was proposed to have a large retractable weapons bay on either side of the fuselage, aft of the cockpit. These would each carry a battery of twenty-five 2in (5cm) unguided air-to-air missiles.

The Central Fighter Establishment (CFE) wanted the interceptor role emphasized with the P.1121 and, with Hawker's consideration that this was the right move, Camm began investigating the Gyron's fuel consumption for the aircraft's low-level operations. This was found to be excessive and discussions were opened with Bristol Siddeley on the possibility of their Olympus 21R being used, for its specific fuel consumption (sfc) figures were far superior to those of the de Havilland engine. Rolls-Royce, too, were approached regarding the use of their Conway, but the Gyron in its PS.26-6 version was the only engine available for the provisional first-flight date of April 1958. Operating in the low-level role with a Rolls-Royce Conway RCo.11R was put in the file marked 'future possibilities'.

The Sandys' White Paper axe was wielded in April 1957, beheading anything, post-English Electric P.1B, that remotely bore the description 'fighter' or 'interceptor': the defence of British airspace was supposedly going to be secure in the hands of ground-to-air missiles. Therefore, officially the P.1121 had nowhere to go but, as it was a private venture, it was immune from government policy and it was very creditable on the part of the Hawker Siddeley Group's management that they continued with the project, in the hope of a market being found.

The summer of the same year produced the first significant setback in the programme. De Havilland had been running a Gyron behind a test-section of the P.1121 intake design and the engine suffered surging long before maximum rpm had been reached. A variety of intake modifications were tried without success and eventually the intake test-section was returned to the manufacturer for redesign. The internal bullet fairing was deleted, internal vanes were introduced and improvements were made to the bank of inlets surrounding the lower half of the intake structure. The redesigned intake was returned to Hatfield, where one of the

Technical Data – Hawker P.1121	
Dimensions:	Span 37ft (11.27m); length 66ft 6in (20.27m) excluding nose boom, 69ft (21.03m) including nose boom; height 15ft 4in (4.66m)
Powerplant:	One de Havilland Dgy.2 Gyron PS.26-6 turbojet, producing 17,000lb (7,700kg) thrust dry, 23,800lb (10,800kg) thrust with reheat
Weights:	Empty 31,000lb (14,000kg); loaded 42,000lb (19,000kg)
Performance:	Maximum speed at sea level Mach 1.3; maximum speed at 50,000ft (15,000m) Mach 2.25; operational ceiling 70,000ft (21,000m)
Production:	One aircraft partially built as private venture

later Gyron variants was removed from the Short Sperrin test bed for employment with the new intake. There was an improvement, but the surging was not completely cured and the programme was delayed when the engine was damaged by ingesting an element of the intake structure, necessitating its removal for repair. During its absence, Bristol Siddeley enquired as to the possibility of an Olympus being used and, when it was delivered in October 1957, it was run with no trouble whatsoever being encountered.

But the Gyron, despite being over-sensitive, was still the only true supersonic engine on hand for the aircraft to meet the maiden flight date, so it had to be accepted. De Havilland promised to continue developing the Gyron, but the P.1121's cost was draining the Hawker Siddeley Group's blood and, with reluctance, they decided that a reduction in expenditure on the programme was necessary, a decision that was passed on to de Havilland.

With the P.1121 placed on a lower level of priority, the Project Office began re-looking at an earlier two-seat P.1121 variant that had been offered when OR.339 was raised, but they did not consider the design viable. (That OR culminated in the TSR.2, one of the greatest political footballs of the age, as described later in this chapter.) In March 1959, the use of the P.1121 as an Olympus test bed was proposed, on the strength of the good results obtained during its testing with the test intake, but this was rejected. Still hopeful of getting the aircraft flying at an early date for true level supersonic testing to take place in Britain, Hawker's management released the purse-strings a little, basking in the optimistic belief that in reaching this goal they might generate some Treasury support. However, getting to that stage would require at least another £1 million of the company's money and they were just

not in a strong-enough financial position to sustain this. Therefore, on 30 September 1959, they had no alternative but to close the project; the following year, de Havilland followed suit with the Gyron.

Building the prototype's airframe had progressed to the stage where the fuselage forward- and centre-sections were complete. Besides the mock-up, a systems-testing mock-up frame had been built to determine the looming and plumbing layouts, but these had not been applied to the section of completed fuselage at the time of cancellation. One wing had also been partially completed, but that was the full extent of the aircraft's construction. In retrospect, it appears doubtful if £1 million would have been enough to get the prototype airborne. The constructed elements were passed to Cranfield for instructional purposes, after which it went into the RAF Museum's reserve collection, but from there the trail runs cold and whether it exists today is doubtful.

From Hawker's point of view, despite their disappointment, it enabled their Project Office to turn its attentions to the principle of S/VTOL, which would follow the technically exciting path that led to the Harrier. But the RAF lost the opportunity of having a British aircraft that, had it been ordered in 1958, would have been in operational service by 1964, capable and strong enough to undertake all that the Phantom was purchased to do, but four years sooner.

Saunders-Roe SR.177
Scheduled First Flight 1958

Even while Saro had the first prototype SR.53 mixed-power interceptor under construction (see Chapter Eighteen), doubts were starting to surface about the aircraft's suitability for the role. In particular, the

Central Fighter Establishment (CFE) expressed the fact that any interceptor designed for future operational service must be equipped with a satisfactory Airborne Interception (AI) radar system.

Saro's Chief Designer, Maurice Brennan, learned from the Royal Radar Establishment (RRE) that the AI.23, developed by them and in production at Ferranti's Scottish works, was what his aircraft required. On seeing the equipment, Brennan knew that not only was it too large to be fitted to the SR.53, but also it was too heavy and the aircraft would be incapable of getting airborne with such a weight up front. The obvious solution was to design a new aircraft on the mixed-power principle, so it was literally 'back to the drawing board'. His thoughts centred around the fact that in the case of the SR.53, the turbojet engine was installed purely to enable it to

return to base after an interception, but an aircraft with a 'normal' turbojet as well as the rocket engine would give an aircraft greater latitude. A longer endurance would be possible, with the aircraft taking off under the power of both units, then the turbojet could be used for cruising, with the rocket motor re-fired purely for the chase and interception.

Brennan calculated that a turbojet producing at least 8,000lb (3,600kg) thrust but light enough to be used in an interceptor was necessary, and there were then two in that class: the de Havilland PS.50 Gyron Junior and the Bristol Saturn. As the de Havilland engine was further down the road to development than the Saturn, the DGJ.10R variant was selected as the engine around which the new interceptor would be designed, operating in conjunction with an uprated de Havilland Spectre

rocket motor. The Saro design team made good progress in converting the basic idea into a larger, tangible aircraft and the company designation SR.54 was pencilled in as its title. It was 15 per cent larger than the SR.53 and not only would it be capable of carrying the AI.23 radar, but it would have a 50 per cent greater fuel capacity.

The design that Saro submitted to the Ministry of Supply (MoS) in the spring of 1955 was a much more sophisticated aircraft, although it retained the SR.53's general aerodynamic appearance and, in order to interest Admiralty House as well as the RAF, blown flaps were incorporated in a 53sq ft (4.92sq m) larger wing. To the amazement and obvious delight of the whole company, the MoS was so enamoured of the proposal that it wrote Specification F.177D around the design, without putting it out to tender, with OR.337 plus the naval requirement NR/A47, being combined within the specification. On 4 September 1956, Saro received an order for nine aircraft, allotted serial numbers XL905 to XL907 and XL920 to XL925, with the first batch of three aircraft being regarded as prototypes. Chronologically, the pencilled-in designation SR.54 should have been applied, but it is believed that SR.177 was chosen because of the specification number, and the aircraft has always been referred to as such.

A year before the contract was awarded, having received an Instruction to Proceed (ITP), Saro started building a full-size wooden mock-up in their Cowes experimental shop, for engineering and the laying-out of systems. They appreciated that for the comparatively small company that they were, they had a pretty daunting task ahead of them. Within the space of three

Saro constructed a full-size wooden mock-up of their SR.177, which showed it was going to be a big interceptor, with large ventral engine bay access doors for the removal and replacement of its proposed Gyron Junior engine.

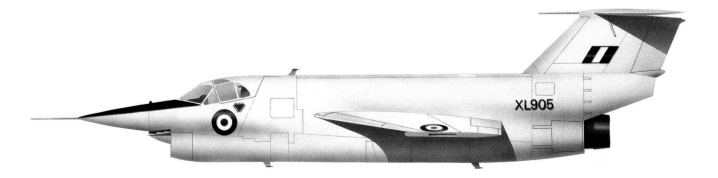

This impression is based on the assumption that, had the SR.177 been built, its finish would have been similar to the SR.53. XL905 was the serial allocated to the first prototype. Author's artwork

years, having initially been completely ignored when Specification F.124T was issued, from which the SR.53 had emerged, they were now going to build just about the most advanced interceptor in the world.

The SR.177 had a rather slab-sided, teardrop-sectioned fuselage, with a broad fin/rudder at its rear, on top of which was a delta-shaped, variable-incidence tailplane, with a 39-degree leading-edge sweep. The fuselage front section contained a sharply pointed nose-cone, in which the AI.23 would be housed, with a deep, Vee-windscreened cockpit on the top and a large semi-circular chin intake below. A conical, fixed centre-body occupied the top portion of the intake, which had the first 15in (40cm) of its lip able to slide forward when the undercarriage was lowered, to allow for the engine's pressure recovery at landing speed, and sliding back to the in-flight position once the wheels had been retracted. The wings, with a 6 per cent thickness/chord ratio and leading-edge sweep of 40 degrees, were set with a 5-degree angle of anhedral. An armament of one *Red Top* air-to-air missile, formerly known as the Firestreak Mk 4 under the code name *Blue Jay*, was carried on a launch shoe sited at each wing tip. A forward-retracting nose-wheel went into a bay that split the engine intake trunking, while the main wheels retracted rearwards, with the oleos turning through approximately 45 degrees, to enable the wheels to fit into a bay between the engine's jet-pipe and the outer skin. A large, retractable airbrake was situated on either side of the rear fuselage section.

The Gyron Junior was to be mounted at an angle of 3 degrees to the fuselage datum line, with the jet-pipe bending up, then down, to the exhaust orifice and reheat unit, set at 5 degrees to the datum. Within the fuselage, above the engine and its long exhaust pipe, the whole top half would contain fuel in seven separate tanks, which would be allocated, from the rear of the cockpit, as follows: two HTP tanks, an HTP collector tank, two more HTP tanks and two kerosene tanks; the final tank's kerosene was for mixing with the HTP to form fuel for the Spectre. An additional turbojet-fuel tank, to be situated aft of the nose-wheel well, would give a total fuel load of 1,290gal (5,805ltr). A non-firing Spectre rocket test unit was installed in the mock-up, mounted between the turbojet exhaust and the fin/rudder assembly.

The construction of the first prototype, XL905, commenced soon after receipt of the ITP and its maiden flight was provisionally scheduled for the summer of 1957. However, by April 1956, the complexity of building the prototype was such that the company, the MoS and the Air Staff realized that this date was quite unattainable. Consequently, it was agreed that the contract would be amended and a new first-flight date was pencilled in as January 1958. Despite this, in September 1956 Saro received a contract for twenty-seven more SR.177s. These were to be distributed as nine aircraft for manufacturer and RAE development trials, nine for the RAF and a further nine for the Navy, all to be used for the separate Services' evaluation programmes. The aircraft were to be identified as the SR.177R for the RAF and SR.177N for the Navy.

Subsequent production was to be farmed out to companies that had greater production capacity than Saro, with both Armstrong Whitworth at Baginton and Marshalls at Cambridge likely to be involved, as both companies had extensive manufacturing and assembly experience. The MoS was talking of production being in the order of 150 aircraft for each Service and West Germany was showing great interest in the product, with their possible requirement being around 600 aircraft. Collaboration with other companies in producing the different SR.177 variants was considered vital, for there was no way that Saro could possibly meet orders of this magnitude on its own.

As has been indicated in many cases in this narrative, the 1957 Sandys' Defence White Paper completely altered everything. On its publication, the RAF immediately cancelled its order, but the Admiralty expressed the desire for the production of their version to continue. The first prototype would be reconfigured as an SR.177N, with arrester hook, catapult points, a strengthened undercarriage and in-flight refuelling capabilities. West Germany, too, were anxious that their variant, the SR.177K, should continue, although the Gyron Junior engine was to be replaced in the SR.177K by a Rolls-Royce RA.24R Avon, which test had indicated, would produce 10 per cent more thrust than the de Havilland engine.

With these assurances, production made good progress and five aircraft were in an advanced state when, in August 1957, the Defence Minister ignored the Navy's wishes and cancelled the SR.177N. Saro had discussions with the MoS that led to the Ministry agreeing to fund the continuance of the five aircraft until the end of the year; the RN requirements would be omitted in order to accelerate the programme.

This turn of events would require West Germany to fund a larger proportion of development costs than had originally been agreed, which was not to their liking at all. Inevitably, in December 1957 they withdrew from the project and Saro's Christmas present was the complete cancellation of all work on the SR.177, with effect from 24 December.

A faint glimmer of light was shed by Japanese interest in purchasing two of the nearly completed aircraft, together with the surviving SR.53 prototype, but, true

Technical Data – Saunders-Roe SR.54/SR.177	
Dimensions:	Span (SR.177R) 30ft 3in (9.22m), (SR.177N) 30ft 5in (9.28m); length 50ft 6in (15.39m); height 14ft 3in (4.34m)
Powerplants:	(SR.177R & SR.177N) One de Havilland D.Spe.5A Spectre rocket motor, producing 8,000lb (3,600kg) maximum thrust and one de Havilland DGJ.10R Gyron Junior turbojet, producing 10,000lb (4,500kg) thrust dry, 14,000lb (6,350kg) thrust with reheat
	(SR.177K) One Rolls-Royce RA.24R Avon turbojet, producing 11,250lb (5,100kg) thrust dry, 14,430lb (6,540kg) thrust with reheat
Weights:	(SR.177R) Empty 14,530lb (6,590kg); loaded 25,780lb (11,690kg) (SR.177N) Empty 14,810lb (6,720kg); loaded 27,340lb (12,400kg)
Armament:	Two de Havilland Red Top missiles
Performance:	Maximum speed Mach 2.35; maximum ceiling 86,000ft (26,213m)
Production:	Five aircraft partially built to Specification F.177D, with serial numbers XL905 to XL907, plus XL920 and XL921. Order for four additional aircraft, plus further order for twenty-seven aircraft, all cancelled

to form in the whole saga, this interest evaporated. All the elements produced up to the final cancellation were put in store, but in 1958 everything, including the five production aircraft, their jigs and the mock-up, were scrapped.

This was the end of a protracted programme that had held so much promise and heralded the end of Saro as a fixed-wing aircraft company. The active helicopter side of the company was taken over by Westland Aircraft Ltd at Yeovil, and de Havilland had bought a 33 per cent interest in the company, with a view to Saro building their Black Knight rocket-propelled missile, but this was cancelled in 1964. The Hovercraft Department had started as part of Saro, but in 1966 this, too, went to Yeovil; today, the former Saro factory has been split up into various light metal companies.

BAC TSR.2
First Flight 27 September 1964

There are few other combinations of three letters plus a figure, that make the blood course through the veins with the velocity that it does at the mere mention of TSR.2. The 'it was right to cancel' and 'it was wrong to cancel' brigades drop their ploughshares and take up their swords to continue the 37-year war of opinion that is still being waged. The roots of the conflict

were formed with the raising of Operational Requirement 339 in September 1957, although English Electric had already been working since October 1956 on an aircraft to replace the Canberra, conscious of the fact that, good as the aircraft was, it could not go on for ever. The result of their deliberations was a twin-engined, straight-winged aircraft, to which they gave the Project number P.17.

As already stated, OR.339 was issued at the beginning of September 1957, carrying the heading Tactical Strike/Reconnaissance aircraft. It demanded a two-seat, high-speed bomber, with the capacity to operate below radar detection, a range of at least 1,000 miles (1,600km), and delivery for squadron service no later than 1964. 31 January 1958 was set as the date when all designs had to be submitted.

On 16 September 1957, possibly one of the largest gatherings of the British aircraft industry's leaders took place at Shell Mex House in London's Strand, to attend a meeting chaired by Sir Cyril Musgrave, the Permanent Secretary at the Ministry of Supply. All the major companies were represented: Blackburn and General Aircraft (Mr M. E. Turner), Bristol Aircraft & Short Brothers' amalgamation (Sir Matthew Slattery), Bristol Aircraft alone (Sir Reginald Verdon Smith and Mr C. F. Unwins), de Havilland (Mr A. Birk), English Electric (Lord Caldercote and Mr H. G. Nelson), Handley Page (Sir Frederick Handley Page

and Mr R. E. Stafford), Hawker Siddeley Group (Sir Frank Spriggs and Sir Roy Dobson), Saunders-Roe (Capt E. D. Clarke) and Vickers-Armstrongs' Supermarine Division (Sir George Edwards). All appreciated that this would be a major project, with very great production potential.

Sir Cyril Musgrave, who had the full authority to speak on behalf of Mr Aubrey Jones, the Minister of Supply, sowed the seeds of what was to be a most contentious issue: OR.339 was too big, he said, to be handled by one company on its own. In answer to an enquiry by Sir Frank Spriggs as to what other new aircraft projects were likely to come up, Sir Cyril said that OR.339 was the only one. Questions were raised as to who would lead any amalgamation, which got no reply, while Sir George Edwards categorically stated that no company could survive on civil aircraft alone. In retrospect, it can be seen that the beginning of the end of the British aircraft industry as it existed, stems from this meeting.

Once the technical enormities of the project had been fully assimilated by the respective project offices, many companies fell by the wayside and withdrew. The Hawker Siddeley Group tried to rejuvenate the Hawker P.1121 project in a revised form, but it was rejected. When the dust had settled, only English Electric had a head start, with their P.17, which they submitted as the P.17A. Supermarine, which had now been fully absorbed by Vickers, proposed two separate projects. These were single-engined and twin-engined designs, known under the old Supermarine numbering system as the Type 571, with both designs using the Rolls-Royce RB.142 turbojet; the single-engined design was soon discarded.

As was to be expected with such a tight requirement brief, both company's designs had many common factors. Government pressure was brought to bear, which officially emphasized Sir Cyril's opinion that no single company could handle OR.339, and the MoS declared that no single company would receive a production contract. This galvanized English Electric and Vickers into forming an alliance, with their reward being received on 1 January 1959 in the shape of the promise to produce a new aeroplane, designated the TSR.2 (Tactical Strike Reconnaissance aircraft number two, although no one explained what was the TSR.1). The Bristol Siddeley Olympus was the chosen power plant, which convinced the engine company

The almost completed first prototype TSR.2, XR219, is in the foreground at Weybridge, with XR220, the second aircraft, partly constructed behind. Derek James

that it should join the two aircraft manufacturers to form the British Aircraft Corporation (BAC); the Corporation was to form a single design team to convert the project into working drawings. The official date of the BAC's formation was July 1960 and Specification RB.192D was issued in August, followed in October by Contract number KD/2L/02/CB.42(a). This called for the production of nine development aircraft with serial numbers XR219 to XR227. Bristol Siddeley received a separate contract to cover their development of the Olympus 22R.

No one would pretend that the English Electric/Vickers marriage was easy. By comparison with Vickers' long pedigree, English Electric was rather a newcomer and such ingrained opinions were hard to dissolve. The setting-up of the management and integration of the two companies posed the question of where the main assembly was going to be undertaken. While English Electric, with its supersonic experience gained through the P.1A and P.1B, felt this gave them an edge, Vickers had Sir George Edwards at the helm, a fact that was not to be taken lightly. His contention was that their Valiant programme gave them the production advantage, possibly conveniently forgetting the great subcontracted Halifax production that English Electric had carried out during World War Two, as well as its post-war Vampire assembly work.

Demonstrating the conflicting opinions that existed in the early days, 'Bee' Beamont received a request from English Electric's Managing Director to lead the TSR.2 flight-testing programme, which would be based at Warton, but this was later amended to Beamont being the deputy to Jock Bryce, BAC's Chief Test Pilot. The fact that the aircraft was going to be the first integrated weapons system to be tackled by Britain's aircraft manufacturers led to a vast number of official committees, each called upon to concentrate on small, individual elements, rather than consider the programme as a whole. There is no doubt that these attitudes were a delaying force, but production of the nine ordered aircraft did start, at Weybridge.

When the design had been finalized, prior to production starting, the TSR.2 was presented as having a low-level design speed of Mach 1.1, with Mach 2 being attainable at high altitude. The Olympus 22R engines were expected to produce 19,600lb (8,900kg) thrust, increasing to

30,600lb (13,900kg) with reheat. Take-off weight was calculated as 95,900lb (43,500kg) and the operating range would be 1,000 miles (1,600km) or more.

The first prototype's maiden flight date was planned for the summer of 1963, but the continual committee meetings enabled the Air Ministry to interject with role changes and requirements, while the static trials of the avionics confirmed what a monumental task the Corporation had taken on. Inevitably the static testing, plus the requirements posed by the multitude of changes that were requested, took time. Time was money, which inspired a concerted review of the aircraft's costs by the Treasury. The outcome of this review

was a request for the RAF to set its sights a little lower in the field of requirements: a suggestion was made by the Treasury for a less sophisticated avionics system to be incorporated, but this was refused by the Service. The slippage in the schedule was new to Weybridge, for they had delivered every Valiant either on, or ahead of, time.

Despite this slippage, on 14 June 1963, Weybridge received another order, Contract number KD/2L/013/CB.42(a), for a further eleven aircraft, for which serials XS660 to XS670 had been allotted. While being welcomed by BAC, this new order could be an embarrassment, for they were realizing that the whole programme was heading into trouble. The Olympus engines

During the maiden flight on 27 September 1964, the landing gear was held in the 'down' position as the retracting system had yet to be cleared for operation in flight. A very visible tip trail was generated, and it can be seen that the airbrakes had not fully retracted. Author's collection and *Aeroplane*

were proving unreliable and difficulties with its control systems just seemed to mount. There was also the unpalatable fact that the project's costs were rising at a rate that made the Corporation wince. The most optimistic forecast for the aircraft entering squadron service was now 1969, five years later than originally proposed, while the sum of £90 million first estimated for research and development had now doubled, with no guarantee that it would not rise any further. This situation had arisen because, in the beginning, the complexity of OR.339 was not fully appreciated by anyone, as nothing like it had been attempted before, but the Air Ministry's ever-changing requirements were also a contributing factor.

Nevertheless, the building of XR219 continued as fast as the shop floor could manage, and in late 1963 it emerged. It was a formidable-looking warplane, having a very long fuselage, cropped-delta wings of broad chord, with marked anhedral on the outboard sections and a vast fin/tailplane assembly. A large air intake on either side of the fuselage had a half-cone centre-body that was adjustable in order to maintain the optimum airflow to the engines, across the whole speed range. A battery of four substantial retracted airbrakes surrounded the rear fuselage section, while up front, the two separate cockpits were set in tandem, with each crew member seated in a Martin-Baker Mk 8VA zero-zero ejector seat. The nose-wheel assembly, which retracted rearwards, had twin wheels side-by-side across the adjustable oleo, while the main wheels were two-wheeled bogies, which retracted forwards into the fuselage. Blown flaps were incorporated in the wings, while the tailplanes were slab surfaces that could operate differentially or in unison. The fin, too, was a one-piece slab unit, that moved in a lateral plane to control directional trimming.

The fuselage centre-section held a large weapons bay, capable of carrying tactical nuclear weapons or conventional bombs. In the reconnaissance role, the weapons were replaced by a pannier equipped with a line-scan sideways-looking radar, plus three vertical cameras; three more cameras were situated in the underside of the nose section. In an overall gleaming white finish, XR219 looked beautiful.

It had already been appreciated that the single, short runway at Weybridge, set in the middle of the old Brooklands racing track, could not be used for the first flight.

Although undercarriage retraction had been cleared, it seems that the airbrakes still did not lie flush with the fuselage. Derek James

On 22 February 1965, XR219 landed at Warton for the first time and shop floor personnel gathered in force to greet it. Derek James

For the Valiant programme, each new aircraft has flown out of Weybridge with a minimum fuel load, to land at Vickers-Armstrongs' test facility at Wisley, about 3 miles (5km) away, but the TSR.2 was an entirely different proposition. Consequently it was planned that the first aircraft would be conveyed by road to Wisley, until the technicians at Warton pointed out that Wisley's one runway was not long enough

for the MoS-controlled flight-test criteria to be met. Therefore, the aircraft would have to be transported to Boscombe Down for its initial flight-testing, as this was the most appropriate airfield. (Warton did point out that their runway met all the requirements, but this was rejected by Weybridge.) There is no doubt that in using Boscombe Down, problems of logistics would arise because of its distance from

Sometime in 1965, English Electric gathered their contributions to post-war British aviation for a photocall at Warton. With XR219 stands Canberra B.2 WD937 and Lightning F.6 XR759. Derek James

the factories at Weybridge and Warton, but this was accepted as being something that had to be lived with. A large flight-test facility was established at the A&AEE, staffed by both Weybridge and Warton technicians, as well as a large building in which the aircraft could be reassembled once it arrived in sections.

These logistic problems created further delays, and although the aircraft was ready for its road journey in April 1964, it was a further five months before it was in a condition to start taxiing trials. Major failures had occurred in the engines being tested at Bristol, while at Weybridge, undercarriage retraction trials had produced another set of problems. However, Roland Beamont commenced limited taxiing trials on 2 September, with Ron Bowen in the rear seat. Being par for the course, fresh complications came to light, in the shape of problems with the reheat, cockpit heating and oxygen supply, hydraulic leaks, plus the inability of the steerable nose-wheel to perform the function of steering. Then, five days later, the braking parachute failed when the aircraft was travelling at over 160mph (260km/h) and the great length of Boscombe Down's runway was fully appreciated.

The two Olympus engines that had arrived from Bristol had a 25-hour limitation and much of this time had been eaten

up with the taxiing. Furthermore, a General Election was due in a couple of weeks, with all the polls indicating a change of government. When Labour was in opposition, it had shown great antagonism towards the whole TSR.2 programme, on the grounds of the technical difficulties that had so delayed the project and, of more importance, the ever-spiralling costs. It was therefore considered imperative by BAC that the aircraft be got airborne as soon as possible, in the hopes that satisfactory flight reports might reduce the hostile attitude.

So, with limited-time, derated engines that could not be guaranteed not to fail, XR219 was given its maiden flight in the afternoon of 27 September 1964. To everyone's undisguised relief, although the undercarriage remained locked down for the fourteen-minute flight as the retracting system had not been cleared, Beamont reported that the aircraft handled beautifully. On touch-down, serious vibrations set in but, on investigation, these were found to be caused by a fault in the reheat fuel pump, which was changed. However, with the two Olympus 22Rs having reached their time limitations, XR219 remained on the ground at Boscombe Down for the next three months before another pair of flight-cleared engines arrived, which led the pessimists in

Whitehall and the Press to conclude that the maiden flight was not as successful as BAC had declared.

The only serious defect encountered in the programme would be the undercarriage retraction system, which was not fully cleared until the tenth flight. The replacement engines had been installed by 31 December and in the afternoon of the last day of the year the second flight was made, but this was not so successful as the first, for the first undercarriage retraction sequence failure was encountered. Further flights could not eradicate the trouble, with the main wheels on the port side not retracting; following modifications, the problem was repeated on the starboard side. On 14 January 1965, late into flight number five, during what was scheduled as the final clearance of the undercarriage retraction sequence, the main wheel bogies on both sides failed to rotate to the landing position. Beamont and Bowen were now faced with a situation that could demand the abandoning of the aircraft, but the decision to continue and attempt a landing was taken, which the pilot accomplished in a very gentle manner. One has to consider Bowen's faith in his pilot, for all he could do was just sit there in the rear cockpit and monitor the fuel gauges.

By now it had been agreed that the main 2,500-hour-long test-flight schedule, required to get the aircraft cleared for squadron service, would be conducted from Warton. During the delivery from Boscombe Down to Warton, the first transition to supersonic flight was made and, with the undercarriage retraction problems behind them, together with fully flight-cleared engines installed, it was considered that BAC now had a really impressive aircraft, which could accomplish the stringent requirements of the original specification. Some of the future test flying was to be in the hands of Jimmy Dell, who had piloted the Lightning chase plane during all the earlier test flights, with Don Knight behind him. They flew seven more sorties during the next few weeks following XR219's delivery to Warton, which completed the initial test-flying programme and Beamont was able to issue the first flight operations summary, which was delivered to the BAC Board and the various ministerial departments. He reported, in very positive terms, that the phase 1 tests had proved the excellence of the aircraft.

The aircraft was withdrawn from the flying programme for the final undercarriage modifications to be made, as the second prototype, XL220, had been delivered to Boscombe Down, ready to join the flight-test programme. It had been slightly damaged when its transporter was involved in a road accident, but examination by BAC technicians revealed that the structure was very strong and the superficial damage incurred could be repaired in a very short time. But, unbeknown to anyone at the time, the twenty-third test flight, made by XR219 on 31 March, would prove to be the last: the aircraft was grounded a few days later for modifications to be carried out, and these were put on hold by political events before they could be completed.

As had been predicted, a Labour government was elected and, during his first Budget speech, on 6 April 1965, the Chancellor slipped in the announcement of the cancellation of the TSR.2 programme. Parliamentary procedure decreed that all announcements had to be fully debated and a vote taken, but the contents of Budgets were approved in a token manner, without any vote being taken on their individual elements. Therefore, through this subterfuge, this most promising of aircraft was killed off, without any hope of reprieve.

Twenty-three flights, totalling 13 hours 5 minutes, had been made, with the longest lasting 1 hour 10 minutes.

BAC received the official notice of cancellation on 6 July, when the position of the whole programme was that XR219 was at Warton for undercarriage modifications, having not flown since the Budget, while XR220 had been delivered to Boscombe Down and was ready to fly. Two more airframes, XR221 and XR222, were at Weybridge, with their avionics testing 90 per cent completed, prior to flight-test delivery. Four more, XR223 to XR226, had been structurally completed and ten more were in varying stages of construction.

The most vindictive aspect of the whole cancellation, apart from the underhanded way in which it was announced, was the decree made that both prototypes, plus all aircraft under construction and all the jigs, were to be destroyed, thereby ensuring that no resurrection would be possible at a later date. XR219, XR221 and XR223 were delivered to the Proof and Experimental Establishment at Shoeburyness, while XR220 was retained at the A&AEE for some time for ground running of the Olympus to assist the Concorde programme. The aircraft was then stored at Henlow before going to Cosford as Instructional Airframe 7933M prior to its scheduled scrapping.

The second TSR.2, XR220, was positioned in Cosford's refurbished display hangar on 23 March 1986. Outside, it passes a Victor, probably XH672, with the H.126, a Meteor and a Hunter behind it. In the distance is a Valetta minus outer wings and rudder alongside Catalina L-866. Inside the hangar, XR220 joins SB.5 WG767, P.1 WG760 and Lightning F.1 XG337. Ian Frimiton via *Aeroplane*

However, underhandedness was not the prerogative of the Government, and 7933M was transferred to the museum at Cosford on 4 May 1975, restored as XR220. XR222 was given to the College of Aeronautics for instructional purposes, with Whitehall's assuming that it would be dismantled in the process, but common sense also prevailed at the College and in 1977 the aircraft went to the Imperial War Museum at Duxford. Today, both aircraft are on display at their respective museums, but I bet the Brooklands Museum would give their eye teeth to have an example there, at Weybridge!

The total cost of the TSR.2 programme was £195 million which, by today's standards, was not excessive. The RAF would have received one of the most effective weapons in its entire history. The government's expressed preference for the General Dynamics F-111K in place of the TSR.2 soaked up £46.4 million, nearly a quarter of the TSR.2 programme costs – and the RAF did not receive that either!

Technical Data – BAC TSR.2	
Dimensions:	Span 37ft (11.57m); length 89ft (27.12m); height 23ft 9in (7.23m)
Powerplants:	Two Bristol Siddeley Olympus 22R turbojets, producing 19,600lb (8,900kg) thrust dry, 30,610lb (13,880kg) thrust with reheat
Weights:	Empty 58,371lb (26,471kg); loaded 79,573lb (36,086kg)
Performance:	Maximum design speed Mach 2.25; maximum speed at sea level Mach 1.1; operating ceiling 54,000ft (16,500m); combat range 1,150 miles (1,860km)

Experimental Aircraft Conservation

Their very existence being for experimental purposes, an understandably large number of these aircraft were lost, either through the ravages of their use or through the lack of consideration for historical preservation that existed in those days. However, a more enlightened attitude eventually prevailed, so that some aircraft do still exist. Their location at the time of writing is listed below.

Aircraft	Serial	Present location
Avro 707A	WD280	RAAF Museum, Point Cook, Victoria, Australia
Avro 707C	WZ744	Royal Air Force Museum, Cosford
Avro Ashton	WB491	Newark Air Museum (fuselage section only)
BAC.221	WG774	Fleet Air Arm Museum, Yeovilton
BAC TSR.2	XR220	Royal Air Force Museum, Cosford
	XR222	Duxford Airfield
Boulton Paul P.111A	VT935	Midland Air Museum, Baginton
Bristol 188	XF926	Royal Air Force Museum, Cosford
Fairey FD.2	WG777	Royal Air Force Museum, Cosford
Gloster E.28/39	W4041/G	Science Museum, London
Hawker P.1052	VX272	Fleet Air Arm Museum, Yeovilton
Hawker P.1127	XP831	Science Museum, London
	XP980	Fleet Air Arm Museum, Yeovilton
	XP984	Brooklands Museum
Hunting 126	XN714	Royal Air Force Museum, Cosford
Rolls-Royce TMR		
(Thrust Measuring Rig)	XJ314	Science Museum, London
Saunders-Roe SR.A/1	TG263	Southampton Hall of Aviation
Saunders-Roe SR.53	XD145	Royal Air Force Museum, Cosford
Short S.B.5	WG768	Royal Air Force Museum, Cosford
Short S.C.1	XG900	Science Museum, London
	XG905	Ulster Folk & Transport Museum, Co. Down

Index